THE SOCIOLOGY STUDENT'S GUIDE TO WRITING

For Casey and Lilli
Because we believe that anyone can write and everyone should

SAGE was founded in 1965 by Sara Miller McCune to support the dissemination of usable knowledge by publishing innovative and high-quality research and teaching content. Today, we publish over 900 journals, including those of more than 400 learned societies, more than 800 new books per year, and a growing range of library products including archives, data, case studies, reports, and video. SAGE remains majority-owned by our founder, and after Sara's lifetime will become owned by a charitable trust that secures our continued independence.

Los Angeles | London | New Delhi | Singapore | Washington DC | Melbourne

THE SOCIOLOGY STUDENT'S GUIDE TO WRITING

Angelique Harris
Marquette University

Alia R. Tyner-Mullings
Stella and Charles Guttman Community College, CUNY

Los Angeles | London | New Delhi
Singapore | Washington DC | Melbourne

FOR INFORMATION:

SAGE Publications, Inc.
2455 Teller Road
Thousand Oaks, California 91320
E-mail: order@sagepub.com

SAGE Publications Ltd.
1 Oliver's Yard
55 City Road
London EC1Y 1SP
United Kingdom

SAGE Publications India Pvt. Ltd.
B 1/I 1 Mohan Cooperative Industrial Area
Mathura Road, New Delhi 110 044
India

SAGE Publications Asia-Pacific Pte. Ltd.
3 Church Street
#10-04 Samsung Hub
Singapore 049483

Printed in the United States of America

Library of Congress Cataloging-in-Publication Data

Names: Harris, Angelique, author. | Tyner-Mullings, Alia,
author.

Title: The sociology students' guide to writing /
Angelique Harris, Marquette University, Alia R.
Tyner-Mullings, The New Community College at CUNY.

Description: Los Angeles : SAGE, [2017] | Includes
bibliographical references and index.

Identifiers: LCCN 2016034258 | ISBN 9781506350486
(pbk. : alk. paper)

Subjects: LCSH: Sociology—Authorship. | Sociology—
Research. | Sociology—Study and teaching (Higher)

Classification: LCC HM569 .H369 2017 | DDC
301.072—dc23 LC record available at https://lccn.loc.
gov/2016034258

This book is printed on acid-free paper.

SFI label applies to text stock

Acquisitions Editor: Jeff Lasser
Editorial Assistant: Alexandra Croell
Production Editor: Kelly DeRosa
Copy Editor: Diane DiMura
Typesetter: Hurix Systems Pvt. Ltd.,
Proofreader: Alison Syring
Indexer: Mary Mortensen
Cover Designer: Gail Buschman
Marketing Manager: Kara Kindstrom

16 17 18 19 20 10 9 8 7 6 5 4 3 2 1

BRIEF CONTENTS

DETAILED CONTENTS

ACKNOWLEDGMENTS

The writers of this fully coauthored volume would first like to acknowledge the contributors to the "Writing in Practice" sections that appear in every chapter (starting with Chapter 2). We greatly appreciate the work they put into their writing and the advice they provided to us and will provide to the students and professionals reading this book. The authors would also like to thank research assistants at Marquette University—Katherine Anderson and Christina Nelson—who helped us conduct research and gather material, as well as assisting with the editing and organization of this project. Additionally, we send thanks to the many college and university professors who reviewed our previous version of this text and provided us with valuable feedback. Finally, we are extremely grateful to our editors at SAGE for their interest in this project and their dedication to working with us during its creation.

Individual Acknowledgments

First and foremost, I'd like to thank my coauthor, Alia Tyner-Mullings, whose insight and partnership were vital to the production of this text. I owe much gratitude to my undergraduate and graduate school professors, who are far too many to name, for their help and encouragement. I thank my past and current professional colleagues for the advice and motivation they have provided me. I'd also like to thank my family and friends for their support through the process of writing this text.

—Angelique Harris

I would first like to thank all my students and colleagues, whose struggles with writing inspired me to embark on this project. I also greatly appreciate the teachers at Central Park East 1 and Secondary School, Oberlin College, and the Graduate School and University Center, City University of New York, whose patience, knowledge, and mentorship gave me the opportunity to become the writer I am today. I would also like to thank my friends and family for their patience—especially my mother, who has spent years dissecting my writing with me and whose advice has allowed me to improve. Finally, I give great thanks to my coauthor, Angelique Harris, for the idea that blossomed into this joint intellectual venture, as well as for the pleasure of her collaboration.

—Alia R. Tyner-Mullings

CHAPTER 1

INTRODUCTION TO WRITING IN SOCIOLOGY

Sociologists can emerge from anywhere. On a basic level, we can all say we are sociologists. Sociology is the study of social interactions, institutions, and how social forces shape our everyday lives. Put simply, sociology is the study of society. Sociologists observe the behavior of people as they interact with others. The true marker of a sociologist, however, is how she observes and what she does with those observations. The sociologist is not simply looking for the existence of these behaviors. The sociologist is seeking to understand why these behaviors happen, what they mean, and how they come to be.

As a sociologist, you translate society, just as you might translate something from one language to another. Your goal is to view social interactions through the lens of sociology, using what sociologist C. Wright Mills refers to as the "sociological imagination"[1]—the ability to make a connection between private life and public issues. A conversation between a woman and a man at the snack table at a party becomes the interaction of gender, race, class, and education. How do her status symbols emphasize her positioning in society? How does he "do gender"[2] and emphasize his masculinity? How might their conversation be different in a different time or place? How do your observations change their interactions?

Sociologists do more than simply describe society as they see it. Sociology is the *scientific* study of society. Sociologists follow the scientific method in their research and incorporate data analysis and tests of theories from research conducted by others. The ability to translate that research into language for diverse audiences is what makes sociologists sought after by employers in so many occupations. Sociologists work in government, human and social services, public relations, advertising, marketing, finance, and entertainment, as well as in many other fields. These fields regularly employ sociologists because people who can read, understand, and, most importantly, explain society are often needed.

To translate society properly, sociologists must be able to communicate with others, and one of the primary ways sociologists communicate is through writing. Writing is how sociology is shared; it is how we are able to learn from the work of others and how we share our own work with others.

This does not mean sociological writing—or any writing—comes naturally. Most of us come from backgrounds where we wrote a paper or two in high school but did not necessarily feel we had enough instruction on how to do so. A teacher might have told you to write a paper about pirates, or an assignment may have prompted you to write an essay about *Romeo and Juliet*. It was not until you tried to write it that you were penalized for not having an introduction, conclusion, or enough supporting evidence. When professors tell students, "You need a literature review," students often struggle to find out what that is, and it may be only through trial and error that students discover what their professors meant. For too many people, this process leads to frustration and the belief that they are not good writers. It is important to remember, however, that no one is born a good writer. We all have to work at writing, and we all can strive to become good writers.

During the process of writing, you will come to realize how it can also help you think. By putting our ideas down on paper or on a computer screen, we can more fully understand and organize them. Writing up our work can give it form. Even if that form needs to be changed through editing and revising, once we have written down our thoughts, the ability to manipulate and make ideas more concrete becomes possible.

In addition to facilitating thinking, writing contributes to other parts of the research and learning process. Much of the work we do in collecting our data involves writing, and whether research is qualitative (dealing with nonmeasureable data) or quantitative (dealing with numerical data), poorly written instruments and fieldnotes can lead to poorly collected data. We use the writing in our research methods and data collection both to communicate with our respondents and informants and to understand them. It is through clear and informational writing that we accomplish this. Without the quality work we collect, produce, and distribute, we are not able to interpret the world of others or translate our world for them.

In our translation, we are able to complete the most important aspect of academic research—the sharing of our work. Once our research is complete (and sometimes before that), we use our writing to share it with our classmates, professors, and sometimes the public. We do this because, as sociologists, our work lacks purpose if it is not shared. We do it for the mission, the grade, the recognition, or the money. If we're lucky, we also get to do it for ourselves. Whether it needs to be revised or accepted as it is, our goal is for our work to be effective—to be seen and understood. The purpose of this book is to help you reach those and all your writing goals.

HOW TO USE THIS BOOK

This book was created as a response to our experiences as students, sociologists, and professors who emphasize writing in our classrooms. The fundamental goal of this book is to introduce students to the breadth of writing a professor might ask a sociology student to do while increasing the quality of writing within the field of sociology. The types of writing we describe in the book, however, can also be found in psychology, anthropology, political science, other social sciences, and even the humanities. When you finish this book, you should be able to effectively share your sociological thoughts and ideas.

The conceptual and organizational approach of *The Sociology Student's Guide to Writing* explores the styles of sociological writing at various stages in the process, from conducting library research and avoiding plagiarism to writing fieldnotes or a scholarly paper. The text also includes a discussion of the writing required to get into graduate school as well as writing outside of the traditional academic sphere—for example, writing for new media such as on websites and in blogs and e-mails.

For Students

The Sociology Student's Guide to Writing is both a reference book and a course book. For a student, the chapters in this book provide a guide for actively participating in the discipline. You can find instruction on most of the writing you will be asked to complete for courses or for other interactions with the social world.

This book also spans the spectrum for writers at different levels. Writers at the beginning of their educational journeys may find the sections on writing letters and e-mails in the next chapter to be extremely useful. As students advance in their studies, they will benefit from our discussion of methodological writing and research papers.

For Professors

The Sociology Student's Guide to Writing is a good course text for any sociology class that includes significant writing or on a suggested reading list for any social science course. If your course requires students to write a final paper, create a survey, or write fieldnotes, this book provides that instruction. If you just want students to pay more attention to their assignments and syllabus or take better notes, this book could also be useful for your class. *The Sociology Student's Guide to Writing* will allow you to focus your course time on other learning, as it will help your students break down, understand, and create the writing you would like them to produce.

THE STRUCTURE OF THE BOOK

Each chapter in this book describes one or several different types of writing in detail. Also featured in each chapter is a section called "Writing in Practice," written by one or multiple sociologists or sociology students explaining her or his approach to the style of writing addressed in that chapter. We include this to help students understand how actual sociologists approach writing and to offer them insight and encouragement in their own process.

Chapter 2, "The Bricks and Mortar of Writing," covers some of the basics. The chapter does not go into detail on aspects of writing such as grammar and spelling, but it describes how a paper is organized and the elements needed to create a document. The chapter begins with a general discussion about building a paper. This includes an examination of sub-sections, sentences, and paragraphs. The chapter also includes an overview of voice, which is also explored in Chapter 6, "Editing and Revising." Chapter 2 ends with a review of note-taking and letter writing, which will be valuable to students, especially those who do not have much experience with writing professional letters or e-mails. More advanced writers could also benefit from a refresher on the information provided in this chapter. The "Writing in Practice" section is written by Dr. Barbara Katz Rothman, professor of sociology at Baruch College and the Graduate School and University Center, City University of New York (CUNY).

Chapter 3, "Writing and the Search for Literature: Proposals, Library Research, and the Preparation of Literature," explores the writing that occurs as you conduct your research. This chapter includes the process of selecting a research topic and beginning to research that topic. It also describes how to write an annotated bibliography as part of the writing process and how to write a research proposal. Cynthia Bruns, an instruction and reference librarian for the social sciences at the Pollak Library at California State University, Fullerton, wrote the "Writing in Practice" section for this chapter.

Chapter 4, "Writing and the Data Collection Process," examines the selection and use of research methods through the writing one must create within them. This chapter is not intended to replace or replicate the information one might find in a research methods text or course. Rather, it is meant to supplement such information by emphasizing the different types of writing involved. The chapter begins with a short summary of research ethics and then goes on to provide a brief overview of research methods. Next, we explain the preparation and process of creating qualitative and quantitative instruments, scripts, fieldnotes, and transcripts. This chapter is one of three in the book that includes multiple "Writing in Practice" sections. For Chapter 4, they cover qualitative and quantitative research. Dr. Randol Contreras, assistant professor of sociology at the University of Toronto, wrote the qualitative piece; Dr. Thurston Domina, associate professor of educational policy and sociology at the University of North Carolina, Chapel Hill, wrote the quantitative piece.

Chapter 5, "Writing for Sociology Classes," addresses the writing assignments that are done for undergraduate sociology courses including reviewing your assignment and syllabus and writing an essay, a literature review, or a capstone project. In the "Writing in Practice" section, Daniel Balcazar, a graduating sociology student at Marquette University, discusses how he approaches researching and writing his course papers.

How we revise and edit our work is the focus of Chapter 6, "Editing and Revising." Important for all students, this chapter provides strategies for quick edits as well as for more extensive ones. The chapter also describes the process in which we all participate to create a first draft, then form and rewrite subsequent versions. Dr. James A. Holstein, professor of sociology at Marquette University and former editor of the scholarly journal *Social Problems*, provides the "Writing in Practice" section for this chapter. Dr. Holstein gives advice for approaching the revision process.

Chapter 7, "Writing for the Public," describes sociological writing intended for a nonsociological audience. Debates continue over whether sociologists should participate in writing for the public, and this issue will be discussed very briefly in Chapter 7. The chapter dissects the process of writing for writing online or creating different types of presentations. Dr. R. L'Heureux Lewis-McCoy, associate professor of sociology and Black studies at The City College of New York, CUNY, begins the "Writing in Practice" section with his piece discussing his views on writing for the public. Dr. Molly Vollman Makris, assistant professor of urban studies at Guttman Community College, includes a "Writing in Practice" section on undergraduate presentations. Dr. Mary Gatta, associate professor of sociology at Guttman Community College, concludes the chapter sharing her experiences on social media in the classroom.

The final chapter in this book provides advice for those transitioning from college into another educational institution or into a career. Chapter 8, "Writing Beyond the College Classroom," describes the writing involved in applying for graduate school and the types of writing one can expect upon acceptance into a program. The chapter does not go into detail on the types of writing used in different careers but does address the writing of curriculum vitae and résumés. The "Writing in Practice" piece for this chapter is written by Christina Nelson, a recent Marquette University alum, who shares the description of her process of applying for graduate school.

The Sociology Students' Guide to Writing provides the resources needed to enhance the skills of budding sociologists. Readers should be able to find a chapter that addresses any kind of writing they might encounter during college. Through the use of this book, we hope your understanding of writing and confidence in your own writing ability will be enhanced and expanded.

NOTES

1. Mills, C. Wright. 1959. *The Sociological Imagination.* New York: Oxford University Press.

2. West, Candace and Don H. Zimmerman. 1987. "Doing Gender." *Gender and Society* 1(2): 125–51.

CHAPTER 2

THE BRICKS AND MORTAR OF WRITING

Writing is more than just organizing words on a piece of paper. It is a process of creating and revising. It is a way to think through ideas as well as a way to express them. Unfortunately, what is in your head does not always reach the paper intact. This can have a dramatic effect on how we understand the thoughts of others and the ways others understand us. This chapter will provide guidance on writing at the level of organization and presentation, ensuring that the final writing product is received as intended.

THE STRUCTURE OF WRITING

For most of us, our first experience with significant writing was the five-paragraph essay. It begins with an introduction, is supported by three paragraphs within the body, and ends with a conclusion. While it often feels as though we are starting from scratch when we write papers at the college level, that basic structure does not change as we advance through our education. What does change when writing becomes more complex are the details within the body of the work, which will vary depending on the type of writing. Those details will be discussed thoroughly over the remaining chapters of this book. Here, we will examine the general structure of writing with an overview of its basic building blocks.

The Foundation of Your House

Building a paper is similar to building a house with a limited budget. Each piece has a purpose, and extraneous pieces should be avoided. The paper is built on propositions—a research question, a hypothesis, and/or a thesis. A research question is the question that guides your research. A hypothesis is the potential answer to the research question based on little research or knowledge. Similarly, a thesis is the potential answer to the research question based on significant research or knowledge. Which of these you include in your paper may depend on your professor and/or the specific assignment, but regardless of how you structure your research question, hypothesis, or thesis, they act as the mortar that holds the paper together. Every so often, a paper will have to return to the propositions and connect that particular brick (a word), row (a sentence), or wall (a paragraph) to the rest of the house.

This means that each paragraph must be properly justified or supported. There should be a reason for each paragraph that is evident within the paragraph itself or in those that surround it. It should be possible to pick out a few paragraphs, or an entire section in a paper, and understand how it connects to the propositions. The length of the paper determines how long you can go without directly referring to your propositions. In a short paper, each paragraph should have a direct justification. For longer works, the document is likely to be divided into sections. In this case, each section should refer back to the propositions. Many writers rely on headings to distinguish between sections. However, headings should not be used as a replacement for transitions—the indicators of change from one thought to the next. It is still necessary both to introduce a section (and its connection to the topic as a whole) and to conclude the section before transitioning into the next one.

Figure 2.1

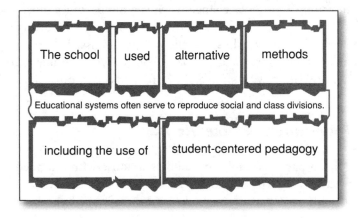

The Walls of Your Room

In any long piece, you may have different types of paragraphs that can be characterized into four types—introductory, main point, elaboration, and concluding paragraphs—some of which do not refer directly to the propositions. An introductory paragraph explains the importance of that section to the overall propositions. The main point paragraph provides and explains the most important point in the section. Elaboration paragraphs provide the evidence and examples that prove that connection. The section ends with the concluding paragraphs, which restate the connection and the evidence and connect that section to the section that follows.

Additionally, elaboration paragraphs will likely fall into two categories: affirmation or contradiction. You can use these paragraphs to develop or support your point further or to present the opposing perspective. To affirm or confirm a point, you should include evidence or expound on previous evidence. In presenting an opposing viewpoint, you should present evidence from other research and explain why your perspective should be considered over the perspectives of others.

Similar to how each section of the paper includes paragraphs that mimic the structure the paper as a whole, each individual paragraph should be written in the same manner. Each paragraph should have an introduction, an <u>elaboration</u>, and a <u>conclusion and/or transition</u> into the next paragraph. In theory, someone should be able to follow a paper at a very basic level by simply reading the first and last sentences (the introductions and conclusions) in the paragraphs.

> Most of the students' complaints about their CPESS experience can be placed in [the college category]. According to the data collected here, 95.8% of former CPESS students applied to college, nearly all were accepted and 89% of survey participants began college. However, sustainability in college proved to be more of a challenge than may have been expected. <u>One of the most significant problems, as discussed earlier in this chapter, is that after spending between two and 14 years in an alternative educational program, students had to return to or, for many students, enter for the first time, the type of traditional educational institution that CPESS had socialized them to resist. Similar to findings in other chapters in this volume (see Hantzopoulos; Bloom), many former students and teachers from the first five graduating classes referred to a culture shock in the process of moving from the sheltered, nurturing CPESS environment into college.</u>[1]

In this example, the reader can gain an understanding of the context of this paragraph and the next one by simply examining the introductory and concluding sentences. However, the elaboration is important for a more complete understanding of the writer's point.

The Lines That Form the Walls

At a basic level, the purpose of a sentence is to describe something doing something. "A woman walked" is a very simple example of this. It begins with a capital letter. There is a noun, then a verb, and it ends with a period, exclamation point, or question mark. A noun is a person, place, thing, animal, or abstract idea and the world is filled with them. As a student you might use nouns such as *analysis, emphasis, approach, summary, result, argument,* and *quote.* A verb expresses an existence, action, or occurrence. *Occurs, equals, critiques,* and *formulate* are all examples of academic verbs.

In academic writing, sentences tend to have more information than what is in our sample sentence in the previous paragraph. From that sentence, we know a couple of things. There existed a woman and she walked. However, there is a lot missing from this sentence. Who is this woman? Why is she walking? How is she walking? Where is she walking? Context clues can often be found prior to or after the sentence, but there is also much space within the sentence for elaboration. For example, you can use an adjective—a word that modifies or describes a noun or pronoun. In our original sentence, the woman could be tall or smart, young or elated. In academic writing, these kinds of adjectives are less likely except when describing individuals in qualitative research. Instead, you might use adjectives such as *alternative, consistent, decreasing, different, important, innovative, hierarchical, high, necessary, possible, primary,* and *significant.* Adverbs can also add more detail to your sentence as they modify or describe verbs or adjectives. An adverb might be added to the sample sentence and lead to the woman walking quickly or slowly. Again, some of the adverbs you might use in academia are *also, even, extremely, further, generally, only, particularly, perhaps, probably,* and *relatively.*

A sentence can also include other parts of speech, such as pronouns, which replicate or replace a noun. Often, we use the last name of an author to refer to that author later in a sentence or paragraph, but pronouns such as *he* and *she* are also used. You can also use gender nonbinary terms such as *they* (as singular), *ne, ey, ve, zie,* for example, but you will want to make sure your reader is familiar with these terms first as these different pronouns are new to many people. You can also use a footnote to explain if you are aware of an individual preference. You will notice in this book that she is used more often than he to refer to a generic person. Prepositions can also be used in your sentences to show the relationship between or among words in terms of direction, place, time, cause, manner, and amount. Examples of prepositions are *to*, *under*, *on*, *at*, *after*, and *by*. Finally, conjunctions connect words, sentences, or clauses. Similar to the prepositions, the conjunctions used in academia do not differ significantly from those used outside of an academic sphere. These are words such as *and*, *or*, *but*, *if*, *after*, *unless*, and *although*. These are also words to note when you are reading or writing as they signal whether the rest of the sentence will be confirming, contradictory, or the next element in a sequence.

In academia, many of our sentences are compound sentences. When we talk about changing the length of your sentences to adjust the flow of your work, you can often accomplish that by creating or destroying compound sentences, which use conjunctions or transitions to connect clauses—a group of words containing a subject and a verb—or sentences. Often this is an independent clause, with a subject and a verb, and can stand alone or be part of a larger compound sentence, and a dependent clause, that cannot function as a sentence by itself. Usually, dependent clauses are preceded by a comma or a conjunction.

A more complicated version of the compound sentence is a complex sentence. This is a combination of several independent and dependent clauses. These are also very common in academic texts. For example:

> If students internalize school cultures as well as what is said in a lesson or textbook, then it makes sense to foster learning environments marked by habits of risk taking, generosity, and understanding of self and others. (DiPardo 2000:307)[2]

These different types and aspects of sentences line up to build the "walls" of a paragraph. While many of the serious edits you make to a sentence often happen during the revising phase (which will be examined more fully in Chapter 6), there are guidelines that you can consider while writing an early draft. As stated above, every sentence tells a particular story. If words are missing from a sentence, pieces are missing from the story. If something is unclear in a sentence, the story being told is unclear to the reader. You should keep in mind the story you are trying to tell when you write and check to make sure it has been told when you are finished.

Clarity in a sentence or paragraph often comes from finding the proper balance of information to place within a sentence. If there is not enough information in a sentence, the reader's picture is incomplete, as in the walking woman above. Some of the information may be included in the sentence(s) that precedes or follows. However, there should be enough information in the sentence that it does not leave the reader with too many questions about what he has just read. For example:

The relationship between family and education has been researched a lot.

If a reader is presented with this sentence, she will have several questions that could easily have been answered by elaborating on the provided information: What is "a lot"? What time period is being referred to? What kinds of results have been found? A lack of answers to these questions is not the mystery that will encourage the reader to move on and might, instead, lead to her interest waning or deciding that the research presented will be elementary or poorly presented. Here are a few possible revisions to this sentence with each including a bit more clarity:

The relationship between family and education has been well researched over the past 50 years.

The results of studies on the relationship between family structure and education have been inconclusive over the past 50 years.

There are more than 1,000 articles from the last 50 years that examine the potential effects of family structure on educational attainment, and the results have varied.

A sentence can also contain too much information and become what many teachers and professors refer to as a run-on sentence. You should try to make only one or two points in a sentence. When you make multiple points within a sentence, the entire sentence is weakened. It is very possible that each point of the sentence is more powerful on its own. In addition, watch for multiple independent clauses within one sentence. If another sentence can be made, it probably should be.

The formation of the United States began in 1776 with the signing of the Declaration of Independence, but the ideals of democracy for all citizens were delayed because African Americans were not officially able to act as citizens until 1965 with the ratification of the Civil Rights Act, even though the Fourteenth Amendment to the Bill of Rights stated that "all persons born or naturalized in the United States . . . are citizens of the United States" (Bill of Rights 1965), many people were prevented from taking full advantage of their rights.

This is an extreme example, but this type of sentence is not unheard of. One cannot expect to explain the history of American democracy and civil rights in one sentence. There are several places within the sentence where the writer could have added a period to create a paragraph composed of more than one sentence. If the reader has to take several breaths to get through a sentence, it is too long. The paragraph above could be edited to create:

The formation of the United States legally began in 1776 with the signing of the Declaration of Independence. However, even though the Fourteenth Amendment to the Bill of Rights in 1868 stated that "all persons born or naturalized in the United States . . . are citizens of the United States" (Bill of Rights 1965), the ideals of democracy for all citizens were delayed. African Americans, for example, were not officially able to act as citizens until 1965, with the ratification of the Civil Rights Act.

The type of run on sentence above can also be the result of the use of speech-to-text technologies. If you choose to use something like this to speak your paper rather than write it, you have to take the next step and edit your work. The program cannot always determine where you would like a period or a comma or even whether you mean "to," "two" or "too." Even quickly reviewing your paper for these common edits (see Chapter 6) can make a difference in clarity.

The Bricks That Build the Walls

The other problems within sentences can come from the words used to build them. To ensure that the meaning a reader receives from a work is the meaning intended, it is important to examine each piece and its interaction with every other piece. One source of common misunderstanding in creating sentences is the use of the wrong words. When writing, and especially when revising, it is important to double-check which words have been used and whether there is a better choice or, if you have misused a word, a correct choice. Many words are easily mistaken for others. *Then* and *than*, for example, are often misused; *then* means following after, while *than* indicates a comparison (see the Appendix for additional examples of confused words).

Words can also be misused because of an uncertainty of the audience you are serving and how to speak to them. Some writers will use every word they know to make their point because they believe that having a large vocabulary makes them appear intelligent. However, you must also know how to use the words properly for them to be effective. If you truly know the vocabulary of sociology, or of the specific area in which you have interest in the discipline, you will be able to use the words economically and not overburden your paper with attempts to display your vocabulary. If you do not yet know the language of your discipline, reading is the best way to learn it. Study scholarly journal articles and read books within sociology to grow your familiarity with the discipline, and its language will eventually become yours. Do not simply use a thesaurus to turn your words into bigger or more relevant words within your discipline. It is generally better for your point to be understood than for you to use vocabulary that you do not understand. In addition, while using the words from an article you read or an assignment given to you by your professor demonstrates that you have at least read it, if you do not understand the words that will also become evident. It is also more likely that you will plagiarize because of that lack of understanding. Make sure you look up any words you do not understand before trying to write using them. Forcing yourself to put a sentence into your own words also ensures a higher level of understanding.

Features of Academic Writing

In addition to the more general structure of a paper, particular attributes are important in the creation of an academic paper.

Formality

Some refer to academic writing as formal, others as semiformal. What this generally means is that the informality that is a part of other types of writing you might do is not present in academic writing. We elaborate on this a little more in our section below on letters, but your writing should generally avoid slang, most abbreviations, colloquialisms (informal words or phrases found in casual speech), and contractions.

Objectivity

While writing in academia usually means presenting a particular perspective, objectivity is still important to maintain. You should always avoid any indications of bias by presenting multiple sides to your arguments. In many cases, the opposing arguments are the foundation of your perspective and you write your piece in response to them. In these situations, an overview of the opposing ideas is typically integrated into the literature review section (see Chapter 5) of your paper. However, even when such an overview does not flow organically from your viewpoint, an objective presentation is important to the legitimacy of your paper.

Caution

Regardless of whether or not your data are qualitative or quantitative, they are usually indefinite. Generally, you can say that "the evidence demonstrates" or that the "data appear to show." It is unlikely that you will come across any information that provides you with something definite. Therefore, your language should reflect that. If you do have some evidence that shows a firm result, you should share that. More likely, however, you will find a suggested relationship, and you should write it up as such. Words such as *should, may, could,* and *potentially* will likely be important in your writing.

Clarity

You should be clear and precise with your language in academic writing. If you are explaining a relationship in your data, your language should reflect that particular relationship. If you want to lead your reader in a particular direction in your paper, use indicators such as transitions to let them know where the story will be taking them. Your vocabulary should also be accurate and representative of what you actually intend to say. We speak more about this when we discuss voice below.

Evidence

Any points you make in academic writing will have to be supported by evidence. This evidence may be data you collected, information you read from what others have examined, or conclusions drawn from analysis of the data of other researchers. All evidence that you include must be properly cited and should be well integrated into your document. This includes both introducing it—a quote, for example—and explaining its place in your work (see Chapter 3 for information on citing and integrating quotes).

Perspective

Academic writing is generally written in the third person. This means that work is done by her or him, sometimes by I (first person), and never by you (second person). This can often lead to passive sentences (see below), but it can also add a level of objectivity (see above), which is important for scientific writing in academia. There is still discussion about the use of the first person in academic writing, and where this perspective is most likely to be seen is in a methods section (see Chapter 5 for more information), especially in qualitative research. Some professors might also ask you to write a proposal or even an essay in first person, so it is important to ask or to examine the work of others to find out if and how first person is used in your school or class.

The construction of your paper with the proper words, an academic structure, fully formed sentences, and well-structured paragraphs can help you build your paper and express your ideas. This enables you not only to be understood but also to share your writing persona or personality with the reader. We refer to this representation of yourself—the personality of your writing—as its voice.

The Voice on the Paper

What a professor refers to as "voice" comes down to two general ideas. The first is when a professor tells you that *you* are missing from the work. This form of voice is about understanding the research and the writer's contribution to his work. The way this type of voice is emphasized in writing varies depending on the type of writing that is created. We will examine it further as we work our way through this volume and the different types of writing. The type of voice we will examine in this section, as well as more fully in the chapter on editing and revising, is more general. Here, we will explore the ways a written piece can be imbued with a voice to make it both interesting and clear—what we will refer to as aesthetic voice.

Aesthetic voice is also about the audience to whom you are speaking. As you will read about in other chapters in this volume, your voice will be dictated to some extent by your intended audience. Writing a paper for a class requires a certain type of formal, semiformal, or academic voice, while an entry on a webpage or blog might use a different voice. You will hear much more about this as we work our way through the book, but most of the types of writing you will find here will be academic. However, our own writing in this text is less formal, as our goal here is to interest our audience in the types of writing in which sociologists participate.

Providing an interesting and clear voice is not easy. While some may be born with the ability to speak beautifully and translate it perfectly to paper, for most of us, it takes some work to create a masterpiece. After much practice, you can reach a point where a first draft will contain a level of aesthetic voice, but until you reach that point, much of the insertion of voice may happen during the editing stage (see Chapter 6).

The first part of including aesthetic voice in a written piece is knowing the audience. Understanding who the audience is, as well as what they expect, allows the writer to speak in a way that resonates with those who are reading. If the audience is your professor or classmates, using the vocabulary and formal structure of the relevant field of sociology will be important. If the writing is for a blog, sociological language can quickly become jargon to the audience.

You should make sure to read the piece aloud. While writing for a presentation and for written formats is different (see Chapter 7 for more information), voice is heard in the minds of the individuals reading the work. If it flows when the writer speaks it out loud, it will probably sound similar to the reader. Several voice edits may happen during your first and subsequent read-throughs, as you may struggle somewhere in your piece or become out of breath and will therefore know it is necessary to change some words or add periods or commas.

If the problem is not immediately evident, there are several places to look to make changes. Many of the structural aspects mentioned above can add to voice when utilized properly. Check your sentences for run-ons or vagueness. Another common problem in papers without a strong voice is a lack of variation in sentences. Writing is very much about flow. Sentences with the same or very similar lengths give the writer's voice an automated tone. Changing the length of sentences might include combining a couple of sentences, inserting a new sentence between existing ones, or adding additional words to refine the sentences.

Example:

The researchers did not agree. One study found positive effects. The other study found negative effects. More research needs to be conducted.

Possible revision:

More research needs to be conducted to explore the topic fully. The two studies differed in their findings, as one found positive effects and the other, negative.

Another way to add variation to sentences is to ensure that the words used to begin or conclude a sentence vary throughout a paragraph or section. *The*, for example, is an easy word to begin a sentence with, and it is just as easy to be unaware of using it repeatedly. If the same word, group of words, or type of word is being used to start every sentence, the sentence should be restructured or, if possible, the structure of the paragraph should be changed.

Example:

<u>The school</u> used alternative pedagogical methods. <u>The students</u> in the classes did much of their work in groups. <u>The teachers</u> emphasized student-centered pedagogy. <u>The administrators</u> protected the teachers from outside influences that might have a negative effect on what occurred within their classrooms.

Possible revision:

The school used alternative methods, which included group work and student-centered pedagogy. Administrators at the school also protected the teachers from outside influences that might have a negative effect on what occurred within their classrooms.

Clichés can also disrupt the voice of a paper. They are considered too casual for most academic papers and should be replaced by words that do a better job of making the same point. Clichés are phrases that use a well-known illustration of an idea, such as "sharp as a tack." Instead of clichés, you should use a selection of accurate and precise words to describe what you are trying to say.

You should also check your sentences for words that are repeated, places where several words have been used when one might work better, and words that may not have been used properly. These modifications will all assist in changing the voice of a paper. Additionally, once you have revised the work by reading aloud, you should look for another person to read it. If that other person can read it aloud, that is even better. Listening to it read by someone else will certainly help illuminate for you any problems in voice.

Recognizing the difference between active and passive sentences can also change the voice of a piece. Passive sentences can make a piece sound flat, while active sentences can add interest or action to your writing. In a passive sentence, the subject of the sentence is being acted on rather than initiating the action. Academic writing is often written with a more passive voice because sometimes there is no subject, the subject is unknown, or the use of a subject comes off as too casual. The third-person perspective that dominates academic writing can also lead a paper to more passive than active sentences. For example, "Research was conducted on the students" is a passive sentence often used to describe methods. While, technically, you conducted the research, some academics believe it is poor form to refer to yourself in an academic paper. Most individuals will accept it either way, but some professors may prefer the more passive version.

A sentence can usually be changed from passive to active by finding the active subject and making sure it is doing the work. Often, in a passive sentence, the subject is missing and/or only implied. If you add the word *by* to the end of a passive sentence, the subject implied after the *by* should be the focus of the sentence to make it active. In the passive sentence, "The test was taken," the invisible subject might be students, professionals, or teachers. To turn the sentence active, make sure the "students took the test."

Form

Some professors will give you a particular format for the overall structure of your assignment. They will tell you exactly how files should be identified and papers should be labeled. This is extremely helpful when you are putting together your assignments as it ensures that you create a document that your professor is comfortable with. Others will give you no information. This does not mean, however, that they have no expectations or that they would not appreciate a particular presentation of your work. Most importantly, any format that you use should be clear and informative.

If you do not receive any instructions, understand that most professors prefer papers that are written in 12-point black font. Do not go below 10 or above 14 in font size. For figures, you can usually go as low as 8. Times New Roman is generally the preferred font but other serif fonts can be used if one is not indicated. Sans (without) serif fonts may be used for figures. Papers should also be double spaced unless otherwise indicated.

There are other formatting preferences in sociology. The margins of your paper should be no smaller than one inch, unless you are writing for publication. You should not use hyphens to separate a word into two pieces at the end of a line and your text should be left justified, which means the left side of your paper (when you are facing it) has text that is even and the right side is jagged. Rather than putting one or multiple spaces between paragraphs, the format recommended by the American Sociological Association (ASA) is indented. Most of your work will only require three levels of headings and subheadings. The first is all capital letters in line with the left side of the paper. The second level is in italics and again, aligned with the left side of the paper. The third level is indented and placed before the beginning of the paragraph, on the same line as the rest of the paragraph.

Unless specifically asked not to, including a cover page is a good way to present yourself as well as information about the assignment. According to ASA, a cover page should include the name of the assignment or the title (if required) and your name. This page should also have the name of the course and the date. Optionally, you can include the name of the professor. A formal cover page should also include a university affiliation (such as a department and/or position). However, this is not likely to be needed for a paper you submit for a course. If an abstract is required (see below for more information), it can follow this information on the cover page.

Some professors prefer that a paper not include a cover page. In this case, the above information (without the abstract) can be written at the top of the first page in two columns on the left and right sides of the header. You can also add a running head which repeats some identifying information on every page following the first one. This header can include your name and the assignment or date. It should not include more than 50 characters and should not be counted in any word or page count. Page numbers can be in the header but ASA format dictates that they are placed at the bottom of the paper.

Similarly, your professor may give you specific information about naming any files that you submit digitally through e-mail or a course/learning management system. If she does not, you should make sure that your files include your name (your last name is probably adequate unless there are other students in your class with your last name) and the name and/or number of the assignment. This will make it easier for you to find and submit assignments and for your professors to identify and grade them. You should also try to keep digital or paper copies of all your assignments at least until you receive your final grade.

Most of this book will focus on writing in your sociology classes, but we begin our instruction on specific types of writing with something that is often a little less formal—the letter. Even though the letter is one of the shortest types of writing involved in sociology, when written properly, the structure of a letter still mirrors many of the other types of writing in this book. We begin with this because it is something we are all familiar with yet still often have trouble completing in an academic, formal, or professional manner.

LETTERS

Letter writing is a very specific type of writing and an art that was once valued and is now, for the most part, lost. It is not the first thing that comes to mind when you think of a sociological guide for writing. However, as a sociologist, in school and beyond, you will have several opportunities to write letters. While some of us may feel we have already mastered the art of writing a quality letter in a professional setting, we can probably all find some helpful hints or suggestions in this section.

E-mails

E-mails are a good place to start a lesson on letter writing, as writing e-mails is something most current college students grew up doing and its format has become second nature. However, few have ever learned the appropriate way to compose an e-mail message. Therefore, it is an extremely misunderstood form of writing.

Since e-mails are generally used for casual conversations, too many people forget that is not their only purpose. Most students understand the respect due to a professor, professional, or other superior in a face-to-face interaction, yet those same people lose that understanding when they are safely behind their computer screens. You should also remember that, while your letter is addressed to a particular person, it is stored on a server and even deleting it does not necessarily erase it. They can be copied, forwarded, and saved. Depending on the laws of your state and institution, they may be accessible to others. They can be very much public. This is a lesson that cannot be taught enough times, regardless of your level as a writer.

For someone who has never had to write and mail a professional letter, saying that writing a proper e-mail should be just like writing a

Figure 2.2

To: Professor1@school.edu
From: HotLips12@isp.com
Subject: HEY Prof!

HEY Prof!

I need to get the homework from today. Can you email it to me ASAP?

Thanks!
Patricia Joy

formal letter is pointless. Instead, looking at an improperly written e-mail can allow us to understand the dos and don'ts of e-mail writing in a formal setting. Here, we will focus on writing a professional e-mail to a course professor. However, the same rules apply whether the e-mail is to a professor or to any other professional or person with whom you have a working relationship.

Information in Header

While this is not exactly an issue of proper writing, it's something to think about if you want to become a professional in any field. When sending an e-mail, make sure to use an e-mail address appropriate for a professional setting. Though the e-mail name you have always used may be hotlips12, it could just as easily be PatriciaJoy12 or PJ.Walker12. Most institutions provide their students with school e-mail addresses (.edu), which would likely make that process easier, but we understand that students do not always keep up with their college-issued e-mail addresses. It is not difficult to create a personal address to use with your professors or any other professional contacts you might have. Most e-mail clients will allow you not only to forward PJ.Walker12's e-mail to hotlips12 but also to send e-mail from hotlips12's account as PJ.Walker12, if you so choose. You can always delete the e-mail account once the course is over, but many people have a main account from which they collect and send e-mails from a variety of other e-mail addresses. Using an e-mail address with your name is ideal. If that is not possible, nonoffensive words or a collection of letters and numbers (such as initials and parts of a date or address) are also acceptable.

Subject

The purpose of a subject line is to inform the receiver of your intent before she opens the e-mail. While not used as often, letters sent through the U.S. Postal Service can also have a "subject line." Sometimes the writer of a letter might write "Re: Your bill" on the outside of an envelope or on a message pad so the recipient knows that the enclosed is "regarding your bill." The same care should be used in an e-mail to a professor or other professional. What is the letter "regarding" or "in reference to"? A basic subject line could simply say, "The homework from May 14th" but, if you send an e-mail with that title, the professor may choose not to open it if she is not ready to grade. If the e-mail is a question about the homework, a more detailed subject line could read, "Question from P. Mullings about the homework from May 14th," and it may receive a response in a timelier manner. Be careful of length; your subject line should not require any scrolling. You should also keep in mind that your professor may get many e-mails from students in a given day and the more detail you can provide, the more likely you are to get the appropriate response.

Greeting

Another concern with the e-mail in the example is the "HEY!" in the subject line. This problem is similarly evident in the greeting. First, you do not want to start a professional letter by writing "hey." You should address a professional letter, specifically one to a professor, with "to," "dear," or even simply the professor's title and name (see the table below for a selection of titles). Unless you already know how the professor would like to be addressed, you should begin with Dear Professor (or Dr.) Monte. You can leave off the last name (i.e., "Dear Professor"), but its use tells the professor that you know who he is, as well as allowing you to be sure your message is going to the right person. Once you have written your first message, you can follow the recipient's lead in greetings and titles. Do not let a professor's use of your name be an example (although you can look at the type of greeting she used). Instead, make a note of how she has signed her letter. If she used her first name, unless she has already told you not to, you can probably use it when you address her in your next e-mail. If she uses her full name, you should address her as you have in previous letters. You should respond similarly if she has not used any name or used just her automatic signature.

Dear:	Can begin almost all letters; can be followed by names (Gwen), titles (Dean), or categories (Hiring Committee)
To whom it may concern:	Should be used only if you cannot uncover the name of the person
Hi, Hello, Hey	Should be used only for informal letters to people you are close to

If you are on a level playing field with the person you are corresponding with, rather than a subordinate to him, you can follow his example in terms of what he calls you and how he signs his name. If he addresses you as Emily and signs his name Mike, you can probably address him as Mike. Similarly, if you would like someone to call you by your first name, you can either tell him so or sign your letter with the name. If you have not been given any particular instruction in how to refer to someone, you should use a title.

Ms.:	For an unmarried woman or if marriage status cannot be determined. Ms. is considered more politically correct than Mrs. Must be used with a last name.
Mrs.:	For a married woman using her married name. It should be used only if you have been told to use it. Must be used with a last name.
Mr.:	For a man with no other title. Must be used with a last name.
Dr.:	For someone with a PhD, MD, DDS, or other higher degree. Must be used with a last name.
Professor:	For someone who teaches at a college or university.
Dean, Director, President, Provost, etc.:	The heads of an office, institute, or institution. Must be used with a last name.

If you need to address two people, you should use both of their names and titles with an *and* in between them. For three or more names, you may use "classmates," "professors," or "students," depending on who will be receiving the letter.

Finishing this section on the greeting, you should never use an exclamation point in a greeting to a professor. In fact, you should try to avoid them anywhere in your e-mail. In the words of F. Scott Fitzgerald, "Cut out all those exclamation points. An exclamation point is like laughing at your own jokes."[3] If you want to emphasize something in an e-mail, use a modifier—usually an adverb or adjective (or a word that acts as one) that adds description to the sentence—and explain your emphasis, rather than trying to elicit the emotion with a punctuation mark.

Body

Unarguably, the body is the most important part of your e-mail. This is why you are writing. This is where you explain yourself, make your argument, or ask your question. Yet even students who know exactly what they need often express themselves poorly in the bodies of their more professional e-mails. There are several important guidelines to remember. While these specifically center on writing professional e-mails, they can also be useful in writing an e-mail to anyone.

Recognize the Reader's Head. This means that, regardless of your intention, the reader will almost always take her mood, attitude, or feelings and breathe that life into the e-mail. If she is angry and there is anything at all ambiguous in your e-mail, she will hear it as angry. People often forget this attribute of letters and can both read emotional states in someone's e-mail that were not present and unwittingly send an angry e-mail to a friend. For this and many other reasons, it is important to read your e-mail before you send it out. Try reading it out loud with a different emotion in your voice. Can your receiver read something completely different in your letter than what you intended? If so, go back and try to change your words into something more neutral.

Additionally, intended emotions can also often be misread or missed all together. Sarcasm should never be in an e-mail to a professor, but if you are sending an e-mail to someone else, make sure you exaggerate the sarcasm. Without the inflection in your "voice," subtle sarcasm can easily be missed.

Don't Yell. Avoiding exclamation points was previously mentioned, but that is only one way your e-mail can seem demanding. You must keep in mind that you are likely sending this e-mail because you need something, yet your professor may not be able to assist you immediately. Avoid demanding terms such as *want* and *need*, and, at all costs, do not use phrases that signify that the receiver should stop what he is doing right away to help you—words such as *immediately*, *today* (except in a descriptive manner), *now*, and *ASAP*. Instead, remember you are asking the recipient to do something for you that may fall outside of her responsibility or course guidelines and that she will get to it when and if she can.

Write Properly. An e-mail to a professor is closer to a class paper than it is to a text message or a chat with a friend. You should follow the same conventions you would when writing anything for your professor. Write in full sentences with proper punctuation, grammar, and spelling. This includes not interrupting a sentence with an exclamation, words, or phrases the professor may or may not understand. Your professor doesn't want to hear that you are "LOL" or if something is "gr8." There should be no "text speak" in your e-mail. Similar to the Fitzgerald quote above, you don't need to LOL at your own jokes. If they are funny, they will be perceived as such. If they are not, no one will know they are jokes.

Follow Instructions. This is less about the actual writing and more about the considerations before you write. For example, in writing to a course professor, be sure to pay attention to what is listed in the syllabus or what your professor has said about e-mailing. If Professor Jones has told you that she will not accept late homework by e-mail, do not try to send it. If she has not given you an alternative, you may e-mail and ask if there is another way to drop off your work.

The structure of the body portion of your letter should mirror an essay in other ways as well. As in a basic essay, the main part of your e-mail should have an introduction, a body, and a conclusion.

The introduction can do many things. Depending on the purpose of the e-mail and how many e-mails you have already shared, you may need to introduce yourself:

My name is Colby Mani, and I am in your Sociology 101 class.

Or you may want to inquire as to how the recipient is doing:

I hope you are doing well.

However you begin, your letter can start with a casual tone but still fit within a formal structure. The body of your e-mail should explain your question, comment, or issue. You should keep it short and get to the point. We will discuss the different ways you might use the body of an e-mail when we discuss specific letters below.

Closing

You should conclude your letter with an appropriate closing or a closing salutation. You can end by wishing your professor well or letting him know that you will be in class for the following session. You can also include something like "best," "best regards," or "sincerely." You should not, however, include salutations such as "love," "yours," and "truly." You should follow the closing salutation with your name, especially important if you have not introduced yourself or e-mailed before, or if your name is not part of your e-mail address.

Appropriate salutations for formal letters include the following:

- Sincerely
- Yours sincerely
- Respectfully yours
- Kind regards
- Best regards
- Warmest regards
- Many thanks
- Take care
- With appreciation

There is a school of thought that e-mails should not have closing salutations because their true nature is more conversational than that of a traditional letter. Many of the messages exchanged among friends and family members are very informal and you will probably forgo much of the formality described here. After several interactions with your professor on a particular topic, she might stop using the greeting or signing the message, you should feel free to do the same. Your first professional e-mail, however, should follow these guidelines to ease the communication for both parties.

Finally, remember that a response may not be immediate, but you shouldn't push it. If the next class session and the office hours have passed and you have not heard anything, you can bring up the e-mail questions in person, but, unless it is an emergency, more than a week should go by before you send another e-mail, if you do at all. E-mails provide a quick way to communicate, but not everyone thinks of e-mails as needing an immediate response. The convenience of e-mails tends to overshadow the problems with them. If you can follow the guidelines in this section, you can be sure that you are able to address those problems.

Formal Letters

As a student, you may on several occasions need to write a business or professional letter. If you apply for a job, for example, your prospective employer may require you to write a cover letter. Some graduate or professional schools may require a cover letter with an application. Additionally, you may have a situation, separate from school, where you need to write a formal letter. Even if your letter is sent by e-mail, it is still important that it is in the correct format.

Writing a business letter was once something all students were required to do to graduate from high school. Now, in this age of e-mailing and texting, students are taught "snail mail" letter writing much later in their educations or never at all. Sometimes, like so much other writing, it is not until they have written a poorly structured letter that they are taught how to do it properly. Yet a well-written letter can assert authority, confidence, and competence.

Similar to e-mails, formal letters can be divided into different sections: header, introduction, body, conclusion, and footer. While the header and footer in an e-mail are often included in the e-mail client's programming, in a formal letter, you will write the header yourself and what is contained within it will vary depending on the type of letter.

The header of a letter usually includes the addresses of both the letter writer and the letter recipient. If you use a letterhead with an address, you do not need to include your address in the header. If there is no address, you should include one on the right-hand side of the header. The street address should be in the first row and the state, city, and ZIP code in the second row in the normal format for addresses. On the next line, the date should be inserted in the form "month, day, year" (although, if you are writing to an organization or company outside of the United States, "day, month, year" might be more appropriate). You may also include the day of the week preceding the rest of the date.

The receiver's information should be on the left on the following line in the same format, but it should also include the receiver's name in the first row. Alternatively, the sender's address and the date can be on the same side as the receiver's address (the left side) with an extra line break

Figure 2.3

```
                                                    123 Electric Street
                                                    New York, NY 10023
                                                    September 18, 2012

Professor B. Johnson
Green Men Consulting
New Haven, CT 06511


Dear Professor Johnson,
```

Figure 2.4

123 Electric Street
New York, NY 10023
September 18, 2012

Professor B. Johnson
Green Men Consulting
New Haven, CT 06511

Dear Professor Johnson:

between each element. Finally, after another line break, you should write a salutation and the individual's title and name. In most cases, that salutation is "Dear," and the title will depend on the individual.

As mentioned above, you should do your best to use the proper title of the person to whom the letter is addressed. If you cannot discover the recipient's gender, and you are using one of the gendered titles, you should use that person's full name. If you cannot find a name, you may use "To Whom It May Concern" (this can be written with each word capitalized or with only *to* capitalized); however, this should be used only as a last resort. Either greeting-plus-name combination can be followed by a colon; the combination that includes "Dear" may also be followed by a comma. See above for additional examples of greetings and titles.

The body of your letter should begin after a line break and, like other types of writing in this book, should be divided into several pieces. The details within each section in the body will vary depending on the type of letter being written, but each will begin with an introduction within which you explain to the receiver your purpose for writing and give a little information about who you are. If you were directed to write the letter by someone or have a contact at the school or organization, or someone you share in common with the recipient, that should also be mentioned in the introduction. In a longer letter, this could be a full paragraph. In a shorter letter, the introduction could be just one or two sentences. However, the meat of the body is where different letter types vary.

Job Letters

The introduction of a job cover letter should explain why you are writing the letter, such as "I am writing to apply for the position of statistical consultant at Green Men Consulting." Additionally, it should give a quick overview of your story and your qualifications: "My experiences in statistical analysis and software qualify me to fill your position."

The body of the letter is where you share the details of your qualifications. You should sound confident and competent. Review the qualifications required for the job before writing your letter and make sure to emphasize the experiences you have had that most closely fit the position in their order of importance to the potential employers.

Think about each of your former jobs, research you have conducted, organizations you have been a member of, or experiences you have had as a series of skills gained, responsibilities held, or activities completed. For example, if you worked as a college assistant, you probably had a lot of different types of responsibilities. You may have had to do administrative work, such as filing, data processing, and written communication. The job might have included research, and/or other knowledge of the school or other schools. It may have also required certain computer software, meeting with other members of your office, or organizing events or meetings. These all become skills you can highlight in a cover letter. Remember that your résumé or curriculum vitae (see Chapter 8) will provide an overview of all of your relevant jobs, skills, and service/volunteer work, so your cover letter should highlight particular experiences and draw the reader's attention to the ways you fit that particular position. In writing up your skills in a cover letter, make sure to emphasize what you actually did rather than what your title or official responsibilities were. It may also be a good place to explain how the jobs you had allowed you to gain the experience that the job you are applying for requires. A cover letter allows you make the link between the jobs you have had and the job that you want especially if that is not entirely clear in your résumé/curriculum vitae.

Organize your letter by skill, and, as usual, make each paragraph its own miniature paper. Introduce the skill, either with an introductory sentence or an example of the skill from your own experience. You then want to support your claim that you have that skill or can complete that task. You should try to avoid using more than three examples. Remember, they will have access to your résumé/curriculum vitae and can get further information from there. Follow up your skill paragraphs with a closing or transition sentence. As you want the receiver of your letter to be excited about you, you should use active words that exhibit your achievements and bring them to life. Rather than saying that you "wrote a few summaries," tell them you "created reports to promote changes in your program."

While much of your letter will be the same from position to position, make sure that you personalize each letter with the name of the school/organization/company and by addressing their particular needs and how your qualifications fit those needs. Also, the different jobs you apply for may have different emphases, so you should consider changing the order of the items in your letter. If you are applying for a position in a research office, you should make sure your research experience is the first thing the receiver reads. If it is a position where you will be expected to help with workshops, your experiences with tutoring or organizing should be addressed early in your letter. If the employer is interested in someone with nonprofit experience, any service work you have done should be mentioned as early as possible. This not only will ensure that the receiving parties recognize you as someone who fits their interests but also will give the impression that the letter was written specifically for them and their positions. While most will know that much of the letter is repeated for others, the effort is often appreciated (see the Appendix for a sample job letter).

Request/Inquiry Letters

In a request letter, your tone is very important. As a sociology student, the request letters you write will most likely be requests for an update, recommendation letters, information, an interview or survey, or help. It is essential that the body of your letter present your request, cushioned by an understanding of the receiver's schedule and the commitment your request might require. This may include apologizing for taking up the receiver's time (unless your request is within the boundaries of his everyday duties). You will then want to present your situation and your request.

You should also be sure that you have done all you can on your own and have included or attached any information she might need to comply with your request. For example, if you are requesting letters of recommendation, a professor will require information on who she is writing to, who you are, and your experiences. Therefore, you should attach a copy of your résumé or curriculum vitae and a highlight sheet (see Chapter 8) that describes your qualifications to your recommenders. Also, a copy of your cover letter may be helpful. Some of the other letters might include an attached survey, interview, or web link. (A sample request letter is provided in the Appendix.)

Thank-You Letters

Thank-you letters, in any form, are a lost tradition. If someone sends you something, meets with you, or writes a letter on your behalf, it is always good to thank that person for her help and time. While you may believe the verbal thank you that you provided immediately after you received what you requested was adequate, it does not hurt to provide something in writing in addition. A thank-you note shows not only appreciation but also manners and, for many people, will add to their impression of you.

If you have primarily corresponded digitally, that is a perfectly acceptable method of sending your thanks. This may be done as either an e-mail letter or an e-card. However, if you have access to an address, sending a physical card or letter is still a good idea. A thank-you letter can be very brief. You should simply remind the receiver of the situation for which you are thanking her and then thank her for whatever action was helpful to you. Because of the short length of a thank-you note or letter, a card can work very well. Sending a thank-you letter shows common courtesy, but if the thanks is for something like a job interview, such a letter can also remind the interviewers who you are and ensure that your interactions with them remain in their minds. Generally, you want to send this letter within a few days of the action, but within a week is probably still okay. (You can see a sample of a thank-you letter in the Appendix.)

Whatever the type, your letters should conclude by briefly reemphasizing the purpose for the letter and thanking the receiver for reading it. If additional items are enclosed, attached, or will be forthcoming, that should also be noted. The conclusion should include your final personalization of the school, organization, company, or person and an invitation for further correspondence. Again, end with an appropriate closing salutation and your full name and title, if appropriate.

NOTE-TAKING

In addition to organizing assignments and writing papers (which will be discussed in Chapter 5), note-taking is an essential skill in your sociology classes. It can also be very important for any other classes you currently take or plan to take in the future and, depending on what you go on to do, for your life after school. However, like much of the writing in this chapter, it is something that students often never learn and, if they do, they do not always learn how to do it well.

There are generally two circumstances in which you may want to take notes: when you are watching and/or listening to something and when you are reading something. Some of the strategies for note-taking remain consistent while others change depending on the context.

General Note-Taking

The most important thing to remember about taking notes is that they are notes. You are not trying to re-create, in its entirety, what someone is saying or what you are reading. You are trying to record the least amount you possibly can without losing any important information. Therefore, notes need to be (1) short, (2) understandable, and (3) retrievable.

Proper organization is one way to ensure that your notes are retrievable. At the very least, your notebook should be divided into sections for each class. A binder that allows you to remove sheets works best because you can remove and reorganize your notes in a way that fits your study habits. You could also have separate notebooks for each class. Make sure that, however you are organizing your class notes, you have space for everything you need, including notes that you have edited, the syllabus of the class, and any handouts you might get. Your notes and handouts should be organized by date or by topic.

Should you choose to organize your notes electronically, you may want to print, e-mail, or save a copy of them to the cloud, in addition to what you keep on your device. The repetition of copying your notes into a word processor or other online repository can help with retention, but it will also provide you a backup should you lose them or lose access to your device. A benefit of storing your notes in an electronic note-taking program or app is the use of tags—the multiple labels that you can give to the work you do. This can help in both the organization and the retrieval of the notes.

Preparation is also important in making sure your notes are short and understandable. If you have read what the professor assigned before class, you will be better prepared to judge what is important. You will also have a record of places where you need more information or where your understanding is strong and can use the information that is shared in class to fill in gaps or expand your knowledge. If you have questions after completing the readings, bring them to classmates, to class, or to the professor's office hours to help find the answers.

Notes From Readings

Most often your notes for a particular class will be a combination of those taken from a lecture or class discussion and those collected from class readings. Most professors prefer that students read course readings before the class in which it is discussed so these are generally the first notes that you will take on a particular topic. To gather information from textbooks and articles, you must begin with active reading.

Active Reading

This may be different from how you have read for school previously. In the past, you may have allowed the words to wash over you and picked out what you could use in class, papers, or exams. To be a writer in in the social sciences and many other college courses, however, your methods of reading have to change from what they once were. We have to be able to engage with what we are reading—to remember it, analyze it, and understand it—and it is through engaging with reading that we expand our knowledge and gain a deeper understanding of how to write.

Your active reading should begin with a preview. There are several places in academic writing that you could examine to understand where the piece is going. These places should also be kept in mind when writing, as the same elements could be read in your own writing as a preview for interested readers.

If you are reading a book, the table of contents is always a good place to start. The table of contents provides the path the writer takes through writing and can also provide information on her theories or the types of evidence she used. Prologues, chapter summaries, and introductory chapters can similarly provide a reader with an explanation of the structure of the book as well as a preview or summary of what is in each chapter. Prologues and introductory chapters often also include some synthesis that may or may not be found in other places in the work.

With an article, the abstract provides much of the important preview information. If written correctly, the abstract can give the reader a basic

Figure 2.5

Abstract: For three decades, Oscar Lewis's subculture of poverty concept has been misinterpreted as a theory bent on blaming the victims of poverty for their poverty. This essay corrects this misunderstanding. Using a sociology of knowledge approach, it explores the historical origins of this misreading and shows how current poverty scholarship replicates this erroneous interpretation of Lewis's work. An attempt is made to remedy this situation by arguing that Lewis's subculture of poverty idea, far from being a poor-bashing, ideological ploy, is firmly grounded in a Marxist critique of capital and its productive contradictions. As such, Lewis's work is a celebration of the resilience and resourcefulness of the poor, not a denigration of the lower class and the cultural defenses they erect against poverty's everyday uncertainty.[a]

[a]Harvey, David L. and Michael H. Reed. 1996. "The Culture of Poverty: An Ideological Analysis." *Sociological Perspectives* 39(4):465–95.

outline of the entire document. A good abstract will include an introductory sentence (or two), a thesis sentence, and sentences on the methodologies and important findings, and can even include implications and suggestions for future research.

This abstract introduces the article with the thesis that Oscar Lewis's culture of poverty theory has been misinterpreted. It goes on to tell us that the article will correct this misperception through the "sociology of knowledge" theoretical perspective by exploring the historical origins of the theory and showing "how current poverty scholarship replicates this erroneous interpretation." The findings are that Lewis's work is "firmly grounded in a Marxist critique" and is a "celebration of the resilience and resourcefulness of the poor" (Harvey and Reed 1996:465).

Headings and subheadings are another useful way to preview an article, but if you are not already familiar with the topic, they can be difficult to follow. Often headings include terms or phrases explained within the body of the document and, therefore, may provide less information for someone who is not yet familiar with the terms. If the reader understands the headings, or if the writer has taken care to create clear and informative headings, these can be a useful road map. If not, it can also be useful to preview some of the vocabulary that could help you to understand what you are about to read and looking up the words you do not understand can also be helpful.

While it is always important to read an article in its entirety, the introduction, discussion, and conclusion sections can provide much initial information on what the writer intends to do, how she has interpreted the data, and what the data mean to her larger questions. This can provide a solid framework for the reading that follows.

In a textbook, there are a few other places you can go to get a preview of what you are about to read. Textbooks generally include a lot of summary information at the end. There may be discussion questions, a list of terms, or a summary. Textbooks also indicate big ideas and new words or concepts through off-set text boxes, bold words or paragraphs, or colored text. This provides the signal that it is something to pay attention to.

Once a preview has been conducted, the rest of the piece should also be read closely. Breaking the work down into some of the structural elements discussed above helps to fully understand what has been read. Remember that each section or paragraph is like its own small paper. It should include an introduction, a conclusion, and the body between them. The reader can also make a distinction between what is core material and what is elaboration. All the material should be read; however, the core material is usually most important and should receive the most attention.

Identifying core material is also extremely important in highlighting or taking notes. You are most likely to need to return to the core material, rather than the elaboration; therefore, the core material is what should be saved. This core information is likely less than 10 percent of the entire document, and your highlighting, underlining, or note-taking should represent that.

Once you have the basic structure and the key ideas, you want to fill in the information that supports it. If there are steps, evidence, or other elaboration, you should go back to your main points and pull those out. You can summarize this information or include a bullet or two on it. You may want to create a separate list for vocabulary or other types of information that does not really fit the core or elaboration classification.

Notes on the reading can also be kept in the margins of books or on Post-Its or other sticky notes made especially for that purpose. Once you remove the notes from the actual reference, make sure that all information is referenced back to its original source.

A particular class assignment may tell you exactly what you should be looking for. Chapter 5 will give you some hints about doing a close reading of your assignment before completing your work. If you have a syllabus that outlines all your assignments in detail, check for the vocabulary words, concepts, and ideas mentioned in the assignment. The homework worksheet described in Chapter 5 includes some of the terms you might come across in an assignment and therefore what you might need to save in your notes. In addition, you should also consider recording the following annotations, depending on the nature of your assignment: important information, new information, answers to questions, elaboration of previous assignments, discussions or readings, and contrary or confirming information. Once you have identified the core and elaboration material, you can use one of the methods below to organize them.

Notes From Auditory Material

As described above, notes should primarily represent core material, whether it is from what you read, what you hear, or what you see. When someone is speaking, it can be difficult to judge what you should be writing and then to keep up and write everything that you will need. Therefore, you will need to pay attention to what is being said and how it is being said to figure out what to write.

First, and most importantly, if you have completed the reading before class, you will be able to listen for concepts and keywords from what you have read. This can provide clarity or elaboration for the notes you have already taken. You should create a new document with the notes from the lecture or video and you can then add them to your notes on the reading in a new document or review each group of notes separately.

In addition to words you may have picked up from the readings, there are other markers that you should pay attention to that indicate important information that you should record and retain. If the professor sets the stage for a list of items using bullets or numbers, you should keep the information in that sequence. If the professor presents contrasting information or makes a point and then follows it up with evidence, that information should be written down. The professor may also signify through words or tone that something is important or significant by speaking loudly, slowly, or using words like *important, essential,* or *significant.* Information can also be emphasized because they are written (on the board or PowerPoint), underlined, circled, or repeated.

As you record the information, try to write quickly, replacing words with symbols or shorthand where possible (see Appendix for examples of shorthand). You can also use your own abbreviations, but be sure to use words that you can understand or keep a key nearby to remind you of what you meant. Try to write as clearly as you can so the information is more easily retrievable when you have the time to do it.

Organizing Notes

Whether your notes are from a textbook or based on a lecture, how you record them can have an influence on your ability to find and recall them. You may choose to create your own system for taking notes or you might decide to use one of the methods described below. An individual's note-taking style is often a modification of a standard method that creates one that better suits your purposes. Those who are more advanced in their careers might even use more ethnographic methods (see Chapter 4) in their note-taking.

The Cornell Note-Taking system was published in 1962 in the book *How to Study in College* by Cornell University professor, Dr. Walter Pauk. It is the most well-known and widely used method for student note-taking. The method includes six R's: Record, Reduce, Recite, Reflect, Review, and Recapitulate. We will primarily focus on the first few as they are most relevant to writing.

The Cornell Note-Taking system organizes your notepaper into three different areas. Draw a horizontal line at about two inches from the bottom of the page. This is the summary area. Draw a second line vertically 2.5 inches from the left side of the page. To the left of this line is the cue or recall area, and to the right is the main notes area.

As you record, your notes should be focused on the main notes section. When you review your notes (ideally, the same day but no more than 48 hours later), use the cue area to write out questions or keywords that you can use to help you recall what is in the main notes area. Figure 2.6 is an example of this.

Following this extraction of review terms, you can summarize the information in the summary section at the bottom of the page. The Cornell structure also allows for quick review of notes as you can cover the main notes area and use the cue area to provide a clue help you recall what you have written.

There are several other note-taking methods that are useful for students. An outline format (see Chapter 3 for more information) can provide a very detailed summary of what you hear or see. It requires you to synthesize and organize the information and for this reason, many people will take notes quickly and then rewrite it into an outline later. In either case, your

Figure 2.6

What is sociology?	Sociology is the scientific study of people in
	groups
Who came up with the term sociology?	
	We credit Auguste Comte with
	coming up with the term Sociology
The definition of sociology and the person who came up with the term	

section headings should represent headings or subheadings in what you are reading or topics and subtopics in what you are hearing. Each of the smaller sections would represent main points or paragraphs within that topic or heading. This method is also useful because it can provide information about how the topics are structured in relationship to each other.

While much of our communication with each other has become fast moving and littered with grammar and spelling faux pas and our notes have become disorganized and forgotten, the space still exists for communication and record keeping in an intelligent and well-written format. This chapter represents the first step on your journey to becoming a better writer.

SUMMARY

This chapter provides an overview of the foundations of writing. We emphasized the following writing issues:

- How to organize the elements of a paper
- The concept of voice
- The writing of e-mails and formal letters
- Note-taking

In our first "Writing in Practice," Professor Katz Rothman describes the process of writing and what it means to her as a scholar and a person. She uses a trip to Germany to frame a discussion of the importance of books, writing, and sharing what is written.

WRITING IN PRACTICE
by Barbara Katz Rothman

Wie schrjft, die blijft.
Who writes, lives.

I really believe that Dutch proverb—writing is a way of living beyond our own space and time. My sociological research consists mostly of book-length projects. One was translated into German and has brought me to Berlin pretty regularly. Berlin is a city so filled with its own history that one cannot make it down a street without stumbling across

(Continued)

(Continued)

memorials—literally, there are "stumble stones" embedded in the sidewalks with the names of people who were taken off to die in concentration camps. A quick trip to pick up a bike map ends up leading to a sign telling you that Eichmann's office was located on this spot. I became used to it, sighed, nodded, and walked on.

But the memorial that brought tears to my eyes, the one that truly made me stumble, was the book-burning memorial. In front of Humboldt University, at the law school no less, there is a memorial marking the spot where the Nazis burned piles of the books they found offensive. You stand on a square of thick glass in the plaza and look down into a small white room lined with empty white bookshelves. I stood there and cried—the books! It wasn't enough they killed all those people; they had to kill their thoughts and their legacy. Of course they couldn't actually kill the books. Bodies go up in flames once and for all, never to return—but books, books hide in all kinds of places around the world. I could order any one of those burnt books and have a copy in my mailbox next week. I'm tempted to go find the list of books burnt that day and do just that right now.

So for me, writing is central—the way we leave parts of ourselves behind and send parts of ourselves forth, the way we enter the larger ongoing human conversation. And writing isn't just something I do—it's something I teach. I work mostly with graduate students, people doing their first major original piece of writing, making their own first contributions to the conversations they have been studying. Helping those people find their own voices fills me with as much joy as anything life has to offer.

This book is teaching you the early steps of finding your own voice. Do think of your writing as your voice, the way that ideas flow through you to others. Think about your "tone" as you write. People pick up "tone" and "accent" from others—ever notice yourself struggling in a conversation not to copy a strong accent? Or try this fun exercise—read Dr. Seuss aloud to some willing kid for a while, and then pick up a novel or textbook and read it to yourself. You'll probably find the singsong Seussian inflection bubbling inappropriately through. One lesson from that: Immerse yourself in the tone in which you want to write. To write academic papers, read a bunch. To write research reports, read them.

The other lesson to be had from thinking of writing as a voice in a conversation is to remember that writing is read as a voice is heard, that it exists in a meaningful way only when it is read. Share your writing—it improves with reading. Give a rough draft of a paper to a few friends and listen to their comments. Before you record that voice for posterity, before you submit it to an editor or to a grader, get it read by people who will let you know what they are hearing in it. We all sometimes say things we don't quite mean, express ourselves awkwardly or badly—and others can help us see that. I don't—even now, having written a respectable small shelf full of books—submit a piece of writing without having a few sets of friendly eyes go over it for me first.

Write. Live. Read and share. Join the conversation.

—Barbara Katz Rothman, PhD, is a professor of sociology at Baruch College and the Graduate School and University Center, City University of New York.

NOTES

1. Tyner-Mullings, Alia R. 2012. "Redefining Success: How CPESS Students Reached the Goals That Mattered." Pp. 137–65 in *Critical Small Schools: Beyond Privatization in New York City Educational Reform*, edited by Maria Hantzopoulos and Alia R. Tyner-Mullings. Charlotte, NC: Information Age Publishing.

2. DiPardo, Anne. 2000. "What a Little Hate Literature Will Do: 'Cultural Issues' and the Emotional Aspect of School Change." *Anthropology & Education Quarterly* 31(3):306–32.

3. Graham, Sheilah and Gerold Frank. 1958 [1974]. *Beloved Infidel: The Education of a Woman*. New York: Bantam Books.

CHAPTER 3

WRITING AND THE SEARCH FOR LITERATURE

Proposals, Library Research, and the Preparation of Literature

This chapter will address the different types of writing involved in the beginning stages of a research project. While writing is not always associated with the early stages of research, properly phrasing your search terms, research topics, and study interests will greatly aid you in the literature search process. This chapter will include developing a research topic and conducting library research, as well as the use of keywords and other strategies used for research both online and in the library. We will provide helpful hints and information on gathering references, reading, evaluating research, and using software to assist in the research and writing process. We also explain how to write from sources and how to properly attribute and include the work of other researchers in your own writing. In this chapter, we also review how to write outlines, summaries, and annotated bibliographies. These writing tools will help you stay organized and focused in preparing for a more formalized writing project. This chapter concludes with a discussion on organizing the literature, such as articles, books, and dissertations that you find to support your research. We begin with how to select and focus your research topic.

SELECTING A RESEARCH TOPIC

From start to finish, writing is an integral part of the research process. Most of us write down our thoughts and ideas, or brainstorm, to help us formulate our research projects and writing. Before you can begin a project, you first need to select a research topic. Your topic will generally be determined by why you are undertaking the project. If, for example, you are writing a course paper, it is likely that your topic will be based on the area addressed by the course—for instance, writing a research paper on racism for a course titled "Race and Ethnic Relations." However, if you are not writing a course paper and/or do not have an assigned topic, developing one on your own can seem challenging.

In selecting a topic, think about an Introduction to Sociology class. A topic or area within sociology likely seemed interesting to you. It might have been a theory or a particular study that caught your interest. For example, do you find yourself paying close attention, engaging in more conversation, and doing additional readings during the chapters pertaining to gender, deviance, or education? Most sociologists have at least three areas of focus or interest within sociology that we concentrate on and examine. If you look through your professor's curriculum vitae, or academic résumé, you will probably see that you can group your professor's publications and presentations into several similar topics within sociology. She may study one type of population, utilize the same methodology in most of her research, or focus on the same theories.

As an undergraduate, you may find that there is only one topic that has piqued your interest. Is there a discussion that strongly engaged you? Was there a personal story included in your textbook that you wanted to know more about? Does your professor have an area of expertise that you also find interesting? These could be a good start.

Generally, to select and develop a topic requires a few steps. The first step is to brainstorm and come up with the areas of interest to you in the field of sociology. You may also be able to combine your research interests into a topic and refine that topic so you can use it as the basis of your writing. Each step is examined below.

Brainstorming

The first major challenge new sociologists must face is figuring out what to study. This is a lot easier if you are writing a course paper or you have been assigned a topic. If you are selecting your own topic, the task can seem quite daunting and may feel overwhelming for a new researcher, as the field of sociology is quite broad. This is also one of the great things about sociology—we can study a variety of different aspects of society, from a variety of different theoretical and methodological perspectives. Below, we present four suggestions for places that will help you think about your topic.

American Sociological Association

One way to help you choose your topic is by looking up research that interests you in specific areas within sociology. One suggestion for doing this is to go to the American Sociological Association's website (www .asanet.org). The American Sociological Association (ASA) is an organization made up of more than 13,000 academics, researchers, and professionals who work to advance sociology as a discipline and who teach in academia or work for nonprofit and for-profit organizations and agencies. The ASA publishes journals and newsletters, and it organizes the largest annual sociology conference in the nation. Many of your professors are likely members of the ASA and it also welcomes student members. On the ASA website, the link labeled "Sections" will take you to the current list of sociology sections—smaller committees focused on specific areas or fields of study within sociology that are tasked with promoting research and interest in those areas. As of 2016, the ASA has 52 sections.[1]

Figure 3.1

Aging and the Life Course	International Migration
Alcohol, Drugs, and Tobacco	Inequality, Poverty, and Mobility
Altruism, Morality and Social Solidarity	Labor and Labor Movements
Animals and Society	Latina/o Sociology
Asia and Asian America	Law
Body and Embodiment	Marxist Sociology
Children and Youth	Mathematical Sociology
Collective Behavior & Social Movements	Medical Sociology
Communication, Information Technologies, and Media Sociology	Mental Health
Community and Urban Sociology	Methodology
Comparative and Historical Sociology	Organizations, Occupations, and Work
Consumers and Consumption	Peace, War, and Social Conflict
Crime, Law, and Deviance	Political Sociology
Culture	Population
Development	Race, Gender, and Class
Disability and Society	Racial and Ethnic Minorities

Economic Sociology	Rationality and Society
Education	Religion
Emotions	Science, Knowledge, and Technology
Environment and Technology	Sex and Gender
Ethnomethodology and Conversation Analysis	Sexualities
Evolution, Biology, and Society	Social Psychology
Family	Sociological Practice and Public Sociology
Global and Transnational Sociology	Teaching and Learning
History of Sociology	Theory
Human Rights	

Source: American Sociological Association. 2016. "Current Sections." Washington, DC: American Sociological Association. Retrieved March 3, 2016, http://www.asanet.org/sections/list.cfm.

There are more areas of sociology that people may be interested in that are not listed above, but for most of us, our interests fall within one or several of the categories listed. You can use this information in a couple of ways. First, if you already have a topic in mind, the sections may provide you some information on other related topics or authors to look for when researching your topics. If you do not have a topic, you will find that the sections present the issues that are examined by sociologists. Go through the list and see which topics interest you or what you may want to research further. Try to select at least three sections that contain your topics of interest.

News and Current Events

As an undergraduate sociologist, it is imperative that you keep up on current events. News stories can change every day, and we are constantly learning more about different aspects of our society. As a sociologist, you should be engaged in the world. Get a newspaper subscription. Read CNN.com, *The New York Times*, *The Boston Globe*, and/or *The Washington Post*. Since you can always find a newspaper to read online (typically for free), there really isn't any reason why you shouldn't be well versed in current events. What issues are timely or of interest to you? For example, obesity has become a major cause for concern in the country, and news outlets have focused on this epidemic.

Are you interested in obesity or other health issues? If so, you could look at the ASA sections and think about which sections are related and which might be helpful for narrowing your topic. You might want to conduct some research on the impact that obesity has on different populations.

Studying Yourself

As strange as this may sound, it is something that many sociologists do quite often. We are inherently interested in the social world, which is why we want to study it, but there are also many, often contested, aspects of our own lives or identities that fascinate us. Maybe you are a person of color and issues of race interest you. Maybe you are a man and men's issues are of concern to you. Maybe you observed something interesting going to the store in your neighborhood or walking to a friend's house. Think about the issues that fascinate you. Think about the aspects of your life or identity that you want to learn more about. For example, if your upbringing by a single mother interests you, then maybe you might want to write your paper on single parent families. Keep in mind that using yourself as an inspiration is not the same thing as writing about yourself. You need to find a broader topic that gives your topic some significance beyond whatever it has done for or to you. Writing a paper about how *your* high school made a positive impression on *you* is generally not acceptable for a sociological paper. Writing about how high schools that are structured like yours, or how specific components of your high school have an effect on a broad population (that may or may not include you), is more likely to be in line with the guidelines for your assignment.

Active Reading

Active reading is the process of reading to enhance your understanding of a topic or concept and it is discussed further in the previous chapter. However, active reading is not only useful for conducting research; it can also be useful in thinking about a topic. While you read for this or other classes or for your own enjoyment, keep note of what interests you. What do you think the authors did well? What could have been done better? Is there another perspective you think is missing? If you are reading an article on math education in urban schools and you think the article is missing the perspective of women, maybe that is an area of interest for you and you may want to think about studying this further.

You should also consider that any questions that you have after completing a reading or during a class discussion can generally be placed into a larger area of interest (and may also coincide with the ASA sections). It may be that you have a very specific question about an article you read—"can anyone be a professional athlete?" for example. Though this question in itself is not necessarily sociological, research on it could be found in several different sociological sections. You will likely need to specify "anyone" (see below for defining a population) and whether it is based on gender, race, age or class; there is an appropriate section in ASA. For "professional," you could be interested in Organizations, Occupations, and Work. Depending on your specific interest, you might find that the Body and Embodiment section might cover "athletes."

Now that you have selected your areas of interest, you may want to come up with ways to combine them into one research topic. While you might keep some areas separate for future research, you may find that combining your areas of interest leads to a more developed research topic. For example, what other kind of project could combine research interests within the areas of "Sex and Gender" and "Body and Embodiment" (as taken from the ASA sections list) into one research topic? One potential research topic could involve assessing gender differences in perceptions of the body.

Focusing Your Topic

Once you have a general topic based on your areas of interest, you will need to focus it. Sociologists tend to organize their research around larger demographic questions (e.g., race, class, gender, sexuality, religion, nationality). Will your topic pertain to race issues? Gender issues? And, if so, which issues in particular do you want to examine? Which gender, specifically, will you study? In what geographic area will you assess this issue? Will you focus your work on the United States, or will you study some issue pertaining to gender in another country? Does a particular age group interest you? Narrowing your topic to a particular population and location can help you to write a stronger research question as well as assisting with your search for articles.

The topic of gender differences and perceptions of the body, for instance, is much too broad. You will need to focus this topic in order to research and write about it effectively. What aspect of society influences or can be influenced by perceptions of the body? One aspect might be the media and their influence on perceptions of the body. Is that a lens you could use to examine your topic? Will you want to focus on women or on men or compare the two? Will you be looking at a particular age group or the differences between multiple age groups? What aspect of the media will you focus on? The more defined your topic is, the easier it will be for you to conduct your research. Ideally, your research question includes your topic of interest (which could be a social issue or a sociological issue or some combination of the two), a population or place, and some kind of relationship between them.

To help focus your topic, you may want to take a look at some review articles. These are articles written to provide academics with an overview of a particular field. Unlike a focused piece, a review article tries to incorporate all the main issues within that larger topic. A review article on the sociology of sports would include sections on the historical and current research on sports and sociology. This may cover issues of race, gender, sexuality, education, resources, deviance, and nationality. A review article can help focus your topic because it can give you the important issues within that topic. The journal *American Sociological Review* is one place to find such articles.

Once you have selected a topic and focused it, you should ask for advice from a classmate, professor, mentor, or advisor. If you are new to research, you should never select a topic to research and study without first seeking advice. Your professor likely knows more about the topic you chose than you do. She may have suggestions on how to focus your project or may already be aware of literature on this topic. This informed perspective could save you a lot of time and frustration.

SEARCHING FOR LITERATURE

Now that you have your research topic, it is time to begin researching the literature previously published on your topic. Your review of the literature will show you the existing work published on your topic, where it is lacking, and where it can be improved. The first place most academics go to begin this process is the library.

Your college or university library is the best place to start your search for literature. As we are sure you have noticed, there are several differences between your college's library and your local neighborhood public library. Although public libraries are great resources for high school students, they rarely provide access to databases that search through scholarly journal articles and other academic texts. Some cities, such as New York City, have what are known as research libraries. These libraries subscribe to social science and other scientific journals, as well books based on research reports and projects. However, chances are you will conduct most of your research at a campus library. Your college or university library has many resources that will help you conduct your research and write up your research report. These resources include databases, research librarians, interlibrary loan, and bibliographic software. Each will be described in more detail below.

School Library Databases

Hundreds of databases exist to help you search through books, articles, newspapers, research reports, dissertations, and theses. The databases you will have access to will vary depending on your institution's subscription plan. As sociologists, we have a number of databases that help us find sources on our topics. Some of the most popular databases include the following:

- Academic Search Complete
- Academic Search Premier
- Anthropology Plus
- Black Studies Center
- Contemporary Women's Issues
- Criminal Justice Abstracts
- Criminal Justice Periodicals in ProQuest
- Dissertations and Theses Global
- ERIC (via EBSCOhost)
- GenderWatch
- Inter-University Consortium for Political and Social Research (ICPSR)
- JSTOR
- LGBT Life with Full Text
- PAIS International
- POPLINE
- ProQuest Central
- ProQuest Research Collections
- ProQuest Social Science Journals
- PsychINFO
- Psychology and Behavioral Sciences Collection
- SAGE Journals Online
- Social Sciences Citation Index
- Social Science Research Network (SSRN)
- Social Services Abstract
- Sociological Abstracts in ProQuest
- Substance Abuse and Mental Health Data Archive
- Web of Science
- Women's Studies International

The nature of your project will also determine which database you examine. For example, if your project explores issues relating to education, you may want to focus your literature search on databases that specialize in research pertaining to education, such as ERIC.

Most databases allow you to search for journal articles, books, book reviews, and even newspaper articles by focusing on a number of fields. Databases also usually allow advanced searches that give you the option of three to five search fields. These fields often are separated by boxes that contain the Boolean search terms *and, or,* and *not.* These will help you refine your search if you are using more than one search term. For example, if you were conducting research on HIV/AIDS among heterosexual Latino men using the Sociological Abstracts database from ProQuest, you would focus on the terms *Latino, heterosexual,* and *HIV/AIDS.* You could separate the words by the terms *and, or,* and *not.* For example, you could search *Latino* and *HIV* or *AIDS*—which would include resources mentioning *Latino* and *HIV* or *Latino* and *AIDS*—and *heterosexual* not

Figure 3.2

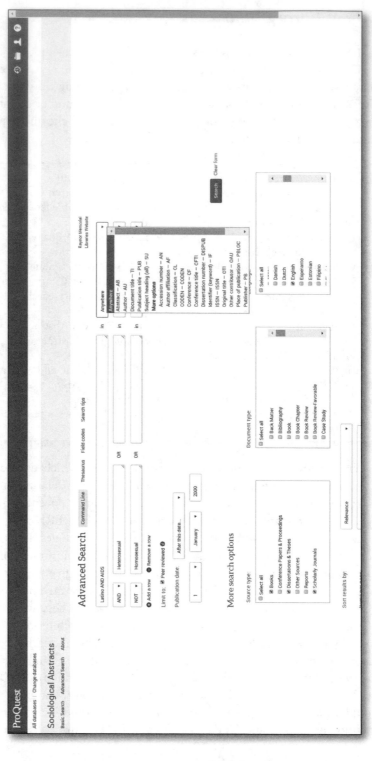

Source: www.proquest.com.

50

homosexual—which would add a focus only on the resources that include the term *heterosexual* and not *homosexual*. Some of the databases have implied Boolean searches, where entering any two terms implies an *and*.

The following fields are usually available to be included in your search:

Document Title—the title of the article or book.

Author—the author's name, usually with the last name first (e.g., "Smith" or "Smith, John"). Some databases will also allow you to search by author's first name or include the first name in the search. Others allow you to search only by last name.

Keywords—These are search terms or phrases that databases look for or filter out to find the appropriate resources for your project. The more appropriate or focused your keyword, the more likely you will find sources on your topic. Keywords are often the nouns and/ or adjectives in your thesis statement/question or overall topic. For example, if you were conducting research on infant mortality among Indian women, you would search keywords *India*, *women*, and *infant mortality*. Some databases will also allow you to see available keywords which you can use in your search.

Author Affiliation—This will allow you to search by the author's affiliation. For instance, if you knew that you wanted to seek out a researcher who worked at a particular think tank or research institute, you could instruct the database to filter for the author's affiliation (e.g., Ithaca College).

Journal Name—If you want to limit your search to a particular journal, you can search through the databases by journal name. If the journal is *American Journal of Sociology,* for example, you can simply type that name into the search, along with any other search terms, and the database will search for key terms and phrases within that particular journal. This is helpful if you have already found an article that may have information you can use and you want to find the journal that it came from so you can check on related articles. It can also be useful if you are looking for a review article on a topic and you want to search in journals that only publish reviews.

Publisher—This allows you search for information by publisher. For example, if you are looking for work by Oxford University Press, you can add this in the search criteria. This might be helpful when looking for literature from a specific region.

Date—You are also able to narrow your search by focusing your work within a particular time frame. The nature of your project will often determine the time frame you will need to focus on in your search and your professor might ask you to search within a particular date range. It is usually ideal to stick with research published within the past 10 years, as the data and the research are more recent and, thus, more likely to still be applicable to your project. An article exploring gender roles within the home that is published in 2016 will likely yield very different findings than will an article on the same topic published in 1966 or even 1986. Keep in mind that while there should not be more than a year between when an article is written and when it is published, a book can take three or more years to be published, so be certain to take even more caution with older books. As sociologists, we study society, and since society is constantly changing and evolving, our research and theories also evolve. As such, if your topic allows, searching for more recent articles will likely be more reliable. However, if your interest involves a historical perspective or changes over time, older documents are acceptable.

Scholarly/Peer-Reviewed Articles—This will allow you to narrow your search to only articles that are peer reviewed. Peer-reviewed articles and scholarly papers are reviewed by scholars in the field before being published, thus giving the work more credibility within academic circles. As will be explained further below, including newspaper or magazine articles in your research is often ill advised because they are not peer reviewed.

After you input your search words or phrases into the database's search engine, you will receive a number of results. If your search produces a book, you will be provided with the book's title, author's/editor's name, year of publication, place of publication, and the name of the publishing house. If your search produces a journal article or newspaper or magazine article, results will include the article's citation, including author's name, title and journal/magazine/newspaper name, date of publication, and issue and volume number so you can find the article, as well as the article's abstract or summary. Depending on the database and what journals your university subscribes to, you may also get a link that will bring you to the actual article online or will provide a PDF or the

HTML link to the article. This will allow you to get your article easily without physically going to the library, searching through the stacks for the journal and specific issue number, and photocopying it. If you are not provided with an option for obtaining the article, there may be options for receiving it from other sources, such as through your university's Interlibrary Loan, which will be described further in this chapter.

The number of search results you receive depends on how specific you are. Depending on your search terms, you can receive no results or thousands. If you find more than 50 articles on your topic, your search terms are too broad and should be better focused. As described above, this could include narrowing to a particular time frame, journal, or even gender of the group being researched. If you find you have too few articles or books, you should include a variety of search terms and phrases to increase the number of results. For example, if you are researching African American boys and school playgrounds in urban areas, you should consider that researchers may have used different words to categorize their research. You may want to search for the broader term *Black*[2], in addition to *African American*. You could also add *yards* to your search for *playgrounds* and *children* or *male* to your search for *boys*. Keep track of the different search terms used in the search fields and their results so you don't keep producing the same books, articles, and other literature in your search.

Additionally, you should also keep in mind that search terms can change over time. The word *Negro*, for example, was used before the 1980s to describe the group of people now often referred to as *African American* or *Black*. Some people who were born before that time may still refer to themselves in that way, and research conducted in the 1950s and 1960s may use this terminology. If you are looking for information on African Americans in previous time periods, considering the change in terms is important. Other terms that have changed over time include *special education, developmentally disabled, bilingual education*, and *adolescent*. Broadening a search may include being aware of or researching the terms themselves. Make sure to include the different variations in your notes on your search progress.

Resource/Research Librarian

These librarians work within college and university libraries, often in a research capacity, to aid faculty, students, and staff with library research and literature collection. Many research librarians specialize in particular areas of study, such as education, medicine, and the social sciences. These librarians serve as excellent resources, as they can help search for books and articles, as well as Internet sources. They can also help you come up with search terms and look for databases. Remember that these individuals have been trained and are paid to help you with your research. You should take advantage of their presence. You can typically make an appointment to meet with these librarians in person, and at some universities, you can also chat with research librarians via telephone or online. The notes that you recorded above can also be used to show the librarians what you have already done.

Interlibrary Loan

If you discover that your college's library does not have a particular book or article, before beginning the arduous task of searching for these sources on your own, find out if your school library participates in an Interlibrary Loan (ILL) consortium. Participation in the ILL will allow you access to sources such as books, journals, theses, and dissertations located at other libraries that participate in the consortium. The ILL consists of a consortium of libraries, typically university libraries, across the country. Not all university libraries are part of a consortium; however, most large universities and colleges provide this service to students, faculty, and staff. With most ILLs, you will need to complete a form with your name and contact information to order the text. Depending on how rare the book or article is, for example, you can receive the source any time from a few days to a few weeks. In the case of articles, many times they can simply be e-mailed to you as a PDF attachment or link.

Bibliographic Managing Software

Bibliographic Managing Software helps you keep track of and store your references. The three main bibliographic software packages are Zotero, RefWorks, and EndNote. These packages allow you to store an unlimited number of references, as well as a limited number of abstracts and notes in a file, often relating to the topic, for easier retrieval and reference. In fact, the software packages even create bibliographies for you in the correct citation style (e.g., ASA style or American Psychological Association style) for inclusion in the reference section of your paper. These software packages are quite similar, but there are select differences. Zotero is a free software program that can be downloaded from the Internet and is available for the Mac, Windows, and Linux operating systems. You will need to save the program to your computer to access your references and you may also be able to get an add-on for your browser to insert any sources you come across online. EndNote is available in two formats; the first is EndNote Web, which only requires Internet connection. The other format of EndNote is known simply as "EndNote" and requires downloading a program, much like Zotero. RefWorks is a web-based program, so you can access your references anywhere you have an Internet connection. These software packages also allow you to export your records so you can share references with other users of the software package, which aids in collaborating on research projects. Again, Zotero is a free software whereas EndNote and RefWorks are both subscription-based services that many universities pay for their students, so be sure to check with your university's library.

SELECTING APPROPRIATE LITERATURE

Not all literature is created equal. You want to be certain that the literature you use as resources on your topic is high quality and, importantly, reliable. Although scholars sometimes cite newspapers and magazines— usually because of their relevancy and timeliness—or theses or dissertations for more obscure topics, most scholars rely on articles published in scholarly journals and books as resources for their work.

Scholarly Journals

One of the most common and well-respected forms of sociological and academic writing consists of research reports or writings published in scholarly journals. Scholarly journals contain research reports or empirical studies based on original research, theoretical papers, and reviews of the literature, as well as review essays and book reviews. The purpose of these journals is to disseminate new knowledge about a particular area of study to other researchers interested in the topic who subscribe to these journals. A manuscript submitted for peer review is first reviewed by the editor to make sure it is appropriate for the journal. Once the submission goes through this initial review, it is then sent out to other scholars in the field so they can review the paper for reliability. If they deem the paper a well written and important contribution to the field, the paper is published.

Scholarly journals are small booklets of varying length; some are quite slim, 100 pages or so, while others can be a few hundred pages or more. Each journal issue contains varying numbers of articles or reviews. Some journals publish several issues a year, while others publish only one. There are also journals that focus on specialized topics and others that are more general.

Larger publishing companies, such as SAGE, or organizations and associations such as the ASA publish research journals. Departments within universities and colleges also sometimes publish journals. Some journals are published in print, and, increasingly, others are being published solely online. If you are ever unsure of whether or not a source is peer reviewed or comes from a scholarly journal, you can always search for the name of the publishing source in a search engine. As journals tend to use the volume number as an indication of years, you can also use the number to find out how long a journal has been in press.

Books

As social scientists, we want to make sure we select the proper books as resources. Most important, we must make sure the work is reliable. It is a little harder to verify the reliability of a book than of an article. Since most articles in scholarly journals are peer reviewed, you can be a little more certain that the article is reliable and a contribution to the field. However, this is not necessarily the case with books. Some books make excellent resources, but literally anyone can publish a book.

The type of research you conduct will likely determine the books you will need. Academic presses tend to publish the most reliable book information. There are a variety of academic presses; some are university presses, such as Harvard University Press, Oxford University Press, University of Minnesota Press, and University of Chicago Press. There are also academic presses that are not affiliated with a university, such as SAGE, Routledge, and Peter Lang. Additionally, there are popular presses, such as McGraw-Hill, that publish academic books. It is always important to note the publisher of the text and to use scholarly sources as your references.

Some books, known as edited volumes or anthologies, consist of a number of essays written by multiple authors that are compiled and edited by one or multiple editors. Anthologies provide excellent resources, as they often focus on more specialized topics and provide a variety of perspectives on the topic. You should check to see if there is an edited volume on your topic when you are beginning your research.

Although books are quite helpful as they provide a more thorough analysis of a particular subject, they are also quite time consuming to read and analyze. You can read a dozen articles with dozens of methodologies, theories, and findings in the same time it would take to read one book. As mentioned above, books also take longer to publish, and, therefore, the information within them is probably older than what you find in articles.

Reference Sections

The reference section or bibliography of a book or article lists the materials and literature referenced in the text. These reference sections potentially serve as great starting points for a literature search, as they already provide a list of materials on the research topic. The reference pages of dissertations and theses are especially helpful. Go through the references the authors cited in their text and you can see if there are any titles or works you may want to examine. This is particularly useful if you have an obscure topic or are having difficulty finding sources. You might also consider reverse-citation searches, which Google Scholar and JSTOR provide. These will allow you to find other sources that have cited the article you are reading. While examining an article's reference section exposes you to older articles, reverse-citation searches open up the field to newer articles. Looking through the references of the various essays included in an anthology can also be particularly helpful because, with all the articles contained in the collection, you may have access to hundreds of potential references on your topic. You don't have to reinvent the wheel while collecting references.

Encyclopedias

These provide great resources if you need an overview of an issue or the background story on a topic. As social scientists, we typically conduct research that is much more focused than what you would find in your typical encyclopedia entry. As useful as a traditional encyclopedia can be, it is not as helpful if you are interested in doing research, for example, on the impact of stigma on the lives of those with AIDS. There are a number of more focused encyclopedias that we use in the social sciences, such as the *Cultural Encyclopedia of the Body* and the *Encyclopedia of AIDS*. Encyclopedia entries often provide a list of the works referenced in the entry or further suggested readings on the topic.

Many general information encyclopedias, like the *Encyclopædia Britannica*, have gone online as, for publishers, editing and reprinting new volumes are expensive, particularly as new information about topics are consistently being produced. Additionally, fewer people purchase encyclopedias since they are expensive, they take up a lot of bookshelf space in the home, and we can now find out so much more information online.

Perhaps the most well known and used online encyclopedia is Wikipedia.org, which is an online encyclopedia of sorts that is produced in a variety of languages that can written and edited by people around the world. It is both a wiki and an encyclopedia. A wiki is a collaborative website that multiple people can create and edit. It is important to remember that, as anyone can write and edit pages, the material on Wikipedia is not always factual and as such, Wikipedia should be used as a reference to help spark interest in a topic or to find additional research and sources that have been verified. As an international wiki, information on random or obscure topics and people can often be found on Wikipedia. Also, since anyone can edit a page, if there are errors on a site, they are often reported and corrected. Many professors will not allow citations directly from Wikipedia. If you find some helpful material from Wikipedia for a research paper or on a project, you should follow the references on Wikipedia back to their original sources and, if they are reputable, cite those. This brings us to our discussion of other material you can find online.

Webpages

Many websites, like Wikipedia.org, contain valuable and reliable information, but many do not. Websites often contain false or biased information and, as such, do not always make suitable sources. There was once a time when professors would caution their students against or even forbid them from using online sources as references in their research papers and projects. As the nature of the Internet has changed, professors have come to realize that some websites can be valuable resources.

Not all websites are created equal. That is, not all webpages are reliable and appropriate for referencing in a course paper or professional report, so you should always cite webpages with caution. As anyone can create a *.com* webpage, we typically advise that such websites be fully researched before citation. With *.com* sites, it is important to check when the website was created and who or what organization or individual created it. Much of this information can be found by checking the page information with the menu on your web browser. You should consider whether the information adds or takes away from the webpage's reliability. American websites ending in *.gov, .edu,* or *.org* are usually more reliable—especially those ending in *.gov*, as they are government websites and contain

findings from government reports and documents. Websites ending in
.edu belong to educational institutions and are typically more reliable
sources (there are a few sites, like Academia.edu, that predate the relationship of .edu with an educational institution), as are *.org* websites, which
are often run by nonprofit organizations. However, *.org* is an open
domain that anyone can use, so it should also be fully vetted. Looking at
the domain name as a whole can also give you an indication of where the
information is coming from. A number of scholarly journals are published
only online, and those may be suitable sources because many of them are
peer reviewed. Keep in mind that some websites are more accurate than
others, and you should always be careful when using online sources.
Below, we present several questions you should ask yourself to help evaluate the potential reliability of a website's information.

- What is the webpage's focus?
- What is the webpage's content? Does it include research the author
  did herself? Is she reporting on a study or describing another article
  that explains a study? What were the methods used to conduct the
  research? Is it opinion or fact based? Does it present multiple perspectives or just one? What evidence is included?
- Is the webpage well written or does it contain many grammatical
  or spelling errors?
- Who created the webpage? Is it a single person, a group or a com-
  pany or organization?
- Is the author an expert on the issues addressed on the webpage?
- What are the author's qualifications?
- When was the website first created? Is it discussing recent informa-
  tion? Does its publication fit within the range of dates for your
  research?
- When was it last updated? Is it updated regularly?
- What sources and information does the webpage cite or reference?
- Can you verify the information? Can you find similar information
  from other sources?
- Can you contact the author?

To find out more about the webpage's author, you can always search
his name using a search engine such as Google.com. You can also look
up his institutional affiliations. In your research, you should look for
someone whose qualifications support the knowledge that he is sharing.
If the person is an engineer, he may not have expertise on racial discrimi-
nation in the school system. However, if you can find a bio or a curriculum vita (see Chapter 8), you may find that he has already published

several peer reviewed articles in reputable journals which means that experts in the field respect his knowledge. Additionally, to verify the content, you can search for the references cited on the webpage in library or online databases such as JSTOR or Google Scholar.

The advice that we provide in the rest of this book about writing can also be important in your evaluation of articles that you find online. If something is not well written, presents a biased opinion, and/or describes research that was conducted by talking to a few friends, that is not an article that you should cite in your research. In the end, you (with the help of your professor) will have to use your best judgment to determine if a webpage is suitable for use and if it will help enhance your research. If you are still not sure about an online source, ask your professor if you can submit a list of your references beforehand and she may be able to let you know which ones are or are not appropriate. You can also choose to focus your research on peer reviewed journals and books from academic presses which avoids some of these issues.

When to Stop

The number of references in an academic piece of writing can range from a few hundred, in a book manuscript, to one, in a summary. For a class assignment, your professor will likely give you a number of sources to include. This is not the total number of sources you should find, however. The first reference you open will not necessarily fit your topic or the perspective you are interested in. You may need to read or skim three, five, or even ten references before you find a reference that fits your paper, so you should become comfortable reading abstracts and be prepared to have a final reference list that does not include all the references you collected.

If your professor does not give you a particular number of references to cite in your reference section, you should not think that you can just include any amount. You should first ask her if there is a particular number you need to complete the assignment but, even if the reference requirements are open ended, you will still need to find multiple sources as evidence. You cannot make a point about a topic or provide evidence for a particular perspective based on what one author has said or done. You do not know if the one author is really knowledgeable, extremely uninformed, or working through some biases with her work. You want to find other authors who agree or disagree with her. You want to find others who make the same point in similar or different ways. In the ideal, you are looking through references until you reach a saturation point— when the authors are repeating what each other have said—for most assignments you are completing for a class, you want to make sure to have at least three.

How many more than three you have, depends on the type of writing you are working on. A literature review or annotated bibliography, for example, generally has a larger number of references as it contains a larger overarching issue—such as how race is portrayed on television—as well as several smaller ones—such as the different theories and/or archetypes found across different shows. For each topic in that example, you would want to have at least a couple of references that agree and/or disagree with your themes. These multiple references are important because they provide legitimacy to the point you are trying to make rather than it being only supported by one person or article. Especially if you select an article that says something controversial, one reference on a topic is never enough.

WRITING FROM SOURCES

Once you have selected the relevant literature for your project, the process of integrating these sources to help inform your research begins. You can incorporate the work of another author or a particular source through the use of summaries, paraphrasing, and direct quotes, and all this must be properly cited. Each discipline has an appropriate way of citing sources, and we will examine how this is done within sociology using the two most frequently used styles, ASA and American Psychological Association (APA). First, however, we will briefly discuss (and caution against) plagiarism.

Plagiarism

To *plagiarize* is "to steal and pass off (the ideas and words of another) as one's own" or "to use (another's production) without crediting the source."[3] This means if a writer uses the words, ideas, or language of another and is not authorized to do so (either under fair usage, which must be cited properly, or by permission), he is committing plagiarism. However, most plagiarism is not intentional but, rather, the result of sloppiness or disorganization. As we will show in several of our chapters, the writer may find that much of the information in the first few sections of his document will be cited information, as the early sections of a paper are where the research gathered has not yet come together to create the writer's own perspective. When something isn't cited, it is usually a known fact or the researcher's own contribution. If there is a question as to whether something should be cited, citing the work is always best. If you remember nothing else, remember this one rule about citations: Every piece of information that is not the writer's must be credited.

Plagiarizing is highly frowned upon in academia, as colleges and universities are in the business of producing knowledge. As a result, the consequences of plagiarism can range from a failing grade to expulsion from one's school or place of employment. Every institution has its own rules, definitions, and guidelines concerning citations and plagiarism. Rules regarding plagiarism can typically be found in the student handbook, the school guidebook, your class syllabus, and/or several other locations on a school's website.

Summary and Paraphrasing

There are several ways to organize and use the information the writer has extracted from academic sources. The first is through summarization. A summary overview is not a common assignment within sociology, but the most common place where a summary is used is in writing an abstract or the summation of a paper or study found at the beginning of a journal article or book chapter. Most other summary-type writing, such as an annotated bibliography, will focus on a particular theme or question and will not be a simple summary of the whole piece.

The more common use of a summary is found in paraphrasing or indirect quotes. Paraphrasing someone else's work is a way to synthesize various pieces of information. Here, the writer has the opportunity to summarize a particular idea or several ideas from one or multiple authors. As these are not the writer's original thoughts, even if the ideas have been put together in unique ways, they must be cited.

Initial quote:

"According to domestic and transnational polls on religious beliefs and commitment, 'American Blacks are, by some measures, the most religious people in the world.'"[4]

Possible paraphrasing:

Research indicates that African Americans are among the most religious racial/ethnic groups in the world (Pattillo-McCoy 1998).

Direct Quotes

Direct quotations are, as the name suggests, directly borrowed from the book or article and included in the writer's piece. The initial quote above is an example of a direct quote. The quote will either be no more than a few sentences—in which case, it can be set in line with the rest of the paragraph—or will be longer and set as a block quotation—that is, set off from the rest of the text in a manner that varies by discipline. In sociology (ASA format), four or more lines of text should be structured as block quotations, which are indented on both sides and single spaced. Short quotations always include quotation marks at the beginning and end as well as a citation, which in sociology is the author's last name, followed by the date, a colon, and the page number. Longer quotes also include citations but not quotation marks. Unlike paraphrasing, the citations for direct quotes must include page numbers.

The exact wording from the original writing should also be used in a direct quote. When it is necessary to edit, the writer must note that changes have been made through the use of ellipses (. . .)—which indicate missing words—or brackets ([ ])—which indicate changed words, when, for example, a personal pronoun must be changed or a word needs further explanation or translation.

Initial quote:

"The school was difficult for me. I really wanted a lot more than I was able to receive there. I felt I put my all into my work and didn't see the rewards" (Jenkins 2008:53).

Possible revision:

According to Jenkins, Jenna's "school was difficult for [her]. . . . [She] felt [she] put [her] all into [her] work and didn't see the rewards" (2008:53).

Below, we provide a passage and show how a direct quote, summary, and paraphrase can be written based on the passage.

"Yet in spite of this gender development, attitudes to female football supporters remain strikingly sexist. One man who witnessed women throwing bottles and punches at Fulham Broadway said female fans only wanted 'to watch Beckham's legs and marry Wayne Rooney.' A policeman regularly deployed at football grounds, who conceded that women were increasingly engaging in disorderly [behavior], rejected the idea that rowdy female fans could be serious about the sport. 'The girls are just trying to impress the boys, aren't they?' he said. 'They've had one too many Smirnoff Ices.'"[5]

(Continued)

(Continued)

Direct Quote	Summary	Paraphrase
According to Wake, many football fans believe that women are interested in the sport only to "watch Beckham's legs and marry Wayne Rooney" (Wake 2008:20).	The article describes the ways female fans of football (nee soccer) are still referred to in sexist ways. According to Wake, women who are fans of football are interested in it only because they connect with the players in a sexual way, believing that they have attractive bodies or are husband potential. Women may also find that interest in the sport attracts the attention of men. Overall, many men tend to look at female fandom with skepticism and, even when faced with female hooliganism, still see it as based on women's relationship with men and not their own interests (Wake 2008).	Researchers have found a lack of understanding of female fandom, such that men often believe women get involved because of their attraction to the players or to get attention from men (Wake 2008).

As illustrated in the above example, remember that when you refer to an author of an article or a book, you do not need to use the name of the article but simply the author's last name. Also, you do not need to keep saying, "he said"; let the audience know who "he" is by referring to the author's first and last name the first time you mention the article and the last name alone for each subsequent mention.

Integrating Quotes

Students often think the use of direct quotes adds legitimacy to their papers and therefore, will include as many as possible. While it is important to include evidence and quote people who support or argue against your hypothesis, the quotes that you include need to have a purpose. The reader is not necessarily going to know exactly why you included a quote, you must tell her. You need to introduce your quote using the author's name (see below for whether a date is appropriate) and provide some kind of transition from the previous sentence or paragraph. The quote should not be randomly inserted. It is part of the evidence for your paper so you will need to explain exactly why you used it. Especially if your quote is ambiguous, different readers may see different things or not know exactly how you are referencing the quote and so your text following or introducing the quote should provide that information.

In-Text Citations and References

Since ASA and APA are the styles most frequently used by sociologists, we will focus on those two styles in this chapter. However, it is always good to have a style guide on hand for more details and to keep abreast of changes in the citation styles when they occur. Each professional organization should have a hard copy of the style guide available for purchase on its website. Some of the organizations also provide access to free digital versions.

American Sociological Association Style

When you use direct quotes in ASA style, you incorporate short in-text quotations into the text of your paper and enclose them in double quotation marks. The accompanying citations are written in this format: ([author's last name] [year]:[page number]). If the quote is indirect or you are referring to the entire book, you do not need to include the page number. There is a space between the author's last name and the year but not between the year and the page number. If you include the author's name in explaining your quotation, you do not need to repeat the name in the parenthetical citation; likewise, if you include the year of publication with the author's name, you need not include it in the parentheses at the end of the quotation. In-text citations in these instances should precede the ending punctuation.

Finally, if one volume has more than two authors, you should include each author's last name (up to three names) with commas between them and an *and* before the last author name. For all subsequent citations for these authors, write only the first author's name and use *et al.* for the remaining authors. If a work has more than three authors, include only the first author's name and use *et al.* for the other authors in the first citation as well as in all subsequent citations. If you are citing multiple works within one set of parentheses, they can be ordered either alphabetically by the authors' last names or chronologically and should be separated by semicolons. However you decide, be sure that all your citations follow the same format.

As described above, block quotations, those of more than 40 words or 4 lines, should be indented with a space before and after the block. They are often single spaced. You should introduce the quotation with either a comma or a colon. In a block quotation, the in-text citation should follow the ending punctuation. If the author's name and the date are included in the quotation, in the parentheses, add a capital *P* for page, followed by a period and then the page number.

Figure 3.3

Citing the entire book:

- Garcia (2003) strongly agrees.

Citing one author—name not in text:

- "the issue with public health" (Garcia 2003:29)

Citing one author—name in text:

- As Julio Garcia suggests **[first and last name used on first mention; only LAST name used afterward]**, "the issue with public health is that time and again funding is often denied to the groups and organizations most in need" (2003:29).

Citing two authors—name not in text:

- (Lopez and Best 2010)

Citing three authors—names not in text:

- (Leon, Pace, and Chang 1999)
- After first citation: (Leon et al. 1999)

Citing four or more authors—names not in text:

- (Leblanc et al. 2010)

Citing multiple works by the same author—different years:

- (Pugh 2008; 2009)

Citing multiple works by the same author—same year:

- (McGruder 2009a; 2009b)

Citing multiple works—alphabetical order:

- (Bartley 1982; Carrillo 2000; Torres 1999)

Citing multiple works—chronological order:

- (Carrillo 2000; Torres 1999; Bartley 1982)

Citing a work with an unknown author:

Use the least amount of information needed to identify the reference in the reference list.

Citing a work with multiple editions:

If you are using a later edition of a volume than its original, place its earliest date in brackets first and then follow it with the date of the volume you used.

Citing a work with an unknown date:

Tyner (n.d.)

The heading for the reference section is generally a first-level heading. Each item should be double spaced and formatted as a hanging indent (first line is left justified; all subsequent lines are indented below it) and in title case. References should list all the articles, in alphabetical order, by author's last name. All authors' full first and last names should be included in the reference section (no *et al.* or initials, unless that is how they have referred to themselves in their document). For multiple works by the same author, list them in chronological order from oldest to newest. If an author has completed both solo work and multiauthored work that you have cited, include the solo work first, followed by the multiauthored work. Be sure that any index letters you use following the dates of works by the same author published in the same year match up with those used in the in-text citations. Even if you are planning on using another citation style, you may want to record all your information as if you are going to use ASA style. We may be biased but because ASA requires the full names of all the authors, it keeps you from having to search for this information later if you change citation styles.

Figure 3.4

Books, one author:
- Anyon, Jean. 1997. *Ghetto Schooling: A Political Economy of Urban Educational Reform.* New York: Teacher's College Press.

Books, multiple authors:
- Attewell, Paul and David E. Lavin. 2007. *Passing the Torch: Does Higher Education for the Disadvantaged Pay Off Across the Generations?* New York: Russell Sage Foundation.
- Bryk, Anthony S., Valerie E. Lee, and Peter B. Holland. 1993. *Catholic Schools and the Common Good.* Cambridge, MA: Harvard University Press.

Edited Volumes (entire):

If there is a volume or edition, it should be after the title and not italicized.
- Arum, Richard, Irenee R. Beattie, and Karly S. Ford. eds. 2011. *The Structure of Schooling.* 2nd ed. Thousand Oaks, CA: Pine Forge Press.

Edit volume (chapter):
- Coleman, James, Ernest Campbell, Carol Hobson, James McPartland, Alexander Mood, Frederick Weinfeld, and Robert York. 2011. "Equality of Educational Opportunity: The Coleman Report." Pp. 120–36 in *The Structure of Schooling,* 2nd ed., edited by R. Arum, I. R. Beattie, and K. S. Ford. Thousand Oaks, CA: Pine Forge Press.

(Continued)

Figure 3.4   (Continued))

Journal articles:

- Battle, Juan. 1997. "The Relative Effects of Married Versus Divorced Family Configuration and Socioeconomic Status on the Educational Achievement of African American Middle-Grade Students." *The Journal of Negro Education* 66(1): 29–42.

- Aguirre, B. E., Dennis Wenger, and Gabriela Vigo. 1998. "A Test of the Emergent Norm Theory of Collective Behavior." *Sociological Forum* 13(2): 301–20.

Journal article with DOI:

- Persell, Caroline Hodges, Kathryn M. Pfeiffer, and Ali Syed. 2008. "How Sociological Leaders Teach: Some Key Principles." *Teaching Sociology* 36(2):108–24. doi:10.1177/0092055X0803600202.

Articles from magazines or newspapers:

- Neergaard, Lauran. 2012. "Use of Condoms Stalls: CDC Issues Report on Teens' Sexual Behavior." *Milwaukee Journal Sentinel*, July 25, p. 3A.

Information posted on a website:

- Botsch, Carol Sears. 2000. "Septima Poinsette Clark." *USC Aiken*. Retrieved July 15, 2012. (http://usca.edu/aasc/clark.htm).

Blog posts:

- Lewis-McCoy, R. L'Heureux. 2012. "58 Years After Brown: More Separate, Less Equal." Uptown Notes Blog. Retrieved May 25, 2012. (http://www .uptownnotes.com/58-years-after-brown-more-seperate-less-equal//).

American Psychological Association Style

APA format is used for publications associated with the APA but also may be found in other disciplines and journals that sociologists might encounter, such as in the field of education. Some professors and sociological journals still accept or even prefer articles in APA format. For these reasons, we thought it was important to include a discussion of APA style in this volume.

When incorporated into the text of your paper, short in-text quotations in APA should be enclosed in double quotation marks. In-text citations of direct quotes in APA format are written in this format: ([author's last name], [year], p. [page number]). If the quote is indirect or you are referring to the entire book, you do not need to include the page number, but APA recommends it. There is a space between the comma after the author's last name and the year and before and after "p." Similar to ASA style, if the author's name is included in your explanation of the quotation, you do not need to repeat the name in the parenthetical citation, and if you include the year of publication with the author's name, it does not have to be included in the parentheses at the end of the quotation. Finally, if there is more than one author for one volume, you include each person's last name (up to five authors) with commas between them and an *&* before the last author. For all subsequent references to these authors, write only the first author's name and use *et al.* for the remaining authors. If a work has more than five authors, include only the first author's name and use *et al.* for the other authors in the first as well as subsequent references. If you are citing multiple works within one set of parentheses, they should be written in the same order they are listed in the references (i.e., alphabetical) and separated by a semicolon.

Block quotations, those of more than 40 words, should be indented half an inch. Most journals will also allow them to be single spaced. You should introduce the quotation with either a comma or a colon. The in-text citation should follow the ending punctuation.

Figure 3.5

Citing the entire book:

- Garcia (2003) strongly agrees.

Citing one author—name not in text:

- "the issue with public health" (Garcia, 2003, p. 29)

Citing one author—name in text:

- As Julio Garcia (2003) **[first and last name on first mention of the author; only LAST name afterward]** suggests, "The issue with public health is that time and again funding is often denied to the groups and organizations most in need" (p. 29).

Citing two authors—name not in text:

- (Lopez & Best, 2010)

Citing three to five authors—names not in text:

- (Leon, Pace, & Chang, 1999).
- After first reference: (Leon et al., 1999)

Citing six or more authors—names not in text:

- (Muhammad et al., 2009)

Citing multiple works by the same author—different years:

- (Pugh, 2008, 2009)

Citing multiple works by the same author—same year:

- (McGruder, 2009a, 2009b)

Citing multiple works by different authors—alphabetical order:

- (Bartley, 1982; Carrillo, 2000; Torres, 1999)

(Continued)

Figure 3.5 (Continued))

Citing a work by an unknown author:

You should use the title of the work in the body of the text or the first couple of words of the title in the parenthetical citation. Use the abbreviation *n.d.* if the date is unknown.

Citing a work with multiple editions:

If you are using a later edition of a volume than its original, place the original publication date first and then the date of the newer volume you used; separate the two dates with a backslash (e.g., 1970/1988).

Citing a work with an unknown date:

- Tyner (n .d.)

The reference heading should be centered at the top of a new page. Each item should be double spaced and formatted as a hanging indent. All major words in paper and journal titles should be capitalized, but titles of chapters, articles, books, and websites should be set in sentence case. References should be in alphabetical order by author's last name. You should use the authors' last names and first initials for all authors up to seven. If there are eight or more authors, follow the sixth name with three ellipsis points, and add the last author's name. If you have multiple works by the same author, list them in chronological order from oldest to newest. If an author has completed both multiauthored and solo works, include the solo works first, followed by the multiauthored works. Be sure the letters that follow the dates of works by the same author that were published in the same year match up with those used in the in-text citations. Books and journal titles should be italicized.

For online information, cite exactly as you would for the print version of the work. If the work is available only online, also include the URL.

PREPARING TO WRITE

Now that you have your topic and a pile of scholarly journal articles and books that you think will be helpful and inform your research topic, you are ready to begin organizing the literature so you can prepare yourself to write. The three forms of writing that will help you prepare your research are annotated bibliographies, proposals, and outlines.

Figure 3.6

Books, one author:

If there is a volume or edition, it should be placed in parentheses after the title and not italicized.

- Goffman, E. (1990). *The presentation of self in everyday life* (15th ed.). New York, NY: Penguin Books. (Original work published 1959)

Books, multiple authors:

- Atwell, P., & Lavin, D. E. (2007). *Passing the torch: Does higher education for the disadvantaged pay off across the generations?* New York, NY: Russell Sage Foundation.
- Bryk, A. S., Lee, V. E., & Holland, P. B. (1993). *Catholic schools and the common good.* Cambridge, MA: Harvard University Press.

Entire book with DOI:

- Author, A. A. (2006). *Title of work.* doi: XXXXXX.

Edited volumes (entire):

- Arum, R., Beattie, I. R., & Ford, K. S. (Eds.). (2011). *The structure of schooling* (2nd ed.). Thousand Oaks, CA: Pine Forge Press.

Edited volume (chapter):

- Coleman, J., Campbell, E., Hobson, C., McPartland, J., Mood, A., Weinfeld, F., & York, R. (2011). Equality of educational opportunity: The Coleman Report. In R. Arum, I. R. Beattie, & K. S. Ford (Eds.), *The structure of schooling* (2nd ed., pp. 120–136). Thousand Oaks, CA: Pine Forge Press.

Journal articles:

- Battle, J. (1997). The relative effects of married versus divorced family configuration and socioeconomic status on the educational achievement of African American middle-grade students. *Journal of Negro Education, 66*(1), 23–42.
- Aguirre, B. E., Wenger, D., & Vigo, G. (1998). A test of the emergent norm theory of collective behavior. *Sociological Forum, 13*(2), 301–320.

Journal article with DOI:

- Herbst-Damm, K. L., & Kulik, J. A. (2005). Volunteer support, marital status, and the survival times of terminally ill patients. *Health Psychology, 24*, 225–229. doi:10.1037/0278-6133.24.2.225

Articles from magazines or newspapers:

- Neergaard, L. (2012, July 25). Use of condoms stalls: CDC issues report on teens' sexual behavior. *Milwaukee Journal Sentinel*, p. 34.

Information poster on a website:

- Botsch, C. S. (2000). Septima Poinsette Clark. *USC Aiken.* Retrieved from https://www.usca.edu/aasc/clark/htm

Annotated Bibliographies

There are two different types of annotated bibliographies. In addition to what we will talk about in this chapter, there are also the annotated bibliographies written and published in research reports and journals to help other scholars ascertain the work in a particular field or area of study. This chapter will discuss those written by researchers in the beginning of the research process, as they help organize the literature on a specific topic.

An annotated bibliography is a list of articles, books, or other research that pertains to your topic, along with the bibliographic citation (generally written in ASA or APA format), a short description, and an evaluation/analysis. The analysis part is very important because it will help you construct your literature review when you write up your research report. Citations in annotated bibliographies are commonly listed in alphabetical order by the first author's last name and are analyzed one by one. However, instead of arranging this annotated bibliography in alphabetical order by author's last name, we would suggest arranging it by theme/concept. This can help you see where your research deficiencies may lie and will help you organize your topics.

Annotated bibliographies save a tremendous amount of time in the writing process, as they help you keep track of the literature you have and, therefore, you won't have to reread all the literature to remember how it relates to your research when you sit down to write it up. Also, if you plan on writing a literature review (see Chapter 5), arranging the annotated bibliography entries by theme will help you begin to organize your literature review.

The structure of the annotated bibliography typically consists of the following: an introductory paragraph; a series of annotations, including the citation of each source; and a concluding paragraph.

Introductory Paragraph

Many annotated bibliographies begin with an introductory paragraph that is about 150 to 250 words long, introducing the annotated bibliography as well as the literature. This paragraph should contain background information on your topic as well as the questions that interest you about the topic and an overview of what you learned from this particular body of literature. Why did you choose to include this literature in the annotated bibliography? Explain the overall themes you found in all the literature presented in the annotated bibliography.

Annotations

Each annotation should start with a full citation of the source, preferably in ASA or APA format. Annotations are generally concise. Each description should range from 150 to 250 words; excess words and phrases should be omitted. Remember, each annotation should be succinct and to the point.

Actual annotation styles can vary, but they generally begin with a brief summary of the article or book. Articles and books already contain summaries either at the beginning or the end of the piece. Your summary, however, should not focus on the whole piece but should pay particular attention to how the book or article relates to your research and your topic. It is important that your annotation is critical and explains the author's argument. Briefly explain how this research relates to, contributes to, or refutes what other scholars have found. This part is particularly important, as it will aid in the construction of your literature review. At the end of the annotation, you should include a few short sentences that explain how this particular work will contribute to your potential project or overall topic. The purpose of the annotation is not just to help you begin to think about the literature but, more important, to help you discover how it relates to your larger research topic.

Concluding Paragraph

After you have listed all your annotations, you should include a concluding paragraph that assesses what you have learned as a result of your literature search, as well as how you will use these resources. This, too, is typically 150 to 250 words long. Importantly, you should include a thesis statement, or what you propose to argue or research as a result of the literature you examined. Explain what research questions you now have and how this literature will aid you in your project. The concluding paragraph should help you form your research question based on your search topics. What has the literature, overall, said about your research topic, and what resulting research question do you now have? This question forms the basis for your project.

For example, if you are interested in exploring the influence of the media on the perceptions of body image for men, you will probably find a variety of sources covering topics such as the types of bodies that are promoted in the media, how body image issues manifest in young men, and the effects of media on body image. Based on your research, you will want to focus your topic into a concise research question. What aspects of the media do you want to focus on? Television? Magazines? Special interest shows or issues? In creating your annotated bibliography, were any of these underresearched, especially interesting to you, or not satisfactorily answered? Additionally, you may want to focus your sample of men by age. One research question resulting from your annotated bibliography could be, "How do teenage boys react to the depictions of the male body on exercise and weightlifting magazine covers?"

Research Proposal

Now that you have your annotated bibliography, or list of readings, and your research question, it is time to develop a research proposal and begin thinking about your thesis statement and/or hypothesis. As discussed in the previous chapter, a hypothesis is an early answer to the research question(s) you developed as a result of your literature search, and a thesis is developed after more extensive research has been conducted. As you focus your topic, think about how a sociologist might examine this issue. As sociology is the scientific study of society, you want to be certain that you examine your issue from a sociological perspective. Recall that a question such as this connects to at least two ASA sections—Body and Embodiment, and Communication, Information Technologies, and Media Sociology. You should begin this process by preliminarily answering your research question. For example, if your research question is,

"How do teenage boys react to the depictions of the male body on exercise and weightlifting magazine covers?"

a statement that answers this question could be,

"Depictions of the 'idealized' male body on weightlifting and exercise magazine covers have a negative influence on the body image of teen boys."

This statement could serve as the hypothesis, or the answer to the research question. To develop the hypothesis, you should first think about the purpose of your project and what you hope to accomplish as a result of your study. Based on your review of the literature, what do you expect to find? Although there could be a number of possible reactions to these depictions, you will need to work to focus your hypothesis so it is neither too broad nor too general. This will help guide you through the rest of the research process.

Writing a research proposal will help you think about the process of developing and proving your thesis statement. Undergraduate students are often required to write proposals prior to writing a research paper or a capstone project (see Chapter 5). Research proposals explain the proposed research and what it will entail. Proposals can be written for yourself as a reminder of what you plan on doing for your project, but they can also be written for professors and different agencies and organizations. Research proposals can vary in length depending on the size and nature of the intended project. Some could be as long as 20 pages, while others could be only 500 words. These proposals help prepare you for your project and keep you on track. Importantly, these proposals are handy in helping you articulate your project to a professor or colleague. Although the structure of research proposals may vary, they contain the following basic parts: an introduction to the problem or issue, background for the problem or issue, a description of the proposed research, and a list of references.

Introduction to the Problem or Issue

The issue is the problem you find, or expect to find, based on a particular research topic. If the topic is the economy, the issue may be the high unemployment rates found within minority communities. This introduction should introduce the reader to the issue. This may seem a bit confusing if you are writing a research proposal for yourself, but you may want to have your professors or colleagues read your proposal for their insight and feedback. An introduction that adequately and briefly introduces the issue should provide the necessary background information for readers. Explain what this problem or issue is and why you are interested in examining it.

Background to the Problem or Issue

Provide a background to the overall issue. Here, you will briefly explain how this issue became a problem. At the end of the description, state your thesis statement and explain how you came upon it. This may include explaining your research question(s) and the resulting hypothesis as well.

Description of Proposed Research

Explain how you plan on proving your thesis. You should have an idea in mind of what kind of data you plan on collecting and how you plan on gathering this data. You can also base this section on a review of the literature if you are not collecting your own data or analyzing secondary data. Describe the methodology you propose to utilize to explore your thesis statement. Given your time and resources, think about what methodology will be feasible so you can explore your thesis. If you are collecting your own data, you don't want to propose a methodology that is too costly or too difficult for you to conduct on your own. Also, think about what has been done before and how. When you look back at those other articles, or the annotated bibliographies you created from them, think about the methods they used. What did you think worked and did not work? Are there ways you could expand on or change their methodology? You will already have an idea of the different work on your topic, as you have conducted a review of the literature and have written about your overall findings within the literature in your annotated bibliography.

References

Provide a list of the key references that helped inform your research hypothesis and that you plan to cite in your research. You do not have to include all the references you plan to use in your project, but you should list the important ones in the area of study. Again, this will be helpful to your professors as they can see which research you have or have not cited. This way, they can provide some suggestions on intended literature.

Outline

Although not necessarily part of the research process, writing an outline is certainly part of the writing process. We are including a discussion of outlines in this chapter because, while outlining does not necessarily help you prepare your research, it does help you prepare to write, and lay out, your paper. Whether you are writing a research paper or literature review, an empirical research report, or a capstone project, an outline should always be part of the writing process. Like the proposal, an outline can help you organize your thoughts and ideas. Ideally, the outline should be written once all research is conducted, or once you are ready to write up your paper. However, some people write outlines as part of their process of thinking through the topic. In creating an outline, you will want to think about how you plan on breaking up your paper and what you plan to include in it. It will be easier if, before writing the outline, you already have an idea of the overall purpose of your paper and already know its structure as well as your intended format. Since there are a number of different types of papers and formats (see Chapter 5), this section will focus on a standard empirical paper (with the following sections: introduction, literature review, methods, results, discussion, conclusion) as an example.

Outlines follow the logical progression of a paper, as they contain some kind of summary of the introduction, the body of the paper, and the conclusion. They concisely state what will be included in each section of your paper and use numbers, letters, and/or Roman numerals to identify how the proposed project is broken up and its subheadings.

You can begin writing an outline in a number of ways. We suggest beginning by listing the sections you know you will include in your paper, organized in a logical order. These sections could also translate into subheadings in your final paper. This will serve as the basic skeleton of your outline. If you were to write an empirical paper, you would include the following sections:

I. Introduction
II. Literature Review
III. Methodology
IV. Results
V. Discussion
VI. Conclusion

Once you have the major headings, you can begin to flesh out the skeleton by listing what you plan to include within each section. Again, this keeps you organized and helps your paper follow a logical progression. Your outline should begin with an introduction to the essay or paper and your topic. Depending on the level of detail you want to include in your outline, you can also explain what specific topics you will address.

I. Introduction
    a. Introduction to topic
    b. Introduction to paper topic
    c. What you will actually discuss in your paper
       i. Issue 1 you will discuss
       ii. Issue 2 you will discuss

You can see that here the general structure is indicated by uppercase Roman numerals, while the details of the introduction use lowercase letters. When you further break down those details, you might use low-ercase Roman numerals, capital letters, numbers, and/or bullet points.

As you further develop the section on literature reviews, for example, you could list all the citations you plan to include in your paper.

I. Literature Review
    a. Introduction to the literature review
       i. Collins (2001); Smith and Rodriguez (1989)
    b. Literature on issue 1
       i. Chu (2011); Goodhand (2010); McGuire (1999)
    c. Literature on issue 2
       i. Keith (1961); Manning (2011)

The various sections of your outline can serve as subheadings as you transition from one topic to the next. Remember, outlines help keep you focused so you know what you will include in your paper and where you will include it. It is also helpful to show your developed outlines to a professor or colleague and ask her for feedback on what you should or should not include in your paper before you actually begin to write it.

After you have completed your library research, review of the literature, annotated bibliography, research proposal, and outline, and you have an understanding of how to cite the literature on your topic, you should have a clear picture of the paper you are about to create. You are then ready to begin the work on that construction. The next chapters in this text explore the various types of writing you are likely to encounter as a sociology student and scholar.

SUMMARY

This chapter examines the common writing styles often used in conducting library research and in the beginning stages of the writing process. We explored the following areas:

- Ways of developing research topics, such as brainstorming for topic ideas, combining areas of interest, and focusing research topics
- Conducting library research and the resources available in a typical university or research library
- How to select appropriate sources, such as books, refereed journals, encyclopedias, and websites

- How to avoid plagiarism and incorporate the proper citation styles into your text
- How to reference sources in ASA and APA formatting styles
- The different types of writing that help you develop a larger writing project, including annotated bibliographies, research proposals, and outlines

The following "Writing in Practice" piece was written by Cynthia W. Bruns. This essay explains her role as a reference librarian. It also provides advice on developing a research topic as well as conducting library research.

WRITING IN PRACTICE
by Cynthia W. Bruns

I am a reference and research librarian specializing in sociology. I have a master's degree in library and information science and a second master's in American studies. As a librarian, it is my job to select the sociology resources and the research databases that the library purchases and to instruct students in the process of effectively manipulating these databases. I work with sociology classes, the faculty, and individual students to assist in the process of discovering the literature of sociology and locating materials on the topics under investigation.

I work daily with research databases, and it is easy to forget that students do not automatically recognize the existence or effectiveness of these resources. I can recall that as a college freshman, I had my first experience with journal articles when I was given the assignment to read an article of my choice. The only parameter I was given was that the article could not come from a magazine. What a shocker! Even though I had attended an excellent high school, I had no idea that journals existed, or how to access one. I don't remember how I was able to locate that first journal article, but I must have, because I passed that class. I have focused on this snippet of a memory to remind me that students do not arrive at a university well versed in all aspects of research and often may not have any awareness of the breadth of quality research information available to them. This is where I can help.

I worked for a number of years as an instructional librarian after receiving my first master's. Assisting the students, I found that the most challenging aspect of researching a paper can be beginning the process.

(Continued)

(Continued)

Narrowing and focusing a research question is a stumbling block for many students and yet is a critical portion of the research process. A poorly chosen topic or a subject that does not interest the student can turn the research process into pure drudgery. Students have told me that when they meet with faculty members, they are generally directed to research a narrower and more focused topic. This is actually very good advice and will make the paper much easier to research and write.

As an instructional librarian, I had watched students struggle with choosing a topic. When I went back to school and started my second master's, I had the same challenges. I knew I was especially interested in researching the changing American attitude toward our environment as reflected in our outdoor recreation choices. However, I needed to turn my interest into a manageable question. Instead, I found myself exploring and reading everything on outdoor recreation and even more on environmental attitudes. First, I started with books, then moved into the popular press, then on to journal articles, and, eventually, started looking at legislation. As a result, I ended up with a great mishmash of everything. The more I read, the more avenues of inquiry opened up for me. It can be a hazard of my profession, having easy access to all types of information. I found it all very interesting but also quite distracting, as I was thoroughly mired in my topic. It was a problem because I was not making progress in producing a thesis. I needed to step back and do what I had always recommended to students: concentrate my research on a concise topic and then stick to my established constraints.

The best way for me to start focusing was to meet with my faculty advisor to discuss my research. I took advantage of the advisor's expertise in the discipline and listened carefully to the suggestions. The questions presented to me challenged some of my ideas, clarified my thoughts, and established the boundaries for my paper. First, I needed to limit my research by time. Therefore, I chose to work with the decade surrounding the first Earth Day in 1970. I also needed to narrow it to one particular type of outdoor recreation. I chose backpacking in the wilderness.

Further, I needed to start taking my own advice. I had always suggested that students start the research process by reading the introductory and background information on the overall topic to develop a global understanding of the larger issues involved. This was really necessary with an issue such as environmental attitudes. After doing so, I knew the dates of significant events, names of people involved, important legislation of the period, and I had an idea of the theoretical framework and a plan of where I was going with my research. I began to see overall patterns, learned the names of some researchers in the area, and found that I was much less likely to spend my research time on tangential issues. Finally, the research began to take shape. The paper would take many more hours of researching and writing; however, after focusing my time on a succinct subject matter, I was able to make effective progress toward completing my thesis and, eventually, was very pleased with the resulting paper.

—Ms. Cynthia W. Bruns, MA, is reference coordinator at Pollak Library, California State University, Fullerton.

NOTES

1. American Sociological Association. 2012. "Current Sections." Washington, DC: American Sociological Association. Retrieved March 22, 2012 from http://www.asanet.org/sections/list.cfm.

2. Although Black is not capitalized in the format of American Sociological Association, we capitalized it here as it, like African American, is used as the name of a category of people. It is distinct from the lowercase black, which indicates a color. It is why we similarly capitalize other racial categories.

3. *Merriam-Webster's Collegiate Dictionary.* 2012. 11th ed. Springfield, MA: Merriam-Webster.

4. Pattillo-McCoy, Mary. 1998. "Sweet Mothers and Gangbangers: Managing Crime in a Black Middle-Class Neighborhood." *Social Forces* 76:747–74.

5. Wake, Katie. 2008. "Uncivilising Influence." *New Statesman*, June 9, pp. 19–20.

CHAPTER 4

WRITING AND THE DATA COLLECTION PROCESS

Similar to the previous chapter, this chapter examines the writing that is part of your progress toward a final project. Chapter 3 examined secondary research—information you collect from work that others have completed. This chapter covers primary research—the work that you do to collect data from people and about cultures or institutions. Though it will not always be required, some class assignments require a research project, and to complete that project, you need to select and use a methodology.

We include this chapter here not to provide a complete overview of research methods but to explain to students who are conducting survey research, focus groups, or interviews, or recording fieldnotes the types of writing they will have to create and some strategies for completing them. This chapter will not replace a book or course on research methods; however, the writing you produce within the methods is an important aspect of writing for sociology, and to discuss it properly, we begin with some background on the selection and use of research methods.

RESEARCH ETHICS

Although the pursuit and dissemination of knowledge is important to researchers, it is also important to ensure that the participation of our human research subjects is voluntary and that participants are not placed at unnecessary risk throughout the duration of, or as a result of, our research. Therefore, before we are allowed to conduct research on human subjects, our proposed project must first be reviewed by a board of researchers and scientists known as an institutional review board, or IRB. IRBs are charged with ensuring that human study participants, or research subjects, are treated ethically and fairly, which entails informing participants of their ability to withdraw from the research study at any time for any reason and safeguarding against adverse effects on human participants.

The purpose of the IRB is to examine the proposed methodology, the handling of the participants' informed consent, the protection of confidentiality, whether there is a high amount of risk or controversy involved with the research, and, importantly, that any benefits associated with the research outweigh the potential hazards. IRBs also conduct annual reviews of research that has already been approved.

IRBs are made up of a minimum of five individuals with a variety of disciplinary perspectives. There is usually at least one social scientist on an IRB committee. All faculty, staff, and students affiliated with an institution that receives federal aid and where members are conducting original research on human research subjects are required to submit their work for review. As a student, your research is considered a classroom-based activity and it may be exempt. You will need to check with your professor or the IRB on your campus to find out. Also, if you want to be able to present your work outside of your institution or would like it to contribute to generalizable knowledge, you will need to go through the process. This means if you, as a student, plan to engage in original research on human research subjects, you will likely have to present your work to your institution's IRB.

To obtain IRB approval, you will first have to submit an IRB application describing your project. This application typically includes a consent form, sample interview questions or protocol, and the results of a test on the ethical treatment of participants that most institutions require you take. It will also ask for a summary of your research, generally written in a way that is clear to those not in the discipline. Not all IRB offices are the same, and, as such, not all IRB applications will be the same. However, since these offices must adhere to federal guidelines, IRB offices generally require the same information of all applications. They want to be sure that the researcher doesn't place her participants in harm's way and that if there is potential harm, participants are aware of it and of their right to withdraw from the study. Your professor will likely discuss research ethics with you in more detail but the most important thing to remember when you are collecting your data, whether or not you go through an IRB, is to be respectful of your respondents[1] and their information. This includes explaining your project to them, if appropriate, and protecting their data, if possible and necessary. For detailed information on research ethics, IRBs, and this process, please see *Writing for Emerging Sociologists*, Chapter 5.

METHOD WRITING

As mentioned previously in this book (see Chapter 3), your project will begin with a topic and library research on that topic. Once you have selected the topic of interest and formulated research questions, a hypothesis, and/or thesis, you must figure out exactly how you will collect the information you need to prove, disprove, or answer them. In sociology, we divide our research into the general categories of qualitative and quantitative methods. Some social scientists would also include experiments as a sociological category, but, as this is more common in psychology, we will not include it here.

Qualitative research allows for an in-depth analysis. Rather than gathering general information on a variety of different subjects, qualitative research tends to focus on a small sample of people and provides detailed information on that group. Qualitative methods are also useful if the research question or hypothesis is not immediately apparent and you would like to explore a particular issue, person, or location in more detail and allow the direction to emerge as the research progresses. This is called grounded research. Qualitative research generally involves speaking to, or collecting data on or from, several individuals, events, or aspects of culture. Whether you collect this information on an individual level or from groups of individuals at the same time, writing must occur to complete the work.

When we examine something quantitatively, we generally begin with one or several hypotheses about the relationship between two or more measureable characteristics (variables). Since quantitative research consists of placing individuals and their responses into certain predetermined categories and relies on statistical analysis, the samples are often much larger than those that would be collected through qualitative methods.

The type of method you choose for your research depends on the questions of interest to you. If you are interested in questions about how an organization is structured or how a society functions, you will probably focus on qualitative methods. If you want to look at a relationship between variables or understand how certain characteristics affect others, you are more likely to use quantitative methods.

When thinking about methodology, you also want to keep in mind what your plans are for the results. If you are trying to tell a story by sharing the lives of individuals, you will want to use qualitative methods. If your intention is to run a statistical analysis on your data to examine an interesting relationship, your responses are going to have to be closed-ended quantifiable data. You may also choose to employ a mixed-method approach, in which you might use quantitative research for a general perspective and qualitative for a more in-depth view.

QUESTIONS

Prior to composing your qualitative or quantitative questions, you must begin with your overall research question. As described in Chapter 3, your research question is what instructs you of the direction in which your research will go. Your research question must exist in the space between broad and narrow. If it would require you to read every article on the topic for the last 10 years across six different journals, it is too broad and will need to be narrowed. If it can be answered in one sentence, using well known facts or information from one source, it is too narrow for a research question but could possibly be used for one of your quantitative or qualitative questions.

While there is a distinct line between qualitative and quantitative methods, there is writing within both areas that includes asking questions of those who play a role in the group, society, or organization of interest. Therefore, this section of the chapter will discuss questions in general and then will specifically examine the ways questions differ depending on your method. Included in this examination are the types of questions used in surveys or questionnaires (generally quantitative) and interviews and focus groups (qualitative).

Preparation

Your assignment may include a required or suggested research methods (often some combination of both qualitative and quantitative methods) but if you enter this stage of your research unsure about which specific methods you will use, or which you will use for what purpose, you may want to begin by thinking about the types of questions you would like to answer with your research. Consider your

Figure 4.1

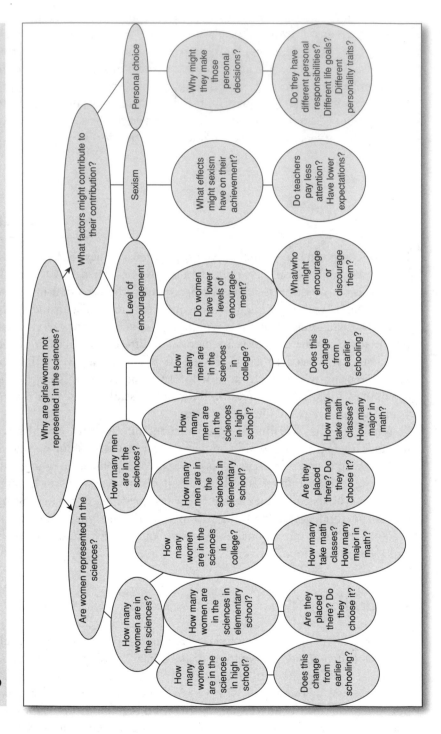

larger research questions or thesis. To answer those questions or address those ideas, what do you need to know? Try building a question tree. Start with your first question and ask yourself what information you need to answer it. Then, look at that second level of questions: What questions do you need to ask to answer them? As you work your way down to the roots of your question tree, continue to break down each question into more questions. Once you reach questions that can be answered with a simple "yes" or "no" (or another one-word response), you should stop.

Examine the terminal questions on your tree: Which questions can the participants of your research actually answer? Separate these questions from those you will need to research through secondary research, document analysis, observation, or other methods. For example, if you are interested in the high school graduation rate for New York City, asking random people in a survey is not going to give you that information. If you want the actual answer, you will need to find the official documents and cite information from them. If, on the other hand, you want to know if a respondent knows what the graduation rate is, this could be an interview or a survey question. You may find that some questions can be answered through multiple methods, and, if the resources are available, you should try as many of those methods as possible. This process is called triangulation, because you collect data through the use of different methods to attempt to find the true value. However, you must make sure that each method is answering the same question. In the above example, researching official documents will give you the answer to the question "What is the high school graduation rate for New York City?" Using the question on a survey or in an interview will give you the answer to the question "Do my respondents know the high school graduation rate for New York City?" The first question will give you a number as the answer, the second will give you a yes or a no.

Review the other questions in your tree. Is there any information that you need that is not covered by one of the questions in your tree? If so, it may be a question that you will have to look up rather than one you are asking. You generally do not want to ask your respondent one of your research questions. You will need to draw conclusions from what they say rather than having them answer the question at the top of the tree. If you ask the question at the top of the sample tree—why are women not represented in the sciences?—you are going to get their opinion, which may or may not be useful to you. If you ask the other questions, and do any additional secondary research, you will have the information to be able to draw a conclusion and/or form a hypothesis which may be more accurate than simply asking them your research question.

Next, you should take the questions that you categorized as interview or survey questions and organize them. Which questions deal with cause and effect? Which are exploring a setting, people, or organization? These will help you think about whether your research is qualitative, quantitative, or mixed. Additionally, once you create and refine your questions, you may find that they serve one method better than they do the others.

Before you can use these questions to gather information, you must operationalize your variables, which is the process of moving from the concepts that you want to find out to the actual questions that you are going to ask. The tree above is the beginning of that but before getting into the detail work of refining your questions, as described below, you should think about the objective of each question. What is the purpose of the question? How does it serve that purpose? If you haven't used the question-tree method, you might instead consider creating questions to serve particular objectives. For example, if your objective is to find out the effect of age on attitudes about technology, you will need to know how old your respondents are as well as their attitudes about technology.

Each of the "better" questions in Figure 4.2 focuses on technology in a different way and is more precise, as is the question about age. In writing your questions, you should carefully consider what you are

Figure 4.2

Objective:	Find out the effect of age on attitudes about technology	
Needed questions:	[age]	How old are you?
		What year were you born?
	[technology]	How do you feel about technology?
Better questions:	[age]	How old were you on your last birthday?
	[technology]	How useful is a cell phone in your daily life?
		How often do you use the Internet?
		How important are air conditioners in your community?

looking for and which questions best fill that need. Consider that in the first question, you are asking your respondents to define both *feel* and *technology*. Does a microwave count as technology? Or are you just referring to more recent technology? Does *feel* refer to their use, their dangers, or more general attitudes?

If you are attempting to conduct quantitative research, you will want your answers to be in an easily analyzable form. However, if you had an idea that age might lead to differing attitudes, for example, but you are unclear what exactly those attitudes might be, you may want to conduct a qualitative study with members of different age groups.

While the research we conduct in college does not always provide us the time to pretest our questions, if you have the time and the resources, pretesting is ideal. Even if you cannot fully pretest, trying out your questions on different types of people that you know and seeing whether their responses fit your goals can help you adjust your objectives and/or the questions that fulfill them. If you have friends in your class doing the same assignment, exchanging and answering each other's questions can help you to refine your work.

Understanding the specifics of the types of questions you might use to create survey, interview, and focus group instruments that fulfill your research needs is important. However, there are some general considerations you should take into account while writing your questions.

Categories of Questions

We have spoken generally about the different types of questions that tend to distinguish qualitative and quantitative methods. Closed questions ask respondents to select their answers from several choices. With closed questions, the form of the response is already determined. This is most useful for quantitative, especially survey, data since responses will have to be in a particular form for you to analyze them. Open-ended questions leave the form of the response up to the respondent. These questions provide the opportunity for unintended answers that can open up new avenues for research. For both interviews and focus groups, make sure you use open-ended questions. A question to which someone can respond with a couple of words will not give you quality interview data, and a survey would better serve your purposes. The types of answers you are interested in should help determine how you frame your questions.

Figure 4.3

[open-ended]	1. What is your impression of your children's school?

[closed-ended]	2. What is your impression of your children's school?

(1) Very positive   (2) Somewhat positive   (3) Neutral   (4) Somewhat negative   (5) Very negative

3. How would you rank your children's school?

(1) High quality   (2) Neutral   (3) Low quality

Each of the questions in Figure 4.3 will give you a slightly different answer. The second question, for example, is called a Likert item and asks you to choose a level of agreement or emotion on a scale generally made up of five or more options. Often, Likert-item questions are clumped together and, as a whole, create a Likert scale, which has been shown to be more representative of an attitude about a particular topic than is an individual question. For example, if you simply ask Question 2, you will get one answer. But if you break the question down as show in Figure 4.4, you can put this information together on a scale and gain a more detailed understanding of your respondent's overall attitude about the school.

With a question like a Likert item, you may also want to consider the utility of a neutral response. Without it, you will create a Likert item with a forced response, and, for this reason, many researchers will leave off the neutral option. Some respondents, when given the chance, will choose to remain neutral rather than taking a stand in one direction or another. However, others will skip a question if they feel none of the answers fit their true feelings. You should think deeply and talk to your professor about the meaning of a neutral answer before deciding whether to include or exclude it.

In addition to the general category of closed- or open-ended questions, other categorizations are used to organize questions. Demographic questions often start or end a survey or interview. These questions refer to facts about the respondents, their lives, or the context within which they are addressing your questions. These questions usually start or end research because they are considered easy questions. Someone can much more easily and quickly tell you his birthdate than tell you what he thinks is the most important part of his community. However, some demographic questions are considered more personal than others. For example, many see income as being quite personal. Age can also be

Figure 4.4

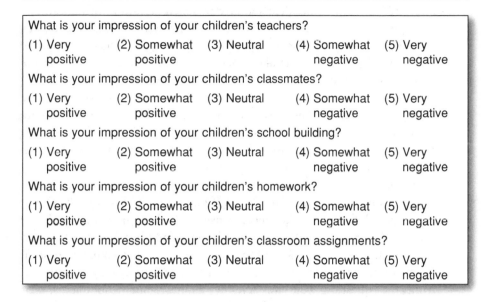

What is your impression of your children's teachers?

(1) Very positive (2) Somewhat positive (3) Neutral (4) Somewhat negative (5) Very negative

What is your impression of your children's classmates?

(1) Very positive (2) Somewhat positive (3) Neutral (4) Somewhat negative (5) Very negative

What is your impression of your children's school building?

(1) Very positive (2) Somewhat positive (3) Neutral (4) Somewhat negative (5) Very negative

What is your impression of your children's homework?

(1) Very positive (2) Somewhat positive (3) Neutral (4) Somewhat negative (5) Very negative

What is your impression of your children's classroom assignments?

(1) Very positive (2) Somewhat positive (3) Neutral (4) Somewhat negative (5) Very negative

a sensitive topic for respondents. Some researchers will move these questions to the end of the instrument because of their potential to make the respondent uncomfortable. Others will put them at the end because they are less important to their research and, if the respondent is not able to complete the survey, it would be better to miss those questions than those on the topic of interest. There are ways to ask some of these potentially sensitive demographic questions so that they are perceived as less personal. For example, asking respondents about social class and year of birth is considered less intrusive than asking about income and age. Be forewarned, however, that while year of birth will give you the respondent's age within a year, social scientists consider social class to be a subjective measure. Not everyone has the same idea of the boundaries of social class, and individuals may have political or personal reasons for placing themselves in one category or another. Most researchers will measure income in a range and, if you do, make sure you choose categories that make the most sense for your research.

Your research will also include other factual questions that are not demographic but may ask a respondent to calculate, recall, or even guess some information where there is a "right" answer. In these situations, you must recognize that you have to take your respondents' word on the accuracy of their answers. Your assumption is that they have answered the question to the best of their ability. It may also be that you are interested in your respondent's ability to recall certain information. For example, if you ask a parent for the name of her 6-year-old child's teacher, and the parent does not know (or gives you an incorrect name), that can tell you something about her relationship to the school. On the other hand, if you ask a teenager how many hours he spends watching television, an accurate response is more important, and you lack the ability to validate his response (except by asking his parents to estimate as well). As with demographic questions, you must rely on your respondent to know the answer but also recognize that he may not even realize he does not know it.

In asking factual questions, it is important to create questions that you believe your respondents can answer. If you intend to find out the size of the national debt, it makes more sense to look it up than to ask the average American. While some may know a number, few are likely to provide an accurate one. Recall that your objective for asking a question (even when the objective is in the form of a question) may be different from the question you are actually asking your respondents. For example, if you are interested in whether the average American knows what the national debt is, you might ask respondents to tell you what the debt is. You would not be asking them because you wanted the factual information but because you were interested in whether or not they knew the answer to the question. You should avoid using the survey as a way to collect facts about American government, of which your respondents may have limited knowledge.

In addition to factual questions, you can ask opinion questions. Often, this and the second category of factual questions overlap somewhat. Some may also rephrase factual questions in the form of an opinion. For example:

> Thinking about all the time you spend in communication with doctors, nurses, pharmacists, and other medical professionals, how many hours per week would you say you spend talking about your health with experts in the field?

This question is both attempting to collect factual information and recognizing that the information you collect is the respondent's opinion. Opinion questions are usually the meat of your work—be it qualitative or quantitative. Generally, you are trying to use your research to capture an attitude, an opinion, or a perspective from your respondents. You want to know how much they are willing to spend on a new stadium in their neighborhood or how they would define a quality television show. You want to know *how* people feel, *what* their opinion is, and *why* they think a certain way. It is through these types of questions that you find those answers.

Compound Questions

You should avoid compound questions at all costs. They come in several different forms. For example, consider this question:

Do you think your mayor is a good person and an effective politician?

If you believe both of those statements are true or false, then you can give a simple yes-or-no answer. But how do you answer if you believe your mayor is an effective politician but not a good person? The solution to this is to make sure that each question asks *one* and *only one* question. The compound question above would more accurately represent the opinions of your respondents if it were divided into two questions:

Do you think your mayor is a good person?

Do you think your mayor is an effective politician?

Keep in mind that both of these questions ask the respondent to use her own definitions of *good* and *effective*. If you wanted to use these questions, you would probably want to either define *effective* and *good* or break these two questions into even smaller questions that would represent a good person and an effective politician for you. For example:

Do you believe that your mayor cares about the environment?

Do you believe that your mayor always puts the welfare of your city's residents first?

Do you believe your mayor is organized?

Do you believe your mayor works hard?

Do you believe your mayor accomplishes her goals?

This similar example of a poorly worded question might lead respondents to give an answer to a question you did not intend to ask:

Is the mayor someone with whom you would like to go to a football game?

Consider what a "yes" answer actually means. It could mean that the mayor is someone you think would be fun to hang out with. It could also mean that you love football enough that you would go with anyone who asked. Maybe you think the mayor would pay and that would make it worth your effort. A "yes" answer to this question may not accurately provide the information you were hoping to gain from it. A better question either would refer to an activity you are sure the respondent finds enjoyable or would directly ask if the mayor seems like someone the respondent might want to spend time with at a social event.

Biased Questions

Also keep in mind that you do not want your questions to lead the respondent in one direction or another. Respondents can often feel as though the questions, even the opinion- or attitude-based ones, have a right or wrong answer. When you are acting as an interviewer or focus group moderator, a participant may try to read your face for evidence that he has said the right thing. With a survey instrument, he may try to use the questions that surround the question he is answering to find out if he is giving the "right" answers. The respondent may ask himself, is the person who wrote this survey asking the questions in favor of the mayor or opposed to him? Does she think this is a good educational policy or a bad one? If your questions are continually in support of a person or policy, your respondent will react to that slant. For example:

Do you believe that this mayor has done more good for the city than any other mayor?

Do you think that this mayor was justified in taking over the schools because he has done so much good work in other endeavors?

Instead, you should take the opinion out of these questions, break them down into multiple questions, or preface them with the person who holds that opinion. If you choose the second option, you should make sure to mix up your questions so the respondent does not know your perspective or what your previous research has already shown you. For the third option, explain that critics of the mayor have said particular things, and ask your respondent if he agrees; then tell your respondent that supporters have said other things, and ask him for his level of agreement. This should present a more balanced perspective to your respondent, which will give you more representative answers. Below are some examples of these different approaches:

How would you rank this mayor in terms of what he has done for the city?

How would you compare your mayor to previous mayors in this city?

Do you agree or disagree with the decision to grant the mayor control over the schools?

In an article published last week, a writer for the *Manhattan Times* said that this mayor has done more for the city than any other mayor in the last 50 years? Do you agree or disagree with this statement? Why?

Additionally, bias can sometimes come from the organizations, companies, or individuals conducting the research. Participating in a survey sponsored by a neighborhood organization that has helped gentrify a neighborhood may automatically get more favorable responses from one group and more negative reactions from another. If you can eliminate that kind of biased information from your research, it can allow your data to be less influenced by it.

Reliability

The reliability of a question refers to the results of the repeated use of the question. A reliable question elicits the same response from different people, and, therefore, any differences in the answers would be a result of differences between respondents. This is the type of question you want to create. If your questions are not reliable, you may be measuring something other than what you are interested in, such as your respondents' understanding of the question. Reliability cannot be completely ensured, but it can be maximized.

Writing clear, well-defined questions can increase reliability. Asking only one question at a time as well as including the other methods we suggest in this chapter can also help. This will increase the likelihood that all your respondents will understand the questions in the same way.

Personalizing questions on an interview or survey—such as including the number of children your respondent has in a question about the amount of money they spend on childcare or the college they went to when asking out their major—can also increase the reliability of your questions.

Validity

A valid question is one that asks the question you are trying to have answered. Reliable questions are also more likely to be valid. Additionally, asking the same question in several different ways can ensure that the structure of the question will not be a barrier between you and your research goals. While it may not have an immediately analyzable effect on your question, including a space for your respondents to explain their answers can help you see whether they are responding to the questions you are asking.

Question-Based Methods: Survey

A survey instrument is the survey document, whether on paper or in digital form (surveys viewed on a computer or other electronic device), that includes all the questions. In addition to the questions, you may provide specific instructions to introduce a question and/or methods for dealing with questions that do not apply to a particular respondent. Keep in mind that unless the survey is conducted online and a help option has been made available, the respondent has no one to whom she can go if she comes across something she does not understand. Any questions a respondent has must be answered by the survey, and any survey directions must be clear, as there is no one to explain problems or fix issues that might arise. If a respondent is confused and cannot reach the researcher when she has a question, she is likely to become frustrated and not complete the survey. As mentioned above, confusion can also lead to the respondent answering a question that you are not asking so clarity is very important.

As we discussed in the beginning of this chapter, survey questions are generally closed and use particular quantitative responses. Closed questions are those that include response categories. These refer to the different answer choices available to the respondent. The structure of the response categories is how we define the question's "level of measurement." At the "lowest" level, we have nominal questions. Nominal answer options give the respondent the choice of categories represented by text and/or nonmeaningful numbers.

When a question's answer choices have a particular order and can be organized from highest to lowest or smallest to largest, it is an ordinal question. However, the distances between the different categories for such a question are not necessarily the same, and you cannot perform mathematics on them.

Figure 4.5

What is your sex? ☐ Female ☐ Male	How would you categorize yourself? (Check all that apply.) ☐ White American ☐ Black American ☐ Latin@ ☐ Asian or Pacific Islander ☐ Native American ☐ Caribbean ☐ European ☐ African ☐ Other

Figure 4.6

What is your mother's highest level of education?

☐ Less than high school

☐ Some high school

☐ High school graduate

☐ Some college

☐ Associate/junior college degree

☐ Bachelor's degree

☐ Graduate degree (MA, PhD, JD, MD)

Please specify: _____

The distance between not entering high school (less than high school) and enrolling but not completing high school (some high school) and graduating from high school (high school graduate) and enrolling in but not finishing college (some college) are not the same. Levels of agreement (*strongly agree, agree, neither agree nor disagree, disagree, strongly disagree*) are another example of ordinal answer categories. While the order is meaningful, you cannot average *strongly agree* and *neither agree nor disagree* and come up with *agree*.

Figure 4.7

What was the first grade you spent at this school? (Check one.)

☐ 7th   ☐ 8th   ☐ 9th

☐ 10th   ☐ 11th   ☐ 12th

Finally, the categories of interval/ratio variables include numbers with values that can be placed in a meaningful order. A response category that represents the respondent's number of children as *1, 2, 3, 4,* and so on is interval/ratio. Someone with four children has twice as many children as someone with two.

While there are ways to treat nominal and ordinal data as interval/ratio, much of the higher-order statistical analyses use interval/ratio-level data. This should not preclude you from using data measured at the other levels, but it is something to keep in mind.

Instrument

Generally, a survey must begin by recording the permission of the respondent to conduct the research. If you have confirmed that you do not need IRB permission for your research, the survey questions will begin on the first page. Otherwise, the first page of your survey will have to be a copy or two of the consent form you created during your IRB proposal process (see *Writing for Emerging Sociologists*) and may include a contact information page.

If either of these forms are included, survey questions should begin on the following page, numbered consecutively, as should the instrument pages. Some surveys also include section headings so the respondent has a reference for what types of questions she will be responding to. For example, a survey that connects high school classroom environment to college experiences might use headings such as those shown in Figure 4.8.

Depending on the structure of your survey, you may also want to use introductory sentences as a road map to lead respondents through your survey's subsections. Your section headings can also fill that role. In addition, you could include other information before a question or section as a prompt to stimulate your respondents' recall and further explain the individual or group of questions. For example:

In thinking about all the time you spent in high school, how many hours in a typical week did you spend engaged in any of the following activities?

Figure 4.8

Demographic Information: This is where the respondent is asked about race, gender, age, location, family type, etc. Social science surveys generally include the big three variables (race, class, gender), since these categorizations can lead to some similarities in experience. It is important to know—whether subjectively or objectively—where people position themselves or are positioned by others. Choosing not to include these variables is a valid personal choice, but one must be prepared for the possible response from the academic community.

Pre-High School Experiences: Your respondent's life before entering high school could be important to your research. These questions might allow you to examine whether the effect on college experiences comes from high school or something previously in the respondent's life.

High School Classroom Environment: These are the questions that begin the essential aspects of your research. Here you would collect as many questions as possible that examine classroom environment from different perspectives. What are the aspects that make up classroom environment as you understand it? Teachers? Students? Paint or pictures on the walls? Clean desks? Private lockers or bins?

College Experiences: Similar to the previous section, these are the other questions that are important to answering your research questions. You should make sure to be clear in writing your questions and consider the connections between these and the previous questions. Are you looking for a change? Similarities? A new perspective? These should all be considered here.

Conclusion/Completion: This is not necessarily a heading in your instrument, as you might not have a concluding page/section. If you feel your respondents would not answer an income question before other questions, it might be included here. You may also have some concluding remarks about incentives, contact information, or where they could go to find out more information.

Since the respondent must be relied on to read and understand the instrument you have created, you should make sure to use language the respondent can understand. The above question could be rewritten if you believe your respondent may read or understand the question differently. For example:

When you think about all the time you spent in high school, how many hours a week did you spend doing any of these activities?

The format of your instrument should be consistent throughout your document. If you ask respondents to check boxes, you should not ask them to fill in circles or circle the correct response later. If you include open-ended questions, decide whether you will use a blank space or underlines, and continue to use that convention.

One place where the opinion on consistent questions may differ is the use of reversed questions. While switching the direction of a question (for example, placing strongly agree at the bottom of a scale after you have used it at the top of the scale in a different question) can help ensure that your respondent is reading your questions and not just filling out the same answer for each question, it can also confuse people who are legitimately trying to answer the questions. The best way to judge whether your respondents are reading the questions is to change the direction of the questions rather than the response categories. For example, instead of phrasing the statement this way:

My child's math teacher does a great job educating my children.

[strongly agree, agree, neither agree nor disagree, disagree, strongly disagree]

Use this statement:

My child's teacher does not do a good job teaching my children math.

[strongly agree, agree, neither agree nor disagree, disagree, strongly disagree]

If you do choose to reverse or change your response categories, be sure to let the respondent know that his level of agreement may be represented differently in those questions. You could write,

Please read carefully, as the response categories have changed.

A good survey also prepares for the possibility that some respondents will not need to answer some questions. To deal with this, we implement branching or skip techniques—rules that tell respondents which questions they should answer and which they should ignore. When you ask a respondent whether he has any children, his answer determines whether he should go on to answer questions about his children's ages or the schools they attend. Be sure that the skip instructions are clear and that page or question numbers accurately reflect the instrument. Explain both what the respondent should do if he does have children and what should happen if he does not.

Do you have children?

If so, please continue with Question 2.

If not, please continue the survey with Question 7 (Page 2).

Utilizing skip techniques saves respondents from reading through questions that do not apply to them. It streamlines the process and personalizes the survey to some extent.

Once you have created your instrument, you will use it to collect data, which you will then analyze. For college courses, this will usually be on paper. For more information on creating a digital instrument, refer to *Writing for Emerging Sociologists*. We will talk briefly about analysis following a discussion on the writing that occurs when working with qualitative methods.

Question-Based Methods: Focus Groups

As the name of the method suggests, focus groups are groups of people who focus on a particular aspect, definition, or understanding of an issue. Rather than concentrating on only one perspective, focus-group moderators (those who lead and organize focus groups and are most often also researchers on the project) are interested in a range of viewpoints, are trying to understand the difference between groups, or want to see how people interact around a particular topic. Focus groups are often used to pilot questions for other research or to assist in understanding the data already collected. Focus groups generally include fewer questions than would a survey or interview. Consider that, during a survey or interview, one individual answers each question. In a focus group, your hope is that one question will lead to a conversation with several participants. So a question that might take a single respondent 5 minutes to answer could take a focus group a half hour or more. For this reason, a 2-hour focus group can include as few as four but should not include more than 12 questions. Keep in mind the following characteristics of focus-group questions.

Open-Ended

First and foremost, like other qualitative methods, focus-group questions should be open-ended. If you ask your respondents a yes-or-no question, you will get a yes-or-no answer and discussion will be difficult.

You do not want to ask, "Do you like your job?" as respondents can immediately answer with a simple yes or no. Instead, think about what you are truly interested in discovering and what type of discussion would elicit that kind of response. You can find out whether your respondents like their jobs by asking them, "How do you feel about your job?" or "What do you enjoy about your job?" Both of these questions will probably give you the answer to the question, "Do you like your job?" but can also provide your research with additional information that could be invaluable even if unplanned.

Easy to Understand

Remember in writing your instrument that focus-group questions are meant to be spoken and are often spoken by someone other than the person who wrote them. Focus-group questions should be written in a way that is easy for the group to understand, as well as for the moderator to say. For example:

How would you categorize the relationship between your children and social networking websites?

This is a little wordy, and what you are trying to say may not necessarily be clear to your group. Instead, try writing the question in a more conversational manner using words that are familiar to your respondents. Also, remember that you are not asking for a single word or a quick sentence, you are trying to initiate a discussion. A prompt such as "Describe how your children use Instagram" might elicit more useful responses.

Instructive

Since focus groups usually include a moderator, you will also want to write clear instructions. If your focus group involves only answering questions, your directions to the moderator need only include the length of time for the entire group and, potentially, instructions for different types of questions. You may also want to include directions for the moderator to read to the group, which could include how long the focus group is going to last, how questions from participants will be handled, any issues regarding privacy and record keeping, and who will be in charge of making sure the conversation flows smoothly. Make sure to distinguish the focus-group creator's directions for the moderator from those directions intended for the entire group. Once you decide on a text format (bold, italics, underline) to indicate each type of direction, remain consistent throughout. Even if you are the moderator, these notes can be good as it may be difficult to think of what to say to introduce the project or a group of questions during a focus group rather than preparing before the group takes place.

You can also include more involved activities in a focus group, in which case you will need to write more detailed directions to introduce each activity. If you would like the group to rank problems in the neighborhood and come to some agreement, you will have to explain whether they are creating their own list of issues or you are giving them a predetermined list, as well as whether you want the group to agree on the most problematic or the least problematic issue. If you would like the group to draw a representation of their neighborhood, you may have to explain that they are allowed to use their imaginations and that artistic skills are not necessary.

Focus-Group Question Length

Focus-group questions should also be short. The amount of information the group has to remember should be limited. It is much better to ask your group a series of short questions than to create a question so long that your respondents have to take notes or ask you to repeat it. For example:

What do you see as the goals of education, and how good of a job do you feel the school your children attend has done in obtaining those goals?

This question could be divided into several smaller questions. First, you could ask a question about the goals of education. You could follow with questions about the school's role in reaching those goals and then whether it has been successful. As this series of questions draws on previous answers, you or the other moderators may want to jot down notes or write answers on poster board so the group can refer to them during the later questions. Be sure that writing notes for the group does not become a central activity, however. If you find that your respondents are pausing to wait for you to finish writing or adjusting their responses to fit your paper, you are likely writing too much. It may be a good idea to write their words down but keep them to the side, bringing them into the conversation only when you need them for later questions.

Using Why

While much of what makes sociology interesting is the questioning of the world through the word *why*, this question can be problematic in a focus group script. Consider these examples:

"Why did you do that?"

"Why did you think that was right?"

"Why don't you like that?"

These questions, while perfectly valid for understanding a situation, can come off as accusatory when used as a follow-up to a respondent's answer. For many respondents in a group setting, the question "Why?" leads them to feel that you are questioning the validity of what they just did or said or that you think they need to justify their behavior. Instead of using *why*, find other ways to ask the same question. Ask respondents to tell you more or explain further. You can even ask them to describe their motivations for a particular act or response.

Start on the Bright Side

Since a focus group relies so heavily on the interactions among members, it is important to keep the group feeling positive while they are still growing accustomed to one another. Therefore, in the beginning, you should try to phrase your questions in a positive manner so your respondents are encouraged to continue telling their stories. Once the group has established a rapport, they are more likely to be comfortable sharing the tough times with the group, especially if they believe they will get support from people going through similar problems.

Once you have created a list of questions (see the question tree), you should go through and edit them, ensuring you have followed all the guidelines in this chapter and are serving the purpose of your research. This will likely include the winnowing down of a long list of questions into only a few. This final list will then become the basis of your focus-group script.

Creating the Script

Your focus-group script should begin with a descriptive title and a number—for example, Math Education (#1). In this way, you can distinguish the focus-group scripts on different topics from one another, as well as from earlier drafts or sessions. You should also include a quick note that gives some indication of the amount of time needed for the entire session and whether there will be a break. It is also helpful to the moderator, or to you, to include a sentence or two reminding about the overall purpose of the focus group. What are the questions you are hoping to answer? What information are you trying to access?

Before you move into questions, you should include a short introduction for the moderator that introduces her as well as the project or class. For example:

> Good afternoon, everyone. My name is Jiani, and I am a student at the University of New York. We are conducting a study on workplace environments. We hope that the research conducted here can lead to changes in employment for many Americans. This is a safe space. For this work to be effective, we ask that you be as honest as possible. This session will be recorded, but your names will not be used in any publications created from this focus group. The whole process should take about 2 hours.

A large part of what makes a focus group work is the group members' interactions with one another and with the moderator. It is therefore helpful to build your questions gradually toward the main goals of your research. By working your way through different types of questions, you should be able to create a good rapport among members of your group.

Opener

To create a comfortable environment for your focus-group participants, you should start with some opener questions. The opener is an opportunity for you and your respondents to get comfortable with each other and for you to begin to hear everyone's voices. However, the development of animosity between group members is also a risk in the beginning. During this time, you should ask people to talk about factual information rather than going in depth about feelings, explanations, and memories. Learning a little about the group and allowing the respondents to connect based on their commonalities is the ideal product of the opener. As previously mentioned, questions about age, income, religion, or prestige can be problematic and can lead to jealousies or biases. These questions, if needed for your work, may be better answered by a questionnaire or later in the process. On other occasions, these questions may be more appropriate. If you have a relatively homogenous group, some of those types of opener questions will be less likely to cause problems.

Think of the opener as that "get-to-know-you" task a professor might have had you do on the first day of class. You were not necessarily expected to provide detailed information about your life. Instead, your professor asked for your name, year (e.g., sophomore, junior), major or area of expertise, and maybe something interesting about yourself. This task does not require a lot of thought or opinion but provides your professor with some information about you, and it works similarly for the focus group participants and moderator.

Introduction

As distinct from the opener, the questions in the introduction section are meant to get the group comfortable with the topic of your research. If you are interested in problems in public schools, you might begin this section by asking about what education means to the respondents or by asking them to describe the daily schedules of their school-age children. If you are interested in their negative experiences with particular data analysis software, your introductory section might include questions on how they understand the software: What does it do? What is it most used for? What do they know about the other software that they do not use?

Primary Questions

These questions are the essential part of your research. This is where you get to the primary focus of the group. The majority of your time and energy should be put into both writing these questions and having your focus group answer them. The script should indicate which questions are the primary questions so the moderator knows how much attention should be paid to them. These questions should represent the essential parts of your research.

Conclusion

Finally, you may want to include a couple of questions at the end to conclude the group. You might simply ask your respondents if you have forgotten something or if they have any questions. You might also consider asking for a final evaluation or conclusion of the topic or group.

Question-Based Methods: Interviews

The basis of good qualitative research is good interview questions. To collect the data you are interested in and to elicit the information you require from your respondents, you need to write quality interview questions and be, or train, a good interviewer. We will not discuss the training of interviewers here, as that is outside this book's scope, but we will examine the creation of your interview instrument.

Informal or Unstructured Interviews

The first decision to be made is how structured your interview will be. For an unstructured interview, you should begin with broad or general questions to generate responses you can build upon. Unstructured interviews are most often used as part of a larger ethnography, as they allow the respondent and the context to dictate the frame of the interview. Unstructured means you are going into the interview with fewer prepared questions and you allow the interaction between the interviewer and the respondent to determine the follow-up questions.

Informal or unstructured interviews are difficult to do well. If you go into your interview looking for particular answers, this format may not be the best one for you. However, it can be much easier to conduct as compared to the other types. The best way for an informal interview to occur is during the course of a conversation. It provides a comfortable, safe environment for respondents to tell you about themselves and their lives while providing you with valuable information.

Generally, an informal interview will occur early in your research process. At this point, you are trying to understand the unique perspectives of your respondents. If, for example, you are interested in charter schools, your first unstructured interview might consist of a walk with a teacher or student around a charter school. You would take note of what she found important, what she avoided, and what she returned to, either physically or in conversation.

Because of the informal nature of the interview, there is not a lot of writing to be done beforehand. For the most part, your respondent leads you through the conversation. However, you may have some general questions you are interested in trying to weave into the conversation. Early in the process, these questions are probably "survey" questions— meaning a general overview rather than a survey instrument—where you ask informants for a "tour" of their world (e.g., "Show me your school"; "What does your neighborhood look like?"). Later in the process, the questions become more specific—focusing on particular structures, people, or ideas.

It is important to remember not to force the informal interview. An interview is not the same as a conversation, as you go into it with at least a vague questioning scope, but you should do your best to allow your questions to emerge naturally. Part of this is being aware of the context. If, in the course of your tour around the charter school, your respondent has a negative reaction to entering an algebra class, that will likely be a good time to ask your questions about math education at the school. If you are sitting down to enjoy lunch, your questions about the nutrition of the lunch program will make a smooth transition.

Finally, similar to focus groups, you should begin your informal interview with general questions before moving on to more personal ones. Ethnography works only when you build a strong relationship with your respondents—"rapport"—and jumping right into extremely personal information can block that relationship from forming. Wait for the invitation to delve deeper into their lives, and then move slowly and cautiously.

Structured Interviews

As an interviewer in college, you will likely start out with a structured interview. The difference between structured and unstructured interviews is similar to the difference between interviews and surveys. While surveys ask respondents to choose from a predetermined set of answer categories, a structured interview asks respondents to answer a predetermined set of questions. An interview provides more freedom in responses than a survey does, and an unstructured interview provides that freedom in the questions asked.

For many researchers, the biggest problem with the unstructured interview is that it is often unreliable (see above) because each interview is different and built from each respondent's answers to her or his particular set of questions. Reliability is more important in statistics, as it is needed for accurate analyses, but is still considered with interviews. Structured interviews have a premade interview frame, which ensures that each respondent will answer the same questions and allows for comparability.

In ethnography, you would most likely use structured interviews as you moved further into your research. Specific questions are more likely to develop as you work with your respondents and learn more about their worlds. If you are using interviews as their own methodology or as a companion to surveys, structured interviews may be ongoing throughout the research.

Similar to the focus group, if you are not doing the interviews yourself, you should include directions for your interviewers as well as instructions to read to your respondents. When you begin a new topic in your interview, it is beneficial to explain the purpose the next group of questions will serve. For example:

These next questions will address your attitudes about mathematics education.

Interviews should also begin with introductory questions. As mentioned previously, these could be demographic questions covering age, race, or location. Income, again, is a question many respondents do not feel comfortable answering and, even if other demographic questions are not, is often placed near the end of the instrument.

Semi-Structured Interviews

A semi-structured interview combines the freedom and adaptability of an informal interview with the organization of a structured interview. In preparing a semi-structured interview, you should begin the same way you would for a structured interview. The difference lies in your ability to be flexible and change, modify, or add questions as needed. In a structured interview, one of your goals is to ensure that each respondent is given the same interview instrument and that any potential interviewer effect is controlled for. With a semi-structured interview, you recognize that each situation is different and some people may require further information, a rephrasing of the questions, or something else entirely. Semi-structured interviews provide a place for that.

Semi-structured interviews are often conducted after informal interviews because the interviewer has developed a few particular questions from observations or informal interviews but may still have some information that has not been revealed. Respondents engaging in a semi-structured interview are able to elaborate and discuss things that are perhaps only tangentially related to the questions, which would not be allowed in a structured interview.

OBSERVATION

Rather than the question/answer format of the methods discussed above, fieldnotes are, very simply, your observations of a place, area, person, or interaction. Fieldnotes, like the unstructured interview, are most commonly associated with the larger method of ethnography but may also be created through the observation that might be conducted when scouting a location for research, getting some background information on an event, or doing a class assignment for a methods class.

Fieldnotes have a built-in scaffolding process leading to the final product (usually the excerpts included in your paper, report, thesis, or dissertation). The process often begins with jottings or scratch notes. These are quick notes you take while on the scene. This is followed by the expansion of these notes, which should occur as soon as possible after the jottings to ensure little data is lost. Finally, the "final" fieldnotes are written.

Reflections and analyses of the data may happen concurrently with jottings, may occur during the expansion of the fieldnotes, or may be done as analysis through the creation of themes and collections of thoughts, images, and documents. Although some researchers publish or make their jottings or fieldnotes available, fieldnotes generally act as data and are not a published product in themselves. However, if you are conducting research for an organization or company, it may require the submission of both your fieldnotes and your work that incorporates them.

What to Write

The purpose of fieldnotes is to capture a detailed written "video" of a scene, accompanied by your own external monologue or your internal voice-over. You want to depict the feel of the scene on a paper and share it with your audience. Anyone who reads your notes or, more likely, the excerpts included in papers, articles, or books, should feel as though they are there—they should see the people and places you describe and hear the conversations you record.

Your fieldnotes should be filled with thick description. Rather than simply saying the neighborhood is suburban, describe what you see that leads you to that conclusion. Perhaps you know that the city of White Plains is a suburb of New York City. You can begin by noting that information, but you also need to include a description of how it is illustrated in front of you. Are there single-family houses? Neatly trimmed grass? Children playing outside in yards? Individual garages? What in your observations led you to the suburban classification?

The purpose of your fieldnotes is not just to describe how an area might be categorized as wealthy or poor, suburban or rural but also to paint a picture of where you are, and where your informants and respondents are. What does the neighborhood look like? Are there parks? Stores? Apartments? Houses? What is the weather like? How does it affect the environment? What time of day is it? What happens in this neighborhood at this time of day? What might you have expected to happen that is not happening? Do you notice particular sounds or smells? Some researchers take a moment to close their eyes and "get a feel" for the place before taking notes.

Thick description does not end with the setting. Your jottings and eventually your fieldnotes should also include descriptions of the people in the setting. You want to notice how people interact with each other or avoid interactions with each other. What are the community members saying to each other? What gestures are they sharing or hiding from each other? What is the context within which they are interacting? All this information provides a vivid image of where you are, which is ripe for your analysis but also serves as the evidence that brings your readers to the people you are studying in a way that other methods may not.

Fieldnotes also can include conversations or informal interviews that you have with respondents. Accurate representations of their words are important. If you change their vocabulary or the order of their words, you are changing their meaning. You will need to be careful in transcribing your conversations with others, and if recording is not possible, you will likely need to take detailed notes of what respondents are saying. Make sure also to take note of your respondents' body language and other reactions to your questions or their answers.

How to Write

The actual writing of fieldnotes eventually becomes a matter of personal preference. You will know how much you can write down without disrupting the scene, how much you need to write to remember it later, how quickly you need to flesh out your notes, and even what types of notes you need to take.

Jottings

For many, the notes taken in the field are distinct from the eventual product. You have only so much time in a community, household, or organization to take notes, and every moment you are looking down at your notebook, computer, smartphone, or tablet is time you are missing something occurring in front of you. Obviously, you cannot be expected to write nothing and remember everything. Instead, you have to teach yourself to take quick notes that will remind you of what you didn't have time to take down in full. Some of the strategies on note-taking in Chapter 2 may be useful.

You will be recording several types of information in your notes, and you will want to distinguish among them. You should begin by indicating time, place, and date. You may want to add a title, the number of the observation, and the name of the observer if you will have multiple people or multiple observations at a particular site. Some people put this at the top of the first page as a header, while others might use the title page format and place it on a separate page.

Setting descriptions are one type of data you will collect in your fieldnotes. These are descriptions of the community, people, and activities. If you think of this in terms of a play, movie, or television script, this would be the piece that tells you how to create the scene or the background action. The setting should include the place, as described above, but also where in the scene the people and whether they are moving, standing still, or something else.

The content of the notes can also include more personal descriptions. More often, this is where you describe the conversations and activities people participate in. You will likely want to create codes for yourself to indicate the people you have observed or interacted with so you can separate out different people's behaviors and speech. You should also skip lines between different people and/or activities to make it easier to distinguish them from each other. In addition, your notes can include other information you might have gained from interviews or conversations about what you are observing.

Finally, you might also record the less objective reflections. These are the ideas you have about what you are observing. While much of this will happen as you are rereading or rewriting your notes, there may be a few reflections you make on the spot that you would like to record. You will want to make sure your reflections and analyses are distinguishable from your observations. When you incorporate your notes into your final document, your reflections are often written within the body of the text, while your observations are slightly offset. Your reflections should also include any particular effect you, as the researcher, might have had on the environment. You will not always be able to tell what your effect is, especially if you have no comparison, but other times, your impact may be easier to discern. Additionally, if questions arise or your observations contradict or change previous conclusions, you may want to include that in your reflections as well.

How you choose to distinguish or separate these types of jottings is up to you. You might want to put them on separate pieces of paper or in separate files. You could also divide your paper horizontally or vertically so each type has its own location on the page. What is important is that when you read it later (or when someone else reads it), you are able to recognize each element.

Fieldnotes

For some, the jottings are just an earlier draft of the fieldnotes. For others, these are two separate processes. Those who separate the two consider the process of creating fieldnotes to also be a process of synthesizing the jottings with additional reflections, ideas, observations, and analyses you wrote down during your note-taking session. You might

also find that you have a gut feeling about something or a general overview of a situation. Some of these will remain in your head for years,
separate from what goes down on paper, but you will want to include
others to ensure that your fieldnotes are as complete a representation of
the field as possible. Since your notes are a shorthand version of what
you observed, part of what you are writing is a more fleshed-out version
of your notes. In addition to this, you will find that your notes will
remind you of things you had forgotten or misunderstood.

The transition from jottings to fieldnotes should happen as quickly after
"leaving the field" as possible. You will know how much time is too much,
but we would suggest not leaving it for more than 24 hours and not sleep-
ing before writing it up. If you wait too long, you will find that data will
be lost, as you will not be able to remember what your symbols mean or
many of the thoughts that were important to understanding your jottings.

Your fieldnotes can also begin to integrate the different sections of
your notes. Make sure to keep the distinction clear between your observations and your reflections because, as you analyze your fieldnotes, you
will need to refer to the places that led you to draw the conclusions you
did. To assemble the story your fieldnotes create, you will want to set the
scene (with your description), present your evidence (with the content),
and share your analysis (using your reflections).

In a class where you are submitting your fieldnotes, the audience is
your professor. In this case, you will need to make sure to spell out any
shorthand and include, and likely distinguish between, the different types
of notes that you have written down. You will also likely need to figure
out how to distinguish between different people and places.

If you are not required to submit your fieldnotes, the audience for
your jottings and fieldnotes is you. They should make sense and build a
scene you can understand. Eventually, they become a part of your larger
qualitative product, though, so your fieldnotes should include enough
information to create a distinct picture for others as well. Your notes
should be clear and informative. If you pick them up 10 years from now,
you should still be able to see the people and places described.

TRANSCRIPTS

Many professors will advise against recording your respondents: It may
require additional permissions, it distracts from your notes, and they can
take a long time to transcribe. For this reason, we will focus here on
organizing your interview notes, rather than creating word-for-word

transcriptions (for more information about audio transcription, see *Writing for Emerging Sociologists*).

To keep your interview records clear, you may want to include some information about setting at the beginning of the transcript. You could include where you were, who was in the room, who your respondent is, and the date and time of the interview or focus group. You might decide to use codes rather than names if you are eliminating names from final documents.

A transcript is generally written in a format similar to what you might find in a script, with some kind of identifier followed by the respondents' exact speech. Some people bold, italicize, or capitalize the name of the person speaking. Others may use a hanging indent, which indents the conversation but sets the name of the respondent or interviewer slightly to the left.

Figure 4.9

Interviewer:	What was your childhood neighborhood like?
Harden:	I was in a quiet neighborhood ... pretty average. You know, not a lot of noise or problems.
MARK (Interviewer):	What is your strongest memory of that neighborhood?
Respondent (#0010):	I remember my bike. I spent hours riding it between and around the houses.

Similar to fieldnotes, your transcript is not just capturing your respondents' words but their meanings and voices as well. Therefore, you should write the respondents' words as close to how they spoke them as possible. This may mean writing down quick notes and editing them later. Transcribers will often use brackets [ ] to note background information, such as a phone ringing. For those who plan to analyze their qualitative data with data analysis software, you will want to write out the interviews as fully as possible.

DATA ANALYSIS

While instruction in data analysis is outside the scope of this book, we would like to take a moment to briefly discuss the technology used for qualitative and quantitative data analysis in the social sciences. As undergraduate or graduate students, you may not have a choice in software. Often, your school will have a license for one type of program, and you will have no recourse other than to use it. However, if you are in a situation where multiple options are available or you are able to choose, please keep the following information in mind.

Sociologists generally choose between ATLAS.ti and NVivo (this program replaced QSR N6 and Nu*dist) for their qualitative data needs. Both programs will allow you to code data—highlight particular themes—which is essential for analyzing qualitative data. However, they both deal with data slightly differently, and one may be more useful than another for your research. Both of these software are now available for both Windows and Mac. If your institution does not have its own license for qualitative data analysis software, you could choose to code by hand or you can see if your professor can request it for the class. There are also several open source packages available online for as a free download.

Your choice of statistical software will also be influenced by the type of project you are working on but may be more influenced by price and availability than will your choice of qualitative data analysis software. Statistical Package for the Social Sciences (also known as PASW and IBM SPSS, although most researchers still refer to it simply as SPSS) has been a staple of many social science departments. It is generally user friendly and produces easy-to-read results. However, even the basic package can be expensive, especially for an individual, and many researchers find it limiting for some more complicated analyses. Some sociologists prefer Stata, which widely used in economics. Stata has also been favored for more complicated or less common statistical procedures. Both SPSS and Stata are available for Windows and Mac.

In addition to these two software options, researchers also consider several others. SAS has been around for a long time and can be good for very large databases (it is also available for both platforms). R is very heavy on the amount of programming required but is open source, which means it is readily available online. Finally, Excel does not have all the complex statistical support of most of the others, but it comes with MS Office and is therefore usually immediately accessible on PC and Mac. It also has very good visual elements available and that is often how you will present this information in a paper. For most papers in a college class, Excel or other spreadsheet software will be enough.

If available, demonstration, trial, or student versions of the software may allow you to get a better idea of which software package you prefer, and, over time, you will develop your own feel for data analysis. Some of the student versions (such as SPSS) will actually give you a limited version of the software for a lower price. Some software will expire after 4 years, while others will remain limited but not expire.

Chapter 5 provides instruction on the proper ways to integrate your written data into manuscripts. Recall that quantitative data are generally more about the summary of information, and you will therefore use percentages, tables, and diagrams to represent them. Qualitative data tell the stories of individuals or groups, so you are including quotes, descriptions, and reflections based on your interactions with or observations of others.

SUMMARY

This chapter provides you with the information to create most of the instruments you will use in social science research. With this as your foundation, your research can address the hypotheses or research questions you are interested in and the chapter can continue to provide important advice as you work your way through the process. This chapter highlights the following:

- Writing questions for surveys, focus groups, and interviews
- Compiling fieldnotes
- Creating interview transcripts
- The use of technology in data collection and analysis

The "Writing in Practice" sections for this chapter are written by qualitative and quantitative researchers. Professor Thurston Domina shares his experiences with quantitative methods, and Professor Randol Contreras describes his thought process in trying to write up his ethnographic research.

WRITING IN PRACTICE

by Thurston Domina

I started crunching numbers and writing about statistics because nobody else wanted to. I was fresh out of college, working as a research assistant to a bunch of lawyers who were investigating the legality of a set of proposed changes to admissions policies at a large, public, urban university. The lawyers were interested in the equity questions the admissions changes raised. But to really address these questions, they needed a quantitative social scientist.

Admissions decisions at big public universities revolve around a sort of regression equation. A student's admissibility is a function of high school grades, scores on college admissions tests, and other extracurricular activities. The university wanted to increase the weight it placed on test scores. My bosses, the lawyers, worried that such a change would have disproportionate negative consequences for students of color. In response, the university released a series of tables designed to show that the consequences would be small and equitable. My bosses didn't believe these tables, but they knew the media and the judges would— and they didn't have the methodological skills to refute them. And that's where I came into the picture. I had no training in statistics, and my math background was mediocre (I just barely squeaked through calculus in high school and again as an undergraduate). But my bosses wanted me to make sense of the university's estimates of the effects of the proposed admissions changes. If the estimates were wrong, they wanted me to figure out why and come up with an alternative set of estimates.

In the weeks that followed, I got a crash course in quantitative sociology. I learned about sampling, weighting, multivariate modeling, and confidence intervals. But, more important, I learned that numbers have great power in our society. When the university released its estimates, it framed the debate around the proposed admissions changes. If my bosses couldn't convincingly refute the university's estimates, their legal arguments would fall on deaf ears. It occurred to me that learning how to produce compelling social statistics and communicate them effectively might provide me with an opportunity to change the world for the better.

The intuition that numbers are powerful continues to motivate my work and guide my thinking about writing in the social sciences. And it's this potential for social influence that makes quality writing so important. To be influential, quantitative sociology must be relevant and accessible. The easy way to be relevant is to answer a question that others are asking. The harder way to be relevant is to convince others to start asking a new set of questions. But regardless of its relevance, quantitative research will have little influence if it isn't accessibly written. Our research is often complex and highly technical. But our writing doesn't need to be. The quantitative social scientists that have changed the world have done so by finding a way to communicate their research to readers who aren't quantitative social scientists. Doing so requires direct and relentlessly
(Continued)

(Continued)

clear writing—writing that avoids jargon but seeks out revealing examples and illustrations.

But clarity doesn't mean simplicity. In fact, it seems to me that the primary responsibility of the quantitative sociologist is to make the process through which we draw our conclusions as transparent as possible. We can be wrong—everybody is from time to time. But if we articulate our methods, assumptions, and findings with meticulous precision, we're less likely to be wrong. Furthermore, if we write carefully and thoroughly, our errors are likely to be identified before they cause harm. Since numbers convey authority, writing that is muddy and ambiguous is potentially dangerous. Like the judges and reporters that my lawyer bosses worried about, many consumers of quantitative research are willing to take our conclusions on faith. Quantitative writing that fails to fully articulate the compromises and decisions that underlie any statistical conclusion enables sort-of reading. By contrast, good quantitative writing makes that sort-of reading impossible, since it takes the reader by the hand and leads her or him through the entire scientific process.

—Thurston Domina, PhD, is an associate professor
of educational policy and sociology at the
University of North Carolina, Chapel Hill.

WRITING IN PRACTICE

by Randol Contreras

After writing fieldnotes, then finding themes and doing data analysis, there comes a point when I, as an ethnographer, have to make some serious writing decisions. I must choose a writing style, or voice, and decide on the amount of analysis and description. I realize that with whatever decision I make, there will be advantages and drawbacks in terms of academic recognition and reader satisfaction.

For instance, in writing up my research on Dominican drug robbers in the South Bronx, I chose to write in a clear and jargon-free style, which general readers would appreciate. I wanted my audience to easily understand the everyday lives of the study participants and not have to decipher complicated ideas in complicated sentence structures (which is the hallmark of most academic literature). And this took lots of work. I spent weeks, and sometimes months, ensuring that I simplified theories, concepts, and analysis while keeping the substance and complexity. It involved rewording and shortening sentences, shaving paragraphs, removing "filler" phrases and words, and replacing long words with short ones. Most of all, it took lots of rewriting. And then more rewriting. The payoff, I thought, was worth it, as readers would experience a memorable, smooth, and enlightening read.

However, I soon found out that there were drawbacks in writing both clearly and descriptively. After reading a part of my book manuscript, a colleague claimed that my research sounded too much like a "novel" and seemed as though I had "made it up." Then he grabbed two ordinary ethnographies from his office bookshelf and offered them to me as guides on writing up "real research."

Initially, I was offended, especially with the suggestion that my work was fiction or "made up." But later I realized that the simplicity of clear writing could put off academic readers who are accustomed to turgid, complicated expressions. Thus, they can interpret clear and simple writing as not being academically rigorous. Worse, they can liken it to journalism, which has no obligation to educate readers *sociologically* but mostly to tell stories of interesting places and people.

In the end, my challenge was to find a writing balance that incorporated description, analysis, and clarity. In other words, I knew I had to not only clearly describe what went on in the field but also noticeably explain it theoretically or conceptually. So in my book on South Bronx drug robbers,[2] I made the sociology obvious—I conspicuously uncovered hidden social meanings and created new concepts to show that there is more than meets the eye. Also, I wrote *clearly* to avoid frustration on the part of readers, who may not have academic training. Last, I provided lots of description so readers have enough fieldwork data to challenge my analysis and also get a powerful sense of this South Bronx social world. In all, I realized that ethnography is just as much about the writing as doing the fieldwork alone.

—Randol Contreras, PhD, is an assistant professor of sociology at the University of Toronto, Mississauga.

NOTES

1. *Informant* is the traditional term for people who bring the researcher into the field. Because of the negative connotation of the word, some ethnographers have now switched to the term *respondent*, which we will use here.

2. Contreras, Randol. 2012. *The Stickup Kids: Drugs, Violence, and the Pursuit of Happiness*. Berkeley: University of California Press.

CHAPTER 5

WRITING PAPERS FOR SOCIOLOGY CLASS

*Essays, Capstone Papers,
and Literature Reviews*

In the second chapter, we discussed the "Bricks and Mortar" of writing and described general approaches to writing. This chapter builds on that by examining the various ways those skills are used and the different types of papers a student may have to write for different undergraduate sociology courses. These papers range from short reflection papers to longer capstone projects. We will discuss the types of papers as well as give suggestions and tips for how to approach these writing assignments. We will review the various essay assignments, ways to approach writing literature reviews and reports, as well as annotated bibliographies. We conclude with the process of reviewing these assignments as well as a Writing in Practice essay written by a sociology undergraduate student.

APPROACHING WRITING ASSIGNMENTS

As described in other chapters in this book, writing is not just about the work that you do but also how you prepare for it. This is also part of completing class assignments. It is not just the paper that you write, it is also ensuring that you are writing the right thing. Before you start writing any of your assignments, you need to prepare for them.

Review Your Syllabus

Within a week of the first class, make sure you review the syllabus from each of your classes to get an overview of your courses and the requirements to complete them. Create a summary sheet that will act as a quick reference guide for each of your classes. Keep in mind, as you are reviewing the syllabus, that there may be assignments listed that do not include a description of all of the steps to completion or might be adjusted over the course of the semester. The important thing is to have a general idea of when assignments will be due. Once you have made individual review sheets for each class, compile the due dates on to one sheet, organized by month. In this way, you won't be surprised at any point in the semester because you have a lot of assignments due. Instead, you can divide the work over the course of the semester and not become overwhelmed. See Appendix for a sample syllabus review sheet and an assignment summary sheet.

Break Down the Assignment

You should begin all of your writing assignments in the same manner as you did your syllabus: by carefully reviewing the assignment and instructions. You should be able to answer these questions: What am I expected to do in this assignment? How much is this assignment worth? What skills do I need to utilize to complete this assignment? What is the due date? Are there any drafts or outlines required beforehand? Do I need to consult with others (e.g., group members, experts in the field) to complete the assignment? All of these do not necessarily determine the amount of effort involved in completing the assignment, but it does certainly help you think about how and when you should approach it. For example, although you want to put a great deal of effort into all of your course work, if the assignment is worth 50 percent of your overall course grade, you will want to pay special attention to it. Doing poorly on an assignment worth so much means that you will likely perform poorly in the overall course. You may want to extract the information on to a separate sheet or underline it so you can easily find it (see Appendix for a sample assignment worksheet).

Review Instructions

Now specifically focus on the instructions of the assignment. You want to make sure to thoroughly read through the instructions so that you are certain that you understand what you are expected to do along with any particular steps you should take in constructing the assignment. Typically, assignments ask students to constructively analyze and think about a topic. You might need to do additional research to complete your assignment or you might simply need to reflect on the content of a lecture, film, or reading, and describe your thoughts and analysis. Make sure you understand the assignment, and if there is any aspect of the assignment you do not understand or are unsure of, immediately ask your instructor during her or his next office hours. It is always better to talk with your instructor in person instead of via e-mail as the question can be lost or unclear online. The office hours are there for you to use them, so take advantage. If you are only able to ask your instructor digitally, make sure that your question is clear and directly addresses any confusion or lack of clarity you have with the assignment. Make sure to write down the response to your questions or any additional instructions you may have received. See Chapter 2 for more information about writing an e-mail.

Make Note of the Due Date

Once you understand what you are being asked to do in the assignment, make sure to note the due date and any additional assignment materials (such as rough drafts). Make sure that the due date is added to your calendar. If the paper is due at the end of the semester, giving you a few months to complete it, you should begin work on the assignment soon after receiving it or check your Assignment Due Date sheet to find a good time to work on it. Typically, when faculty gives you an entire semester to complete a writing assignment, that instructor has high expectations for the assignment and would expect you to spend a great deal of time constructing it.

For a longer research paper, it is always wise to try to review the paper with your instructor before the due date. Beyond asking your instructor questions about the assignment, if you have any, you want to make sure that you write multiple drafts of your paper before turning it into your instructor. It is important to remember that your instructor is grading your assignment when you turn it into them. You want to make sure that your papers are always free of spelling and grammatical errors and that you follow all instructions. Many universities have writing centers on campus where writing tutors, who may be graduate or fellow undergraduate students, will review your papers and assignments. You can always have your friends and classmates, particularly the ones in the class with you, review a draft of your paper as well. It is always good to get a second, or third, or better yet, even fourth pair of eyes on your papers before turning them into your instructor. Your instructor's job is to not only provide guidance but to also evaluate your work and the more time you give yourself to approach the assignment, the more time you will have to be certain that you are submitting a quality paper free of spelling and grammar issues (see Chapter 6 for more information on editing and revising).

COLLEGE PAPERS

Here we will provide a general overview of the types of assignments students can come to expect in college classes. Keep in mind that this is intended to be general information and, again, we suggest you speak with your course instructor and work closely with them to ensure that you are following all instructions for each of your assignments. As mentioned in the second chapter and above, you will need to follow the instructions closely. The most common types of course papers assigned in undergraduate sociology classes include essays, research/term papers, and assignments that require data collection, such as writing up fieldnotes or a capstone paper. These are writing assignments that tend to have a logical progression and begin with an introduction, body, and conclusion. The introduction typically states what the paper or essay will address, with the body addressing it. The conclusion reviews what was addressed in the overall essay (see Chapter 2 for more general information on paper structure). The assignment's prompt and instructions will provide you with detail on how exactly to approach and structure the paper. There are a few different types of college papers. We will use the popular terms below but know that your professors may use those words differently. You may want to ask your professor if his assignment fits any of these instructions. Any direction they provide should be prioritized over what we include here.

Essays

These are typically shorter writing assignments (two to five pages) that do not require a lot of additional library research or background information. Essays are often assigned as exams in order to assess your level of knowledge on a particular topic. There are four types of essays that students are often assigned and what these essays require you to do is in their name: analytical, argumentative, compare and contrast, and reflection essays. Remember that with all assignments, particularly essay assignments where you are often not using a lot of additional research to support your claim, you want to make sure that your logic is clear and the reader can easily follow it. Any evidence that is available to enhance your essay or that the professor asks you to include should be cited, whether it is course material or research that you conducted at the library or online. Just as other writing in this book, each of these essays should begin with an introduction and end with a conclusion. The specifics of those sections and the details of the body is where these pieces differ.

Analytical Essay

The purpose of this essay is to thoroughly think through a particular idea or concept. You will be expected to analyze a given concept and provide your response to it. You will begin with a research question but unlike the argumentative essay below, you will not necessarily have a particular perspective when you begin the essay. Analytical essay assignments often include the word *analyze* but might also use *examine, investigate, consider, explore,* or *dissect*. For example, a professor might ask you to "analyze how race is represented in *Buffy the Vampire Slayer*."

You will be expected to explore this topic and, through that exploration, your hypothesis may change. You will need to follow a logical progression so that your readers can understand the points you are making in the paper. The best way to begin is to answer the question to the best of your ability. Then, you will need to find evidence from allowable sources to support that answer. As you delve deeper into this topic, you may decide that your initial answer doesn't hold up or make sense. You will then need to rethink it, return to your hypothesis, and collect evidence again. In an analytic essay, you will likely be graded on your ability to write a hypothesis and support it with evidence in a logical way.

In your introduction, you will need to introduce the paper and your research question or topic. The body will be your analysis where you identify and incorporate evidence that supports your response to the question. This might include direct quotes, paraphrases, or summaries, depending on the assignment. You will then need to appropriately conclude your essay.

Argumentative Essay

This essay is similar to an analytical essay, but it will have a special emphasis on creating and supporting an argument. You will usually need to use course material and additional research to support your argument. Make sure to clearly explain what your argument is in the beginning of the essay and spend time breaking apart and providing evidence for each element of your argument so that it is clear to the reader.

An argumentative essay assignment will generally ask you to take a particular perspective which may be left up to you or may be assigned to you. Words such as *argue*, *debate*, *claim*, or *dispute* might be used in the assignment description. If you are not given a perspective, you will need to first determine your perspective and then use the same skills as above to break down that perspective into the evidence you will need to support it.

Similar to an analytical essay, you will first introduce the essay and topic, then list each piece of your argument and your evidence supporting it. You will likely need to present opposing viewpoints as well and explain why that perspective is not correct, accurate, or valid. Afterward, conclude the essay by restating your thesis and connecting it to the evidence you just shared.

Compare and Contrast Essay

These essays require you to present an argument or topic and then review another topic based on elements of the first. You are comparing (showing how topics in the same or in two separate essays are similar) and contrasting (showing how they are different). You will want to make sure that you dedicate particular portions of the paper to each example and that your comparisons and contrasts are clear and make sense to the reader.

The assignments will likely include the words *compare* and *contrast* but could also ask for *differences* and *similarities*, *associations*, *commonalities*, or a *relationship*. Your professor may ask you to look for a particular theme—such as race, class, or gender—across the two or multiple pieces (studies or time periods), or she might ask you to find one or several similarities or differences across them. Once you know what the common and distinct elements are, you will need to select or identify the ones that you will be focusing on and then collect the evidence that demonstrates it.

You will start by introducing the topic and paper, then present the multiple issues, theories, and so forth, and show how they are similar and how they are different. You can either organize your paper by the issue or theme—including information about each document in the sections—or you can organize it by document—describing all the elements in each document before going on to the next one. Either way, you will need at least a few sentences to connect the different documents before you conclude the essay.

Reflection/Expository Essay

Reflection essays, often known as expository essays, can be of any length, so be certain to ask your instructor if there is a page or word requirement. Often, your professor will give you a specific question or list of questions to answer, but you may also be assigned a reflection essay with no or limited questions.

Unless given other specific information, your essay should be a reflection on the main points of what you have read, seen, or done, and how it has had an effect on you or what you are doing in the class. Has it changed how you think about anything or what you believe? Does it connect with experiences, assignments, or discussions you have had? Is there anything missing or anything you would like to learn more about? Most reflection essays will use the word *reflect* but could also ask you to *consider, contemplate, ponder,* or *think about.*

To complete this, you should begin by picking out the main points from whatever you are supposed to reflect on and briefly summarize it. If the professor has not attended the same event, completed the reading, or seen the film that will be written about, you will likely need a significant summary. If she or he has, then it does not have to be as long. Following the description, clearly note how the film, book, or event made you feel, and in particular, how it relates to class lectures and materials. A reflection essay should make you do just that—reflect on the assignment. You will also generally need to provide examples from the material and literature before you conclude the essay.

Annotated Bibliography

Annotated bibliographies were discussed in Chapter 3 as being an integral part of the writing and research process, but they are also written as class assignments and can be published in journals or sometimes on webpages run by social service organizations and agencies. Many of the same rules apply in writing an annotated bibliography as part of your writing process as in writing one for submission to a professor; however, there are some differences. This section will address how annotated bibliographies can be written for an assignment while helping to increase your understanding of a particular topic or area within the field.

Most annotations are very short, typically 150 to 250 words long—about the length of an article abstract. As a result, you will have to be as concise as possible in writing each annotation. Don't forget—the purpose of the annotated bibliography is to summarize, as succinctly as possible, a book or article and to evaluate its relevance to a particular topic. Since the purpose of your annotated bibliography is to find books and articles that pertain to one area of study, you do not need to summarize the work in great detail. Annotated bibliographies that are written for instructors, or for inclusion in scholarly journals or other publications, should be written in a complete and clear but succinct manner, much like an abstract.

Introduction: Annotated bibliographies typically begin with a paragraph describing the purpose of the annotation. This introductory paragraph provides background information on your topic as well as a discussion explaining the parameters of your literature search and why certain similar topics were omitted from your search.

Citations: Citations are typically written in full American Psychological Association (APA) or American Sociological Association (ASA) format. Similar to ASA and APA reference sections, the citations are listed in alphabetical order, with the annotations following.

Annotations: Again, although overall annotations vary, most annotations contain the same information—a summary of the book or article and its connection to the larger topic. Annotations often answer the following questions:

- What is the author's subject?
- What is the author's main focus?
- What is the author's scope?
- What do you think the author hopes to accomplish by writing this piece?
- What is the author's background?
- What are the author's qualifications? Do you find his work credible?
- Who is the intended audience?
- What relationship, if any, does this work have with any other works in this field of study?
- What conclusions are reached by the author?
- What is your assessment of the reading? How does this book or article compare to the other books and articles included in your bibliography?
- Are there any limitations or biases in this work? If so, what are they?
- What are your overall conclusions concerning this source?

Conclusion: Many annotated bibliographies often contain a paragraph after the annotations with an overall review of all the books and articles discussed in the bibliography.

What to Avoid: It is important to stress that each annotation is very short. To make the most of your word count, avoid the following:

- Generalizations and/or imprecise modifiers (*really*, *very*, *bad*, *good*, and *excellent*).
- Beginning each annotation with, "This article . . ." or "This book . . ."

- First person ("I").
- Referring to the article or book by its full name multiple times in the annotation. To save space, refer to the author's last name instead.
- Repetition of information that can be found in the title. For example, in a review of the book *Gender and the Social Construction of Illness*, you would not need to say, "This book explores the impact that gender has on the social construction of illnesses." That is implicit in the title, and it is a waste of space to repeat it. Since the topic of the book is already clear in the title, the space in the annotation should instead be used to describe the book and provide an evaluation.

If you use this as a precursor to a literature review, you should put together your research by focusing on relating these articles and books to one another. What do these articles and books have in common? Do they contradict one another? What is missing from the literature? Are there important methodological or theoretical concerns that should be addressed by the literature that aren't? How will you do it in your research? Make note of *how* this literature supports your argument. Organize your findings by subtopics—as the example below demonstrates with asthma—which can address a particular methodology, theory, or finding.

   I. Subtopic 1 (increasing rates)
- Article 1
- Article 2
- Article 3
- Article 4
- Article 5

  II. Subtopic 2 (reducing rates)
- Article 1
- Article 2
- Article 3
- Article 4
- Article 5

 III. Subtopic 3 (difficulty reaching subjects)
- Article 1
- Article 2
- Article 3
- Article 4
- Article 5

The number of subtopics you include or address in your annotated bibliography will depend on your research project or your assignment requirements. You may address only two or three subtopics, or you may have several. However, be certain that the literature you include in your annotated bibliography informs your assignment, contributes to the discussion on this topic, and explains to the reader how you arrived at your topic. Again, be sure to focus the annotated bibliography you create around the subtopics you find in your literature as opposed to going article by article, summarizing each one. You may find that some of your articles fit several of your subtopics. Check with your professor, but most will let you include them in discussing multiple subtopics. If you find that you are referring to the same article in every subtopic, pick the strongest point or two that the article makes and find other articles for your other subtopics.

Literature Reviews

Annotated bibliographies and literature reviews are similar in that they are both collections of the literature organized around themes and subthemes. However, an annotated bibliography is more organized around the articles while the focus of a literature review is the subthemes. An annotated bibliography is a good way to prepare to write your literature review, but the description of an article in a literature review may only be a sentence long, specifically illustrating how it relates to the theme.

In college, you might come across literature reviews in a couple of places. They are most often found as part of a larger project (such as the capstone project described below), but they can also be assigned as stand-alone assignments. These literature reviews are often referred to as research papers. A literature review is a critical review and analysis of research on a particular topic or area of study. Literature reviews focus on different themes and arguments found within the research and are most frequently used to help the writer formulate a research hypothesis. Literature reviews are typically written as a research paper or included within research reports, master's theses, doctoral dissertations, and scholarly journal manuscripts. Where the literature review is included will often dictate its length and structure, with longer literature reviews found in dissertations and books and shorter ones found in articles. For a class assignment, your professor will likely give you a length for the paper and may also ask that your literature review be a particular length, include a particular number of references, or cover a particular number of subtopics.

Your literature review should be written as an essay in which you explain to the reader how you came to your research topic and hypothesis. Just like any essay, your literature review should contain an introduction, body, and conclusion. We suggest creating an outline first, similar to the ones discussed in Chapter 3, with a focus on the literature. This outline should trace the development of your argument based on the literature you found. If you are hypothesis testing, the annotated bibliography you compiled to prepare for your study will greatly help you in writing an outline and, ultimately, your literature review. As the annotated bibliography doesn't just provide a summary of relevant articles and books, but also contains your review of each individual article and how it relates to the other articles you collected, it can be the foundation for any argument you are making. In your annotated bibliography, you should have made note of what theories or methodologies may be problematic or missing in previous research. Again, this can help give you possible ideas for research projects. As mentioned in the previous chapter, this saves you from having to go back and read the articles again to decide what to include in your assignment.

We mentioned in Chapter 3 that you should concentrate on scholarly articles and books, and this is also what you should include in your literature review. From the annotated bibliography, select the articles and books that informed your research. What omissions from the literature inspired your research? Is there something in the literature that your study refutes? How could the literature be combined in a new way to support your theory? Again, the purpose of your study should determine which literature you select to include in the review.

Once you have selected the literature from your annotated bibliography, think about how you plan to structure the body of the review. The structure of the review will likely be determined by your research question(s) or assignment. Reviews are typically structured in one of three ways: chronically, methodologically, or thematically.

1. *Chronological Review:* As the name suggests, chronological reviews are arranged in chronological order by either date of publication, time period analyzed, or how a topic or area of study has changed over a given time. For example, articles and books published during a particular time period would be grouped and discussed together in different subsections of the body of the review. If you were examining the history of education reform, you could categorize the changes according to time period, such as examining changes in access to education before and after the 1954 *Brown et al. v. Board of Education* ruling.

2. *Methodological Review:* A methodological review is organized not by the research topic but by the methods used to conduct the research. For example, if the literature review examined the different approaches to studying religiosity in the United States, research that utilizes a quantitative approach would be grouped separately from research that utilizes qualitative methods.

3. *Thematic Review:* Thematic literature reviews are usually organized by the themes or concepts found within the literature on a given topic. How is the topic discussed or analyzed within the literature? What ideas or themes do you find emerging from the literature? For instance, a project studying literature on civic engagement might focus on the various forms of civic engagement and then on the demographics of those who would most likely participate in these activities.

Regardless of whether the literature review is thematic, methodological, or chronological, reviews should be organized by like concepts presented in the literature, such as trends in time periods or themes found in the literature on your topic. Do the articles or the research on your topic have a similar methodology, theory, or population type? What work do you feel is relevant to your project? Are there studies that you want to refute or support with your research? What research enhances your theoretical framework? You don't want to select too many different themes or subtopics, as it will confuse the reader. Instead, stick to the ones that most informed your research.

Keep in mind that the purpose of the literature review is to give the reader an idea of the journey you took through the literature that helped you develop your research project and hypothesis. If your research project explores the rates of asthma among the urban poor, for instance, you will probably find many articles and books on that topic. These articles and books address a number of issues or subtopics, also known as themes, within the literature that tackle this issue from a variety of perspectives. These subtopics, as described above, range from what causes asthma within this group, such as secondhand smoke or pollution, to the increasing rates of asthma within this population. Research may examine the work done to reduce these rates. Research may also explore the difficulty in reaching subjects to participate in studies on asthma rates. You might find articles that focus on a particular age demographic, such as children or the elderly. You will also find articles that will address how the rates influence a particular racial/ethnic group within urban populations. As mentioned above, one article could cover several themes and different articles will address the same themes. Once subtopics are identified, organize the literature or sections of the literature into those subtopics. Remove the annotations you did not use.

As described above, a next step could be to reorganize your annotated bibliography into one that selects and summarizes the pieces of literature most relevant to your work and explains how these selected articles relate to one another and what is missing from the literature. After your subtopics have been identified and the literature has been arranged by subtopic, you can then begin the process of fleshing out your annotated bibliography and molding it into a literature review essay.

You will begin the literature review essay by introducing the reader to the review. In the introduction of your literature review, just like in the introduction to an essay, you should provide the reader with an overview of the types of literature you examined for your research, the way the review will be structured, and, importantly, the themes or reoccurring issues you found in the literature that pertain to your topic. You can also provide any definitions for terms found and examined in the literature you will present. For example:

This research concerns how a social problem is framed (Spector and Kitsuse 1987) and how issues relating to health and health care can be framed based on themes and ideas that resonate with its target population (Kolker 2005). The idea of "framing a problem" is quite relevant to the social sciences. This concept can be applied when addressing a number of social issues, such as missing children (Best 1987), labor disputes (Babb 1996), and even understandings of White separatism (Berbrier 1998); furthermore, it holds great relevance to the development of health social movements. The use of frames is especially important in the case of the Black Church, whose congregants were not targeted by mainstream AIDS awareness campaigns (Harris 2010).[1]

Once you introduce the literature review to readers, you should then move into the body of the review. Regardless of whether you organize the body of your review chronologically, methodologically, or thematically, you will have to present your literature in an organized manner based on concepts or subtopics found in the literature. To make your literature review more organized, we suggest providing subheadings for some of the larger subtopics you found in the literature that informed your project. These subheadings provide a very clear visual breakdown of the literature review and the topics you will cover in the review. If you do not want to use subheadings, you should still be sure that you have constructed clear transition sentences so your readers can follow your discussion as you move from one topic to the next.

After your introductory paragraph, you will present the research in order of subtopic. Again, you are writing a literature review, not an annotated bibliography, so you do not want to go article by article in your analysis and summation of the literature. You are going one step further in your literature review than you would if you were writing an annotated bibliography. Explain how these articles relate to one another and *omit* the summary of each article. If a number of articles make the same point, you should summarize or put their overall point or argument into your own words and cite the authors whose points were included in this summation. In the example on pollution provided above, the author could state under the "Increasing Rates" subheading:

Rates of asthma have been increasing among the urban poor (Jones, Collins, and Smith 2009; Martin 2006; Williams 2005).

The rest of that section of the literature review should examine what the literature says about increasing asthma rates. As opposed to describing what each of the three articles says about pollution, this example summarized a common point about asthma rates among the poor. Since they all provided the same overall finding, you can cite the works together. You can break your subtopics up by paragraph or you can provide separate subheadings within your literature review. If your paper is on pollution, your subheadings could be race, class, increasing rates, for example—whatever subtopics informed your project. Again, your literature review is based on what you learned from the overall literature, not necessarily what each piece of literature says. As a result, you do not go source by source but, instead, write an essay and use the literature to support your claim or argument. There will be a lot of citations throughout your literature review. Don't be worried if it seems as though every other sentence has a citation. This section is called a literature review for a reason. Ultimately, the argument you present in your review of the literature demonstrates to your readers, professors, and yourself the need for and importance of your research.

After you have gone through your various subtopics and referenced the pertinent literature, you will inform your audience of how it led you to your research topic. This is where you will discuss your hypothesis. Again, the purpose of the literature review is to place your research into a particular research area. You should use this section to talk about the ways the holes in the research that has been conducted directed you to take on your project the way you did. What was missing from previous work? What subtopics did you synthesize to develop your hypothesis? This discussion of your hypothesis also serves as a conclusion to your literature review. You want to be certain that you provide enough information in your literature review so that the reader can clearly see how you arrived at your hypothesis.

CAPSTONE PROJECTS

Projects are increasingly becoming popular as the final assignment in a number of master's programs, most often in applied sociology graduate programs. However, capstones are also used in undergraduate classes as the culmination of a college career. All the research and courses you took while in your program becomes a project that serves as the capstone of your education. Projects vary based on program requirements and student research interests, but in sociology, they are typically the application of theory to fix or provide advice on a problem or issue within an organization, institution, community, or some other social setting. Capstone projects are those that encapsulate your whole sociology education. You will want to show that you can understand and incorporate sociological theory as well as use sociological methods (qualitative or qualitative) in your work. It serves as a way for the department to know that you have learned as a sociology major in the department.

Capstone projects can take a number of different forms, depending on your department's requirements. Some capstone projects consist of oral presentations while others are written. Capstone projects might take the form of papers that consist of large literature reviews or they might require you to collect original data or analyze data provided to you. The following will provide instruction on writing a capstone paper based on original data collected. The suggestions in this section will also be applicable to a capstone paper written from secondary data (or data collected by another researcher). As described several times in this book, papers typically have different sections: introduction, literature review/background, methods, findings/results, discussion, and conclusion, and may also include an abstract and reference page. We will review each section in detail below.

Introduction

For a capstone paper, the introductory section is typically only a few paragraphs long, as the primary purpose of this section is to provide the framework for your paper. Here the author introduces the reader to the paper and the topic. In your introduction, you want to make sure you clearly state what your paper will address and how you will go about exploring the topic. The introduction to your research has three main functions: setting the stage, stating the problem, and responding to the problem.

Setting the Stage

Introduce your topic and your reason for analyzing the topic. Although it is safe to assume that your instructor will be somewhat knowledgeable about your topic and the issues surrounding it, you shouldn't build your paper on that assumption. You could start with a striking opening line. Think of a good book or an interesting magazine article you have read. They often start with an opening line or phrase that captures the audience's attention. Below, you will find illustrations of some well-known opening lines from books you may have read:

It was the best of times, it was the worst of times, it was the age of wisdom, it was the age of foolishness, it was the epoch of belief, it was the epoch of incredulity, it was the season of Light, it was the season of Darkness, it was the spring of hope, it was the winter of despair.

—Charles Dickens, *A Tale of Two Cities*[2]

It is a truth universally acknowledged, that a single man in possession of a good fortune, must be in want of a wife.

—Jane Austen, *Pride and Prejudice*[3]

It was a bright cold day in April, and the clocks were striking thirteen.

—George Orwell, *1984*[4]

I am an invisible man.

—Ralph Ellison, *Invisible Man*[5]

Some of these lines are long and descriptive, while others are straightforward and to the point. Either way, these opening lines draw in the reader and set up the story. You want your opening line to do the same. Your introduction should grab the reader's attention. You may want to begin your paper with an interesting fact or statistic about the issue you plan to examine. A researcher exploring diabetes within Latino communities could start his introduction with the following:

> The Centers for Disease Control and Prevention[6] estimates that the rates of diabetes among Latinos in the United States have increased dramatically in recent years.

Although not enormously striking, an opening sentence such as this not only would let the reader know what the paper will be about but also would highlight the importance of the issue you plan to address, as well as the importance of your paper.

You can also begin with a quote from a notable scholar or theorist. For instance, if you were conducting research on the response of a sample of residents to the high unemployment rates in their city, you could begin your paper with the following line:

> More than 50 years ago, C. Wright Mills (1959)[7] wrote, "Nowadays people often feel that their private lives are a series of traps" (3); it would appear that today, very little has changed. Unemployment rates are increasing in both urban and rural areas throughout the country.

You can even begin with an interesting anecdote or story about your experience with the subject. This could be particularly helpful if your project is based on ethnographic research or some other firsthand account. For example, if you are writing about your experiences observing student–teacher interactions in a classroom, you could use a passage from your fieldnotes, or notes taken during ethnographic field study, to start the paper.

> Mr. Smith beamed as the students in his fourth-grade class raised their hands, both anxious and eager to answer his question: When did Columbus arrive in the Americas? Students jumped in their seats and called, "Oh, oh," as they frantically waved their hands back and forth, hoping they would be the one chosen to answer.

The author could then put this scene into context and explain to the audience how it is important to the work or representative of the issues pertaining to the research question.

These are just a few ideas for how you can start off your paper. The primary goal is to make sure you set the stage and provide enough background information about the issue for your readers. An opening sentence that is straight to the point not only informs your reader about the paper and topic but keeps you on track.

Stating the Problem:

Once you set the background or let the reader know a little about the overall topic, your next goal will be to state the problem. Be clear for your readers (and reviewers) when you explain what the social problem is. Again, the purpose of writing the paper is to address a particular social issue or problem. You need to clearly define for the reader what this issue is and why it is important. You should be able to articulate clearly, in one sentence, the overall point of your paper. In fact, you can simply write:

This paper will address . . .

The nature of your project will determine how you state the problem. For example, if your manuscript is based on empirical research where one or more independent variables were manipulated, clearly explain to the reader which variable you tested. You could write:

This study explores the influence that the [independent variable] has on the [dependent variable].

Let's say you are studying the influence of fast-food consumption on the body mass index, or BMI, of teens. The independent variable in this case would be food consumption. The participants' BMI would be the dependent variable. The dependent variable is the variable influenced by (dependent on) the independent variable. For example:

This study explores the influence fast-food consumption has on the BMI of a sample of youth between the ages of 13 and 17.

The above example clearly explains to the reader the issue that the paper will address.

Responding to the Problem:

Now that you have set up the background, provided the context for your reader, and described the problem, you are ready to explain how your research explores or responds to the problem. You are not necessarily explaining what the large-scale response to the problem *should be*, just how *you* respond to the problem with your research. This is the point in the introduction where you explain to the reader what your paper is about. In this last part of your introduction, you tell the reader why your paper is worth reading. In essence, you should be able to explain your theoretical premise and how your paper will address it. What do you think is contributing to this problem? How do you go about explaining it in the research you present in this paper? This is typically where the author would describe and introduce readers to her hypothesis if she were hypothesis testing. If your paper were to explore the influence of fast-food consumption on the BMI of teens, you would first want to notify the reader of the relationship being examined:

This study explores the influence fast-food consumption has on the BMI of a sample of youth between the ages of 13 and 17.

You could then tell the reader what you expect to find.

This project posits that increased levels of fast-food consumption will be positively correlated to higher BMIs among teens.

Some authors include in the introduction whether or not their hypothesis was supported by the research, while others wait until later in the paper to inform the readers of this. Don't worry about spoiling the surprise, as the reader already knows what you will find—you already identified your findings in your abstract (discussed later in this chapter).

You could also begin with a question and answer the question in your paper. For example:

How does fast-food consumption influence the BMI of a sample of youth between the ages of 13 and 17?

Then inform your readers that your paper will explore the response to the proposed question.

Again, these are basic ideas about writing the introductory section of your paper. You could also seek out examples of introductions (for example articles in the journals from which you collected references) for ideas on how to organize and structure your introduction. It's important to remember, your introduction does not need to be too detailed, as you will explain your literature, methodology, findings, and analysis in the body of the paper.

Literature Review

Literature reviews, as complete research papers, were discussed in great detail earlier in this chapter but we will focus here on how they are often written as just a part of a research paper. Research studies and empirical research typically require that your paper contain a review of the literature on your topic. Sometimes, a literature review can also be included in the introduction of the paper or within a background or context section (a brief section often found within the introduction that provides the historical framework for the study). Either way, you need to show that you reviewed the relevant literature on your topic.

The purpose of this section of your paper is to discuss what previous research has said about your research topic. It also describes the literature used to develop your research hypothesis or questions. The literature review explains to the reader what literature informed your argument. Literature reviews are usually found in the beginning of the paper and should be written as an essay (as described above), with an introduction, body, and conclusion. The literature you present should be a review of the most pertinent literature on your research topic, and it should help you organize and justify your research project.

A majority of literature reviews for research papers typically utilize the thematic literature review format. In this case, you will organize your literature review section by themes found in the literature. Each theme should be discussed separately, with effective transitioning sentences or subheadings separating each theme. Most literature reviews cover several different themes found within the literature. Remember not to go article by article but, rather, theme by theme, and focus on the links found between the books and articles. Since the literature review for capstone papers are relatively short—these types of papers are usually around 20 pages long—the literature review should be focused and straight to the point.

As we mentioned before, the nature of your capstone paper, the instructions from your professor, and the methodology employed may determine the structure and placement of your literature review. Grounded theorists collect and analyze their data before the literature is examined and look for the theory to emerge from the data. The idea is that this reduces researcher bias when it comes to data analysis. The researcher lets the data speak to her before consulting the literature to explain the observed behavior. If you are taking a grounded approach in your project, you should look for themes to emerge from your data in a similar fashion as you would in looking for subtopics in your review of the literature. Once you have identified these themes in your data, conduct a review of the literature to see how previous research has addressed what you observed in your findings. The more literature you examine, the easier it will be for you to present your explanation and theoretical analysis, which should be incorporated within your literature review.

As explained above, your literature review will likely be organized by subtopics that address particular aspects of your research project. The way the articles are presented in a literature review will depend on the purpose that the piece of literature serves for your larger project and the type of literature review you are writing. When an article makes multiple points related to the research you are doing or you are focused on something that requires more space to discuss, you might have to use a paragraph to describe an article. See the sample breakdown below of the organization of a literature review on the promise of education leading to social mobility.

I. Subtopic 1 (Cultural Explanations)
   - Point 1/Reference 1
   Cultural explanations often center on aspects of the culture of minorities and low income people. John Ogbu and Signithia Fordam have produced well-known examples of this focus on individual or group culture. Based on their fieldwork, they conclude that Black students are faced with "the conflict inherent in the unique relationship of Black people with the dominant institution: the struggle to achieve success while retaining group support and approval" (Ogbu and Fordham 1986). Obgu's thesis, often referred to as "the burden of acting white" posits that Black students underachieve because of the stigma they face embracing the norms, which in this case is productive participation in schools, of the dominant group.[8]
   - Point 2/Reference 2
   Based on research in low-income communities in Puerto Rico, Mexico, and New York, Oscar Lewis (1966) described a "culture of poverty" in which poor people are trapped and it produces conditions where after the age of four or five, regardless of changes in the environment, individuals are unable to change their behavior. This might lead to an interpretation of his work which would preclude the investment of funds into poverty areas for basic social infrastructure such as neighborhood schools, commercial areas, parks, or housing.

As demonstrated in this example, often there are several related points in an article which would encourage using an entire paragraph to discuss it. However, the relationship is still maintained between the points and there is a connection to an overall theme. There will likely be a few articles in your literature review that will be organized in this way. What is more likely is that you will be pulling from a variety of different sources to support a particular point. In this case, each paragraph will include multiple refer-ences. In fact, even a sentence might be supported by different authors.

I. Subtopic 1 (Cultural Explanations)
   - Point 3/References 4-8
   - The Moynihan Report, *The Negro Family: The Case for National Action* (1965), named for its author, former New York Senator Daniel Patrick Moynihan, is an example of this type of reasoning. According to Moynihan, the African American family, marked by the prevalence of female-headed households, shows "an unmistakable influence" on the underachievement, dropout rates, and general "pathology" of the African American community. In contrast to the theories described above, Juan Battle and others have demonstrated that the effect of family structure on education and cognitive ability varies and can be influenced by additional variables such as income, mother's mental health, and multigenerational households (Battle 1997; Carlson and Corcoran 2001, Deleire and Kalil 2002; Ginther and Pollak 2004). For example, Battle found that among African American families at lower socioeconomic status (SES) levels, students with divorced parents "scored significantly higher on standardized achievement tests than did their counterparts from married households" (Battle 1997:37).

The second to last sentence is an example of what much of your litera-ture review will look like. Though it doesn't specify which reference refers to which point in the sentence, together they support the point that there are other variables that influence the relationship between family structure and education.

In contrast, Juan Battle and others have demonstrated that the effect of family structure on education and cognitive ability varies and can be influenced by additional variables such as income, mother's mental health, and multigenerational households (Battle 1997; Carlson and Corcoran 2001, Deleire and Kalil 2002; Ginther and Pollak 2004).

As shown in these examples, the literature review is not summaries of the different articles but references to particular points emphasizing the ways the articles connect to each other and the subtopic. Incorporating theory is also an important part of the literature review and is often required in capstone papers, as it explains to the instructor how you developed the theoretical framework for your study. In incorporating theoretical perspectives, you want to make certain that you not only understand the theory but also can explain how it relates your research. Through the process of reading the research and theories presented in the literature, you will then be able to develop the theoretical framework you will use to test your hypothesis. This framework can either be incorporated into the literature review or can be a separate section presented after the literature review. However, the purpose of this framework is to explain how you came about the theory used to dictate your project.

Pay special attention to the following:

Be selective. You should be as thorough and exhaustive as possible in your initial review of the literature. However, when you write your paper, you should include only the literature that informed your project.

Focus on scholarly journal articles and books. Scholarly journal articles and books offer the best resources to help you develop your hypothesis, as they have been reviewed by other scholars in the field and have been deemed an important contribution to the field. Also, if you do not use any scholarly articles and books, you have not performed a proper review of the literature, and this may reflect negatively on your overall grade. We advise against including too many references to webpages, magazines, newspapers, and encyclopedia entries, but if you do include these sources, use them with caution. See Chapter 3 for more information on conducting research.

Don't go article by article; go subtopic by subtopic. As described in detail above, your literature review should be written as an essay. Do not move from one article to another, evaluating each one. Instead, present the literature based on the subtopics and analyze the articles found within those subtopics.

Focus on recent literature. While you may have begun the research project with a collection of resources, we suggest that you continue to examine current research during the entire research and writing process. In fact, you should keep looking until you write your final draft. You will also need to show your instructor that your paper is timely and fits within the current dialogue on the topic. Don't forget, new papers are published every day.

Don't quote too much. Try to use your own words in defining something or providing a description. Your instructor wants to read your voice and your interpretation of the readings. You will provide a list of all the books and articles you used for your project in your reference section, so if your instructor wants to know exactly what other authors said about a topic, she or he can find that particular article. Keep in mind that if a student quotes too often throughout his literature review, it is often a signal that he didn't understand the material well enough to put it into his own words. See Chapters 2 and 3 for more information about quotes and research.

Do not cite citations. Use primary literature. If you find an article or book that directly quotes or cites another source—a source that defines a particular sociological term, for example—and you want to incorporate that term or definition into your paper, do not cite another researcher's citation. Instead, seek out the original article and cite that instead.

Make sure you cite the proper article. Keep track of the different articles and books you use throughout your review of the literature. Be organized so you don't mix up research, forget to attribute a theory to the correct person, or mistakenly leave out a citation. While many students and professionals wait until they have completed their paper before they organize their references, the process always takes longer than you think it will and it is best to add references as you use them. See below for more information about the reference section.

Methodology

Now that you have introduced the instructor to your topic and project, reviewed the literature, and explained your hypothesis, you must inform her of how you went about proving or disproving your hypothesis or answering your research questions. Here, we will explain how research methods are most frequently described in research papers. The methods section explains the what, who, why, when, where, and how of your data collection process.

- *What* methodologies were used to collect the data?
- *Who* is included in the data? Who was spoken to? Observed? Surveyed?
- *Why* were these data used or these respondents chosen?
- *When* were the data collected?
- *Where* were the data collected?
- *How* were the data collected?

The purpose of the methods section is to describe to your instructor the methods used to address your research question and, importantly, to justify your methodology. The methods section also usually explains how data were analyzed. However, you can sometimes opt to include this in the results section of the paper instead. Remember, your methods section should provide enough information that another social scientist following your methodology would find similar results. This makes your research stand up to scientific inquiry.

The structure of your methods section will be determined by the project itself and the instructions provided by and approved by your capstone instructor. The methods section describes your research plan as well as your data, including the data collection process and analysis. There is usually a difference in how qualitative and quantitative researchers present their methodology. However, the write-up of both methodologies describes the research plan and the study participants and materials used as data. Either way, you will need to present your methodology in a clear and organized manner.

Research Process

Describe the data and briefly discuss your research plan or the process by which you identified and gathered the data. What specific methodology did you employ to gather your data? Did you conduct a content analysis, ethnography, or interviews? Did you distribute surveys or questionnaires? Here you will describe your unit of analysis (what you are actually studying) and identify the study variables and how they were measured. You will also want to explain what your research design is and, importantly, *why* this methodology was chosen.

Sample

Describe your data and your reason for selecting these particular subjects or materials to obtain your data. If it is quantitative data, you may also have to explain your sampling procedure.

Study Participants

Explain who your study participants are, why they were selected, and how you were able to access them. Essentially, what criteria were used to select your study participants? How are these participants representative of the issue you want to examine? How many participants do you have? You can opt to include demographic information, such as race, gender, age, sexual orientation, or religion, for the subjects in the methods section of the paper. Other writers opt to include this in the results section, as any findings concerning demographic information are a result of data analysis, which is usually discussed in the results section.

Materials

Explain what materials (such as books, newspapers, magazines, films, diaries/journals, pictures, artwork, etc.) were used, how they were selected, and how you were able to access them. List and describe the materials you used. If you performed a content analysis of Western films of the 1950s, you will need to list each film and explain why these films were selected. You may also want to provide more information about these movies, for example, in the endnotes or appendix of the manuscript (we provide a more detailed discussion of the appendices and endnotes at the end of this chapter). If you analyzed brochures, you will need to let the audience know what you looked for and how this will help you explore your hypothesis.

Data Collection

Once you have described your sample, you will need to describe your process of obtaining the data from the study participants or materials. You will not just describe how you collected data but the specific procedures for data collection Do your data consist of an analysis of the transcripts collected in a focus group? Do they consist of a historical narrative? Whether you used secondary data (data collected by someone else) or have collected your own data, you will need to describe your data in detail to your readers. Did you conduct interviews? What were the interview questions? How long were the interviews? Consider providing sample interview questions in the text of the manuscript or even providing the whole instrument in the appendix of the paper.

Location

Describe your research site. Where did you go to find your study participants and collect your data? Did you conduct an ethnography? Depending on the nature of your project, you may want to provide a description of the neighborhood or community in which your study participants reside. Did you conduct phone interviews? Did you interview people in your office? Did you interview them in their homes, churches, or places of employment? Where did you go to distribute surveys? Did you try a location that didn't work? You have to describe where your study participants came from.

Time Frame

Identify the time frame for data collection. Identify the number of weeks or months it took you to gather the data. You may also want to explain how long it took for your participants to complete the surveys or interviews. If you conducted an ethnography, how long were you in the field?

Response Rate

The response rate is the percentage of people who actually responded to the request to participate in the study. Discuss how many people were initially approached, how many agreed to participate, how many people were actually interviewed, surveyed, and so on. Response rate is very important to a research study.

Analysis

The discussion of your data analysis can appear either in the methods section or the results section. However, it is typically found in the methods section of your paper, as data analysis is part of your research methods. What method did you employ to analyze the relationship between the variables? Explain how you will analyze your data. Was your project quantitative? Which statistical software package (e.g., SPSS, SAS) did you use to analyze your surveys? What statistical tests did you use? Did you perform a simple bivariate analysis or a multivariate analysis? Was your project qualitative? Which qualitative software package (e.g., ATLAS.ti, NVivo) was used to analyze your interview data? Did you analyze your qualitative data by hand?

It is also appropriate here to explain what the unit of analysis is. What were you looking for? Did you explore certain themes or concepts? Let your instructor know what these are so they know what to expect when you present your findings and your analysis of the findings. Keep in mind that you are writing about how you conducted your analysis here, not what you found after conducting it. See Chapter 4 for more information about the writing involved in research projects.

Results

This section, also often labeled "Findings," explains the results of your study that are relevant to your research hypothesis and questions. This section should be written in a straightforward manner. To start off this section of your paper, you will want to restate your hypothesis to remind the audience, or your instructor, what you planned to look for and what you expected to find. You will then proceed to discuss your findings. It is important to emphasize that this section is where you present your findings to your audience, not where you interpret or discuss your findings. Save that for the discussion section of your paper. You will, however, report your results and explain whether or not your hypothesis was supported. Here you will also describe how the descriptive variables, such as race, age, and gender, influence your findings. You should present your findings organized around the various codes or themes you used to analyze data, keeping all like information together. As it is possible that your research might reveal an unexpected but important relationship, you can also include that here. You could also provide separate subheadings for each section. It is important to present your work in a clear and organized manner. If you used a mixed-methods approach (both quantitative and qualitative) in the data collection, you should try to present the results yielded from your qualitative analysis in a different section from the results yielded from your quantitative research. Scholars typically write and present the results of their quantitative and qualitative research differently. However, the incorporation of quantitative and qualitative research will vary depending on the nature of your project and the assignment.

Quantitative Research

For quantitative researchers, it is very important that the results section be written in a way that clearly explains the statistical procedures and measures conducted. You will want to remind the audience, or your instructor, of the statistical tests you performed and report the results. Explain the direction of the results and/or levels of significance. You may also need to explain the critical values and degrees of freedom. The purpose of conducting a statistical analysis is to ascertain the probability that the variance between the items in your data is a result of actual differences between people, rather than errors in your findings.

In your description of your statistical procedure and results, it is important to word your findings properly. Present the results of your test in sentence format. Explain in words what is being evaluated and what kind of effect those factors have. What was the significance level of the interaction? If an item is statistically significant, it means there is a higher probability that your findings are the result of the independent variable rather than random error. You should also inform your audience of the alpha level at which your data were statistically significant. For example:

Data were statistically significant at the alpha level of .001.

As you may remember from your research methods class, the lower the alpha level in your results, the less likely that some random error caused the findings. To illustrate:

Gender was statistically significant at the.05 level in predicting one's perception of household chores.

This example would demonstrate that the relationship between gender and household chores was likely not a result of an error in the data or the particular sample that you selected but that women and men actually perceive chores differently. Make sure to include your major findings in the results section. Include any descriptive and/or inferential statistics you may have found. How did the respondents' demographic characteristics influence the relationship between the dependent variable and the independent variable? If it is important to your research, you will want to explain this in detail.

Qualitative Research

Papers based on data gathered by qualitative research methods (e.g., focus groups, interviews) tend to allow for a bit more freedom in how work can be presented compared with the way quantitative researchers write their reports. Qualitative papers often blend the methods and results sections, as often the way researchers gather data *is* the data.

Another major difference between presenting qualitative vs. quantitative research is the rich description often used in explaining research settings or sites. Data collected through qualitative research methods, such as interviews and focus groups, tend to describe the subjects individually and in much more detail. This is done in part because qualitative researchers may not have as many respondents as quantitative researchers do. More respondents decrease the probability that the findings were influenced by error or sample selection alone.

Qualitative research is more exploratory and, as such, provides the audience with a more in-depth understanding of the experiences of the study participants. Here, description is critical. You should include demographic information about the respondents, such as their age, race, and gender. You may want to describe what your study participants were wearing, the settings in which you interviewed them, and their professions, for example. This is especially helpful the first time you introduce a respondent to the reader. Knowing more information about study participants may provide some context for their responses to your questions or for your analysis of the social issue(s) being examined. The following is a quote one might find in a qualitative paper on the influence of small-classroom size on student learning:

One respondent, Ms. Simmons, stated: "The more time I spent with students, the better they read!"

This example provides a deeper description of the participant:

Ms. Simmons, a second-grade teacher who has been teaching in the Los Angeles Unified School District for more than 45 years, believed that spending one-on-one time with students helped improve their reading skills. After one particularly busy class, Ms. Simmons exclaimed: "The more time I spent with students, the better they read!"

This description helps put the quote in context. The fact that Ms. Simmons has been teaching for 45 years may add some authority to what she said. Would you think differently of her quote if she had taught for two years? Providing more of a description of the participant helps provide legitimacy to both the participant's quote and your analysis of it.

In qualitative projects, interview quotes or descriptions of the data (for content analysis, for example) should be presented as data. Taking the above example, you could write:

A majority of the respondents in my sample indicated that the more time teachers and staff spent with students, the better they did in school. Ms. Simmons, a second-grade teacher who has been teaching in the Los Angeles Unified School District for more than 45 years, believed that spending one-on-one time with students helped improve their reading skills. After one particularly busy class, Ms. Simmons stated: "The more time I spent with students, the better they read!"

The quote simply provides an example of what other study participants have indicated. As qualitative researchers typically analyze written documents, such as fieldnotes, diaries, and journals, as data, incorporating the text into the results section is customary. It is common to see passages from a researcher's fieldnotes used as data to describe a location or respondent. This helps add depth and give the reader a better understanding of the data.

Tables, Diagrams, Graphs, and Charts

Tables, diagrams, graphs, and charts that can better illustrate your findings are typically included in the methods or results section. Including these graphics allows others to visualize the relationships between the variables. A variety of charts and tables can be created, and the type of visual you create, as well as the format, will vary depending on the research method performed, type of analysis, software program, and even paper assignment. The visual most frequently used within are tables. As such, we will focus here on how to incorporate the discussion of tables into your writing.

Tables are most frequently found in papers that utilize quantitative methods and are used to provide a visual of the statistical information and findings. Tables are often used to chart information such as independent and dependent variables, demographic information, percentages, mean, standard deviation, significance tests, alpha, and regression coefficients (see the example below in Table 1). A well-constructed table allows for the reader to visualize information easily in a compact presentation. Tables can be constructed from the output of statistical software packages such as SPSS or manually created in programs such as Microsoft Excel. As mentioned above, the structure and format of the table vary depending on the nature of the project and what you are trying to convey through the table. The sample table below illustrates statistical findings explaining on- and off-campus community involvement among a sample of college students.

Be sure to label the chart appropriately so it corresponds to how you refer to it in the text. Check with your instructor about inclusion and

Table 1 Unstandardized Regression Coefficients for On- and Off-Campus Community Involvement Among College Students

	Dependent Variables On-Campus Community Involvement (N = 453)		Dependent Variables Off-Campus Community Involvement (N = 453)	
	Model I	Model II	Model III	Model IV
Independent Variables Community				
Connected to college campus	.284*** (.335)	.278*** (.328)	.230*** (.252)	.225*** (.246)
Connected to off-campus community	.130*** (.037)	.123*** (.131)	.072† (.071)	.073† (.072)
University faculty/staff support	.006 (.009)	.009 (.013)	.038 (.053)	.026 (.902)
Comfort in campus communities		.112*** (−.024)		−124*** (−.164)
Comfort in off-campus communities		.017 (.025)		.078* (.107)
Constant	1.285***	1.273***	1.536***	1.460***
Adjusted R	.160	.158	.088	.091

Notes: † p ≤.10 * p ≤.05 ** p ≤.01 *** p ≤.001; (*betas* in parentheses)

placement of tables, charts, and other figures before including one in your paper. For example:

As illustrated in Table 5.1, the rates of obesity have declined among . . .

Wording of Findings

Be sure to word your findings properly. Your findings are based on a sample of people, books, films, for example—samples you hope are representative of the general population with those same characteristics. As such, you cannot use sweeping generalizations to describe your subjects or results. For example, in reporting your survey findings on perceptions of race in the United States, you cannot say:

Despite Barack Obama's presidential victories, Black people believe they are still oppressed in the United States.

Although all the Black people in your sample may have reported that, it is important to clarify that you are referring only to the Black people in your survey, not to all Black people. If you are not precise in your language, it reads as though all Black people believe this, which is clearly not the case, as you did not survey all Black people in the United States. This could be rewritten more accurately:

Despite Barack Obama's presidential victories, the Black people in my survey believed that they are still oppressed in the United States.

Thus far, we have written up the important literature on the topic and the research hypothesis. We have discussed how you need to explain to your audience the methods you used to prove or disprove your hypothesis. You learned how to present your results and inform your audience whether or not your hypothesis was supported. Now it is time to talk about the analysis and interpretation of your results, and this leads us to the discussion section.

Discussion

After you present your findings and explain whether your hypothesis was supported or not, you will want to analyze your findings. You will need to support your summation based not only on data but also on where the data are positioned in the literature you reviewed for your paper. The discussion section is the most important section of a research paper. As we mentioned above, the focus in your results section is on presenting your results to the reader, without interpreting their meanings. The discussion section is where that interpretation occurs. There are a few key parts of discussion sections that, regardless of the methodology used to gather the data, you may want to include.

Restate Hypothesis

To begin, restate your hypothesis and what you expected to find as a result of your project. It may feel as though you keep repeating your hypothesis, but it is important to remind your reader of your hypothesis, and the repetition also helps keep you on track and focuses your paper. If your hypothesis was supported by your research, explain how it was supported and what factors you think influenced this. Similarly, be sure to explain why and how you think you obtained these results if your hypothesis was not supported. Inform your reader of what these results mean and what the larger implications may be, not just for your research but also for the field of sociology. Again, the purpose of good research is to contribute to a particular area of study, so you want to clearly explain *how* it contributes to the field.

Connect to the Literature

After you discuss your hypothesis, you should then discuss the important results of your project. Inform the reader of what these results mean and the implications for your research. The same way you broke down various topics, subtopics, and library findings in the literature review may be helpful here. You can provide subheadings to keep yourself organized so you go topic by topic. It is also important here to tie your findings back to the literature and the theories you discussed in your literature review. Was the literature supported, or did your findings refute a previous study? Here you will have a dialogue with the literature and explain how your findings/research contribute to field.

Larger Implications

As sociologists, much of our research addresses some kind of social problem or ill. Many of us write with the intent of influencing public policy or the community in which we study. For instance, our findings can be used to reduce health disparities or increase the quality of education, not only for our respondents but also for others in need. In your discussion section, you should explain what public policy and even practical implications your research has. Explain why people should care about your findings.

Areas for Improvement: Flaws and Future Research

No research project is perfect. How would you improve your study? Many papers that you've likely examined include a description of the "flaws" in their research and even label them as such. We, on the other hand, encourage you to think of them as "areas of future research." View any "flaws" you may find in your research design or methodologies as an opportunity for you or someone else to replicate the study. If your project explores the relationship between fathers and their children and you obtained your sample of 15 fathers from a list of fathers active in the Boy Scouts, this could be problematic. Even though you may think you have a really good sample based on race, class, and education level, your project is still biased. Who is to say that the opinions and behaviors of the 15 men are really representative of the typical father? Does the typical father participate in the Boy Scouts? While there will always be sampling bias with most forms of data collection, it is important to realize what these biases are and honestly report them in your paper. It is part of the research process. While addressing flaws may seem discouraging, this is how we keep conversations going within our field.

Conclusion

As with the literature review and the introduction, we often combine the discussion and conclusion sections of a paper. Much of the information you can include in the conclusion of your paper you could also include in the discussion section; yet for the purposes of clarity, we will examine the conclusion separately.

Your conclusion is where you do just that, conclude the paper. Just as you introduced your research to your audience in the introduction, you will conclude the discussion on your research in this section. Start off by restating your main point and the overall purpose of your paper. Was your hypothesis supported? If so, briefly explain why and how. Remind your reader (or your instructor) why your project is important. Additionally, some researchers opt to include policy implications and areas for future research here, instead of in the discussion section. You should end your paper by answering the question, "So what?" This question explains why your research was important and the contributions it can make, not only to our field of study but to the larger social picture.

ADDITIONAL PAPER SECTIONS

Abstracts

Abstracts are short, one-paragraph (or so) summaries of the various sections of your paper. Abstracts are typically 100 to 300 words in length. Most research papers within the social sciences contain the following summarized information in their abstracts: the research question/problem, the methods used, the results, and a sentence or so explaining the study's larger implications. In writing the abstract, be sure to provide a thorough summation of your important findings and conclusions. Think of the abstract as a brief synopsis of your paper (see Chapter 2 for more information about abstracts).

Titles and Subtitles

Ideally, your title will accurately represent your project and jump out at the reader. Be creative. Your title can be a play on words, a famous saying, or even a quote from a subject. It is customary for social scientists to create subtitles as well. A subtitle is often used to describe the actual issue being addressed in the text. Providing a subtitle that clearly explains the project to the reader can be especially helpful if the main title is catchy but vague. This can also be reversed, where the subtitle is catchy and the title explains the topic. In your title, you want to provide as much information as possible without creating an extremely long title. Ideally, you should include information related to your hypothesis or conclusion and your sample (Chapter 7 also includes information on titles). Examples of titles and subtitles from some well-known sociological texts include the following:

- "There She Is, Miss America": The Politics of Sex, Beauty, and Race in America's Most Famous Pageant
- Black Picket Fences: Privilege and Peril Among the Black Middle Class
- Stigma: Notes on the Management of Spoiled Identity

References

Your reference section is based on the literature you actually referenced throughout your paper and should be included with every paper written where literature was cited. This section comes at the end of your paper.

Be sure to check the formatting guidelines dictating the proper citation style. As previously mentioned, most sociology faculty require references in ASA or APA format. The citations should be listed in alphabetical order by the first author's last name. Be sure not to change the order of the names for each article or book. The names should be listed in the exact order they were presented in the original work, as they are either in alphabetical order or positioned to indicate who did a majority of the work on the project or who the primary investigator is. As a result, they get first billing.

The reference section should include only the literature you referenced in your paper. Make sure you check with your professor to find out how they want the reference section formatted (see Chapter 3 for more information on formatting the reference section appropriately).

Footnotes/Endnotes

Footnotes and endnotes are also used to cite information or to include a little note or background information on a topic that, although it relates to the issue, does not fit in the main text. The primary difference between endnotes and footnotes is their placement within the text. Footnotes are found at the end of the page on which the related citations appear. Endnotes, more frequently found within journals and books, are placed at the end of the paper, article, chapter (in an anthology), or book. Do not try to create your own footnotes or endnotes by using a superscript. Most word processors have a function that will do that for you. Often foot- and endnotes are separated from the rest of the text by a line and they are sometimes in a smaller font

Use footnotes/endnotes sparingly, as you should try to include only pertinent information on your topic in your paper. Footnotes and endnotes should be used only if you think they will provide context or additional information for some readers that does not necessarily fit within the actual text. Ask for professor which, if any, they prefer.

REVIEW YOUR WORK

There are a few steps you want to take before you submit your paper. Remember, make sure to follow all instructions and review them before submitting your paper to your instructor. Presentation is everything! When you review your work, do not look only for grammatical errors (although you do want to check for those) but also check for the soundness of your argument. As usual, thoroughly review and revise before submitting anything for evaluation. Ideally, your work should be extensively reviewed by at least two other people (see Chapter 6 for more about editing and revising). Review the following aspects of your paper in particular.

Argument. You should be able to identify your thesis quickly. Is your argument sound? Do you support your thesis with adequate evidence from your data? Do you provide a clear and logical argument concerning your analysis of your findings? Make sure your paper is focused and that you stick to the subject and examine only what is relevant to your thesis.

Terminology. Be certain your wording and use of terminology is correct.

Transitions. Make sure the paragraphs flow together and that you have proper transition sentences or subheadings in your text.

Grammar/spelling. Check for errors in sentence structure, punctuation, spelling, passive voice, and citations. You should avoid contractions when using your own words and are not quoting someone who used contractions in his work.

Format. Check for margins, font size and style, spacing, indents, structure, charts, citation style, in-text citations, and end-text citations.

Word count. Be sure to stick to the word count or paper length. If you feel as though your paper will go over this range, contact your instructor and ask if it will be acceptable. Sometimes instructors will allow you to submit a longer piece, while others will stop reading once you reach the limit. Be sure to check if the reference section is often included in the final word count or page limit.

Tense. Methods sections are typically written in the past tense; however, fieldnotes are written in the present tense. Literature reviews can be written in both past and present tense, but much of that depends on the literature you are describing. The discussion section is typically written in the present tense. The conclusion section can be written in the past or present tense. If you are unsure as to which tense to use, ask your instructor for suggestions.

First person. Debate exists concerning how much professional distance should be maintained in your work. Some writers argue that writing in the first person is unprofessional and that you should maintain a professional distance from your research. Others argue that placing the researcher into the work grounds the project and allows for the researcher's perspective to come through in the writing. Typically, qualitative researchers write in the first person (*I*, *me*, and *we*) and quantitative researchers write in the third person (*he*, *she*, and *it*). In qualitative research, particularly ethnographic work, the researcher is often an active participant in the data collection process. As such, it makes sense that she writes in the first person. Again, make sure to review this with your instructor if you have questions concerning this in your paper.

SUMMARY

Course papers are often the first forms of writing that sociologists compose. Different types of course papers were discussed in this chapter, including

- different types of essays,
- annotated bibliographies,
- literature reviews, and
- capstone/research papers.

The "Writing in Practice" piece for this chapter is written by Daniel Balcazar. Daniel is a recent graduate of Marquette University who majored in sociology. In this essay, Daniel explains how he approaches researching and writing his course papers.

WRITING IN PRACTICE

By Daniel Balcazar

Before tackling any sociology writing assignment, you have to first learn sociology. Learning and understanding comes before writing, much like how you learn to walk before you learn to run. This may sound rudimentary, but it is imperative. *Sociology* is, by definition, a discipline about the world around us; therefore, as "sociologists," it is not only important to read the mandated course materials, but it is also vital to learn about the world and attempt to understand it. This includes reading about history, staying up to date on international and local news, and learning and getting involved in the your community. I am a community organizer as well as a student. I am on the board of an immigrant rights organization and would argue the experience has benefited me as much as my classes this semester have. Firsthand experience is invaluable and cannot be achieved solely through books. It is one thing to read about oppressed communities and use Max Weber's theories to analyze oppressed powerless communities; it is another and far more holistic approach to include direct experience working alongside community members to empower communities. When writing a research paper on health disparities for Latinos in my city for an upper level sociology course, I decided to include in the portion on a social innovation program design, a health clinic at the headquarters of the organization I am part of. I reasoned that the location was optimal and that the organization already had the infrastructural capacity, social capital, and community trust to adequately reach the most vulnerable of the community, including undocumented immigrants who tend to have the worst health outcomes among Latinos. Without my firsthand experience in the community, my ideas would have been superficial. Understanding and learning about the world and your communities are vital steps needed to successfully write well before you even write down any words.

It is also important to find your comfort zone and infuse writing with personal interests. This being said, when beginning to write sociology assignments for introductory courses, you must break out of your initial comfort zone and uncover find your interests. Few career sociologists come into introductory sociology courses knowing what will ultimately be their lifelong passion. So, as undergraduate students, we should use the sociology assignments in our courses to test the waters and uncover what area we love writing about. If I have a four-page paper to write on Pierre Bourdieu's forms of capital and their application to social media for a sociological theory course, as someone who gravitates toward conflict theory, I will shape the thesis to accommodate my perspective and intertwine Bourdieu's notions of the forms of capital with Karl Marx's economic notion of capital. As an emerging sociologist, try and find your comfort area; this can be done by exploring perspectives, theories, and topics. You may find that you have already developed one—it may be the perspective you find yourself most referring to in your papers, reading about in your free time, or experiencing in your life. What drew me to critical theory was that when I was younger, I loved when my father told me stories about growing up in Colombia in a dangerous political era and the history of guerrillas and socialism throughout Latin America. When I began taking sociology courses at the university level, I found myself most comfortable writing using a critical perspective.

Tackling sociology assignments can be difficult. Whether you are writing an analytic paper dissecting the arguments of George Mead's symbolic interactionism, or writing a literature review on prominent Black feminists during the 1960s, juggling the myriad of different theories,

(Continued)

(Continued)

concepts, and theorists can be cumbersome. But reading critically, learning about your community, staying up to date with the world, and writing toward your personal interests have made the task manageable for me. As undergraduate students, we are constantly juggling many courses, and often different areas of study; we strive for clarity during the time of exploration and growth in our lives that is college. Taking the above suggested steps should hopefully aid you in that endeavor, as they have worked greatly for me.

—Daniel Balcazar, BA, is currently a graduate student in the Masters of Public Health Program at Emory University and has his undergraduate degree in sociology from Marquette University.

NOTES

1. Harris, Angelique. 2010. "Panic at the Church: The Use of Frames, Social Problems, and Moral Panics in the Formation of an AIDS Social Movement Organization." *Western Journal of Black Studies* 34(3):337–46.

2. Dickens, Charles. 2010 [1859]. *A Tale of Two Cities*. Alberta, Canada: Qualitas Publishing.

3. Austen, Jane. 2002 [1813]. *Pride and Prejudice*. New York: Penguin Books.

4. Orwell, George. 2003 [1949]. *1984*. New York: Plume.

5. Ellison, Ralph. 1995 [1952]. *Invisible Man*. New York: Random House.

6. Centers for Disease Control and Prevention. 2011. "National Diabetes Fact Sheet: National Estimates and General Information on Diabetes and Prediabetes in the United States, 2011." Atlanta, GA: U.S. Department of Health and Human Services, Centers for Disease Control and Prevention.

7. Mills, C. Wright. 1959. *Sociological Imagination*. Oxford, UK: Oxford University Press.

8. Tyner-Mullings, Alia R. 2008. "Finding space: Educational reforms in practice in an urban public school," City University of New York, ProQuest Dissertations Publishing. http://search.proquest.com/docview/193652672

CHAPTER 6

EDITING AND REVISING

R evision is one of the most important parts of the writing process. This is a point in writing that can be both the easiest and the most difficult to overcome, as well as a part that is often not given the proper amount of attention or forgotten all together. Revision is included in this book because we want to make sure that doesn't happen. This chapter is placed near the end because that is often where we place revision within our writing process. But that does not need to be where it stays.

Revision is an iterative process that is constantly occurring and ultimately changes your final product. You may go over a paper numerous times, changing something during each iteration. Sometimes you revise while you are writing, and other times you wait until you have completed something before editing and revising and editing again. It is important to remember that revision is not just something you do when you have the time; revision is something you are always doing. We hope this chapter will improve on your ability to revise and make the process the second nature it should be.

FIRST DRAFT

Writing always begins with a first draft. For students, procrastination can prevent moving forward in the drafting process. In many cases, the first draft becomes the only draft, as we run out of time to make revisions, decide it is not important, or lose interest once a version has been written. There is no particular attribute that makes a draft a first, second, or final draft. There is not a specific structure for a first draft.

For some, a first draft is little more than an outline fleshed out. It can include the vague headings and subheadings you created to organize your research, along with notes to expand on each of your headings. It can be a new organization of your annotated bibliography (see Chapter 3). For others, a first draft can be more like a stream of consciousness. In this context, a stream of consciousness is a written illustration of your thought process. Rather than worrying about creating grammatically correct sentences, full paragraphs, or a coherent argument, you follow your ideas where they take you. Often, this includes questions you may have for yourself, places where you would like to follow up with more research, or even notes to remind yourself to speak to people who may have relevant information. Your first-draft stream of consciousness becomes a display of every thought you have about, around, or concerning the topic. Yet, there are others who feel that a paper needs to be complete in structure before it can be considered an actual draft. Again, there is no standard for a first draft.

What is most important about this step is that you get something down on paper. You cannot write until you have written. If that first step is difficult for you, you might want to try free-writing or stream-of-consciousness methods to start. Consider these questions: What do you know about your topic? What questions still remain on your topic? What brought you to this topic? What did you learn that you didn't know before? You can write this as a letter to yourself, a journal entry, or a series of notes. Write it in a way that is comfortable for you, and don't worry about structure or spelling or grammar. Just write. Once you have collected and organized your thoughts on paper, you will have a better idea of what you know and what you need to know. This may also help you think about how you have organized your research in your head.

For those who write with a little more structure, an outline (see Chapter 3) is an important foundation on which to build. Your first-draft process can begin with an outline as your basic structure. You create your draft by slowly filling in the meat on top of the outline's bones. Even if you simply have an outline with some notes, quotes, or places to look for notes, you can still consider this to be a first draft.

FIRST REVISION

Depending on the level of completeness of your first draft, you may or may not want to share it with others. Writers tend to be protective of early drafts, and the point at which you allow them to leave your hands is a matter of personal choice. If you have a group of friends or classmates also in college, you might consider starting a study group and, if you are able to be more focused, a writing group. For many projects, this will be more useful if everyone is in the same class together but for writing, anyone can be in the group. Most classes will require some kind of paper writing and, even if your group mates don't understand the details of the topic, they still can provide feedback on what you have written and what works or doesn't work. In fact, sometimes it is better that they don't know the topic because your paper will have to do the job of teaching them. A writing group is also beneficial to its participants because reading and reviewing other students' work can help to improve yours. However, if you are unable to create a group, being able to at least bounce ideas off of or read a draft to someone is important to your writing process. It allows you to see how other people understand your work and provides you with feedback on what you have written so far.

If you do have a writing group, you may want to set guidelines as to what constitutes a first draft. An outline may be sufficient for your group to read, as may be a stream of consciousness. In other situations, you may have a group where documents closer to completion are more appropriate, and, in that case, you may want to go through a revision or two on your own before you share with your group. As a college student, much of this will probably be determined by your time and whether you are able to look at someone's stream of consciousness or can only help if a paper is further along. Whatever you decide, make sure it's reciprocal. If you give someone a basic outline to read, you should be accepting if they do the same. It may also be useful to have smaller groups for earlier drafts. If you only have to look at earlier work from one person, it might help with the workload.

Once you have written your first draft, it is important to take a break from it. As a college student, you might only be able to take an hour or two to distance yourself from your work but if you can, you should. You can take this time to work on a different type of assignment for another class, eat a meal, or complete another task. You will find that the quality of your work will go up as a result of taking the time to do a second read-through with a clear mind.

QUICK EDIT

Even a quick read-through can catch some common problems and produce a second draft; so many of the strategies included in this chapter can be modified for when time is at a premium, as it often is for college students. However, the guidelines in this section are specifically for when you have only a few moments to revise your work. It is better to edit quickly than not to edit at all. In addition, if a course includes a first and final draft, the expectation is that there is some difference between them. Even if you received a good grade for the first draft, you should still address any edits or comments the professor provided. If there were none, send an e-mail or have a conversation and find out what you should do. Make sure to pay close attention to anything your professor says is missing or could use some revision.

Check Punctuation, Spelling, and Grammar

As mentioned in the previous chapter, if nothing else, your readers appreciate a paper free of spelling, punctuation, and grammatical errors. Too many people present themselves as significantly worse writers than they actually are because they do not take enough time to catch the little mistakes made throughout the paper. Read through your entire document, out loud, with a pen (or a mouse, touchpad, or touchscreen) in your hand. Where you pause, add a comma; where you stop, add a period. If a word looks odd to you, put it in a spell check, search engine, or use a dictionary and find out if it's correct. Most word processors also have incorporated spell and grammar checks. If they do not automatically indicate to your misspellings and grammar errors, you should, at the very least, run these checks to ensure that such problems are handled. However, keep in mind that spelling and grammar checks are not perfect. They will not always catch a word you missed or used in the wrong context. Also, if the language of your document and the language of your word processor are not in sync, it will see many more mistakes where there are none. Make sure this is not your sole method of editing.

Main Point

Be sure that the paper addresses what it needs to address. If you were given a question to answer, make sure what you have written provides an answer. If there are multiple points or questions, they should all be addressed in your writing assignment. It may be helpful to return to the assignment checklist you made of all the aspects of the assignment and check them off after rereading your work to make sure you did not miss anything. You may also want to rewrite the question you were supposed to answer in a separate document and then cut and paste your answer and see if the two align. If there was an assigned first and second draft, take note of the requirements and guidelines for both versions of the assignment as they may have different constraints.

Supporting Evidence

You should be able to draw a web through your paper, connecting each thing you write back to the main point. The more secondary points you have to draw your line through—because a particular point supports a secondary point rather than a main one—to reach your main point, the more complicated your piece is and the higher the potential for confusion. Your reader should not have to go back several pages to figure out how to connect, for instance, promotion opportunities in the workplace with the lines at women's bathrooms. Even if you are writing an elaboration paragraph (see Chapter 2), the reader should be able to trace a direct link to a secondary point, which would then lead them back to the main point.

General Structure

Not all assignments call for an introduction and a conclusion, but unless you are simply answering a question posed to you, it doesn't hurt to include them. You can see Chapters 2 and 5 for instructions on the general structure of a paper and writing introductions and conclusions, but even a simple sentence that describes the route you will be taking the readers and another that tells them where they have just been provide useful bookends or a road map for the body of the paper and raises its quality level.

Often the first draft of your paper can include other structural aspects that can make it look sloppy. You should make sure that yours does not include:

- Sentences with random capital letters—They should begin with one and should only include additional capital letters for proper nouns and *I*.
- Multiple spaces between words, lines, or punctuation—Unless instructed otherwise, there should be only one space between words and after periods, commas, and other punctuation. There should be no space before punctuation. If it is within the assignment guidelines to double-space your paper, you should allow your word processing program to do this, rather than trying to do it manually.
- A diversity of formatting for paragraphs—Paragraphs should either be indented or have an additional space between them, not both. Sociology papers generally use the indent method.
- Any inconsistencies with the assignment—Make sure you are within the page limit (some professors will stop reading once they reach it), and that the font size and type are constant and within the guidelines given.

EXTENSIVE FIRST EDIT

Depending on the state of your first draft, it may need more than a quick glance to become a document you can share with others. If your first draft was only a meaty outline or a stream of consciousness, you will have to turn that first edit into a formal paper. While everyone has her own writing process, the first step in forming a second draft from a minimalist first draft is to find out what you have and what you still need to add to your document. Outlining, or re-outlining, is a good way to do that. In your outline, you should make sure every paragraph of your draft is accounted for. If you have used subheadings, you can use the same ones in your outline, and within those, the subsections of your outline can represent each paragraph. In a smaller paper, you might give titles to each paragraph and use these as the outline subheadings. Using headings or titles will help with your organization and you should move any paragraph that doesn't fit within the heading you have used for that section.

In creating your new outline, review the points you need to make and the evidence needed to support those points. Even if you did not write it into your first draft, be sure there is a place in your outline for each part you intend to write and the evidence needed to support it. In some cases, you might use a heading or a question as a placeholder for research you still need to do. You might also use a quote or a citation if you have evidence but have not properly integrated it yet. This way, you have a clear record of what you have done and what has yet to be completed. Once you have combined your outline with your stream of consciousness/free write, you can follow a lot of the same guidelines for other editing; just make sure to expand any bullet points into full sentences.

GENERAL REVISION

Ideally, revision should happen over several readings. You are examining a few different aspects when you revise, and it is difficult to do them all in one read-through. The more revising you do, the more likely you are to find you have a personal preference in terms of what kinds of revisions you do and when you choose to do them. When you are asked do a peer review as part of a class, the professor will likely give you some instruction on the process she wants you to follow. If she does not, these methods should serve you well.

Much of what you will read on revising will divide the work into content and form. Some people will prioritize one over the other and say that you cannot properly address one until the other has been perfected.

Yet, consider a paper that is filled with evidence but consists of sentences that do not follow each other logically, or a perfect five-paragraph essay in which each paragraph covers a different topic. Content and form work hand in hand, and in editing, it's important that both get the appropriate amount of attention.

Generally, revision is a spiraling process that can be never-ending if you allow it to be. You can ask almost any writer about a work he "completed" and he will tell you about a mistake he made, something he wished he had done differently, or edits he made too late. Some academics hate to read their past writing because they know they are going to find those mistakes they missed. Others look back on their previous work as an opportunity to learn from their missteps. Revision is really never complete, but once you are comfortable with your writing, you can make a decision on when to stop.

Regardless of when it ends, revision always begins with a read-through. As mentioned above, this is best done after you have put the piece aside for a period of time. A week or more is ideal, but if this is impossible, a few days works well or, at the very least, an hour or two. Without that time to give your mind a break from your work, you are very likely to miss errors, and you lose the ability to recognize what you have excluded because it may still be present in your mind even if it isn't in your paper.

As you read through your work, be prepared either to edit or to make note of where to edit. For some of us, especially those who did not grow up completely immersed in a digital culture, editing is easier by hand. Without the same level of editing software on tablets or smartphones, a pen or pencil and a hard copy allow for mobility that a computer or laptop may not.

Word-processing programs are equipped with different supports to assist in your editing process. For some, especially those who edit others' work or have others edit their work, add-ons such as Microsoft Word's Track Changes feature are invaluable (see Figure 6.1). Track Changes allows you to insert or delete pieces of text without losing them completely. Depending on your settings, Track Changes will either strike out deleted text or place it in a "bubble" alongside your text. This allows your changes to be temporary until you have accepted or rejected them. Track Changes will also keep track of who has added which edits and when. Google Documents now has a Suggestion mode which works like Track Changes and provides an option to see what changes you or others have made to your document before accepting them. There are also now several apps that will allow you to read track changes as well as a smaller number that will allow you to create them.

Figure 6.1

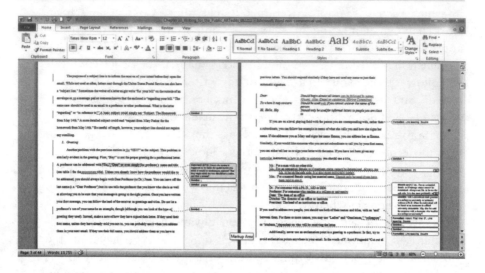

For those who choose to edit by hand, copyediting symbols (see Figure 6.2) are often used to note changes to be made to the structure of the document. Though you may have your own shorthand (or you might create your own), using something like copyediting symbols means that, if someone else does your edits, there is a common language shared between you and the copy editor so you can understand what the edits mean even if you're not together.

As we move into the further digitized nature of the written word, mobile devices become another possibility for editing. This is not yet a norm, but as more people use e-readers, tablets, and phones to read their documents, especially longer ones, they will also use them more for revision. While much of the technology currently available does not allow for complex editing, such as that available on a computer, you can always take notes on what to enter into a document later or simply change the document without saving your process over the original document, if that option is available. Tablets and smartphones can connect the digital age with the editing we do by hand, and you may also be able to find word-processing-based applications to assist in the process.

When revising, remember that you are trying to make the document into something another reader can understand without you having to hold her hand. The reader will not know what you meant by something unless you explain it. She will not know what your voice sounds like or how you meant to set up your argument unless you do it. For this reason, having someone else (or yourself after some time away) read your document can be very informative.

Figure 6.2

Proofreaders Marks

Insertion	Symbol	Explanation		Example
	⊙	Insert period		The authors disagree on outcomes⊙
	⌃	Insert comma		Following that logic⌃the research was flawed.
	⌃ or ⌃	Insert colon		We had three problems⌃the site, the data and the research plan.
	;/ or ⌃	Insert semi-colon		The majority of students were unaware of the school⌃they learned about it by word of mouth.
	⌄	Insert quotation mark		According to Jenkins "students struggled in the school⌄"
	⌄	Insert apostrophe		Johnson⌄s research indicated positive outcomes.
	⌄	Insert single quotation mark		During an interview, Julie explained, "the woman said ⌄how can you be so disruptive⌄ "
	⌃ ⌄ ⟨/⟩	Insert parenthesis		While there were several problems (and residents were not satisfied , the policy seemed effective⌃.
	⌊	Insert bracket		"[she⌊thought that the neighborhood was unsafe."
	? or ?	Insert question mark		What was the effect of the policy on the residents ?
	=	Insert hyphen		Seventy⸗two
	⌃	Insert (general)		⌃

Other	Symbol	Explanation		Example
	#	Insert space		There#search led to several different conclusions.
	ℓ	Delete letter or work		We wrote up the ℓ data.
	⌒	Close-up		Our research was⌒completed a year ago.
	¶	Begin new paragraph		¶
	No ¶	No paragraph		No ¶
	⌢	Transpose (switch)		I her told that she has the wrong idea.
	Caps or ≡	Caps		beginning in 1978, roles were redefined.
	lc / lower case	lower case		lc We created several interview instruments.
	(wf)	Wrong font		(wf) Several of our respondents agreed.

Revision works best when you recognize all the pieces of your document and how they work together to support the whole. This is likely easiest when you start with the larger pieces and work your way down to the smaller elements.

FULL DOCUMENT

When considering the paper as a whole, ask yourself whether it serves the larger goals of your assignment, research question, or hypothesis. The most important question for each section of the paper is "Does this answer the question?" You want to be sure that by the time someone has completed your piece, he has the answer to the question you posed or has received an adequate reason for why the question cannot be answered and/or how it might be answered in the future.

As sociologists, the questions we research cannot be answered with simply a yes or no; they are questions that explore how and why things happen and the relationships between various elements. So, when considering whether your question has been answered, you need to consider not just the simple yes or no but the explanation of the relationship—not only the who, what, where, and when but also the why and how—and recall that the last two are generally the most important to sociologists.

If the question has not been answered, what is unclear or missing from your work? What would answer the question? This may be the most difficult thing to judge if you are editing your own work, as the answer to the main question may seem clearer to you than it would to your reader, which is another argument for having someone else take a look. Once you can say that your question has been answered, you can go on to the next section. Keep in mind that you may need to come back to this question after you've gone through the rest of your revisions to ensure that your paper still fulfills its purpose.

SUBSECTIONS/SUBHEADINGS

We have examined, especially in Chapter 5, the types of sections, headings, and subheadings you might need for your paper. These depend on what you are writing, as each section exists to support the overall purpose of the document. The sections should serve as landmarks or signposts leading the reader through the map of your document. In fact, you should be able to take only the introductory and concluding paragraphs of each section and know exactly where you are going, where you've been, and why. Each section should begin with a paragraph that explains where you are taking the reader, why you are taking her there (what does this have to do with the main purpose of the document?), and where you are taking her next. A good exercise during revision is to create an actual document map, which includes the introductory and concluding paragraph in each section. If you can follow the path of your paper through those paragraphs, it likely holds together well. If you find that once you don't have access to the meat of your subsections, you can no longer follow your argument, you will need to clarify the confusing paragraphs.

While headings and subheadings are intended to provide directional arrows for an individual working his way through your work, they are not an excuse for ignoring transitions between paragraphs. You should avoid, or edit out, all unnecessary turns into a new topic (or a new take on an old topic) without some kind of proper indication of what is happening. Transitions between paragraphs are built on transitional words. Are you building on your previous point (*additionally, secondarily, next, finally, as well as, furthermore, similarly*)? Are you presenting an opposing viewpoint (*alternately, however, conversely, in contrast to*)? Are you providing a conclusion or evidence for the point you just made (*therefore, it follows, as a result of, consequently*)? These particular words do not need to be present every time you make a transition, but the idea behind them should be, and some type of indicator needs to be used to tell your reader where to go.

Introductions and conclusions are specific types of subsections. Although the body of your work will change depending on the type of writing you are doing, these sections will be present in every academic piece you write. For many writers, the introduction and conclusion are the hardest pieces of the writing process. Introductions and conclusions ask you to take the heart of your paper and turn it into something more manageable. They also force you to take yourself outside of the specifics of your work and connect it to something larger in your field, in academia in general, or the world at large. Often, it is during the revision process that these pieces get the fair treatment they need.

You want to think of your introduction and conclusion as an hourglass. You begin your introduction broadly, bringing the reader in by making a connection to a larger issue or problem. Then you become narrower as you approach your hypothesis, thesis, or research question. Following the explanation of your topic in the body of the text, the conclusion brings your work back to your research question or thesis to ensure you have addressed it and then broadens again to a larger issue or the application of your work. Chapter 5 goes into further detail on the composition of an introduction and conclusion.

Once you have completed the paper, you should always return to the introduction and conclusion. You want to ask yourself, what are the larger issues this research addresses or could be applied to? Did I mention them in the introduction? Did I explain how I addressed them in my conclusion? Ask someone to read your introduction and conclusion. Can she tell what the rest of the paper is about? You may need to completely rewrite your introduction and conclusion once you've written your paper, as a paper can sometimes go in unexpected directions, but don't be afraid of that process. It is better to rewrite than to keep an old introduction to a paper that turned out completely different than you originally intended.

From the introduction and conclusion, you can move into even smaller subsections. Each paragraph is used to build your piece, and the paragraphs themselves are built by words and sentences. In an ideal editing situation, you should go through your piece to ensure that every part is necessary.

Does every paragraph support the subsection or document as a whole? Does every sentence support the paragraph? Could this be done better? Does each word support each sentence? Could this be accomplished in a better way?

Recall that each paragraph should be a mini paper within itself. Each should have at least one introductory sentence, and the body of the paragraph should end with concluding sentences that transition into the next paragraph. While you may not have accomplished this during the original writing, you have an opportunity during revision to address these areas to create a better flow in your document.

If you have made any major revisions, you should return to your larger questions. Is your piece still on topic? Does it still serve the purpose you had intended? If not, make sure to review the changes you made to maintain the overall meaning.

DETAIL WORK

Finally, students often face common problems in writing academically. We have mentioned some of these in other places in the book but they are worth repeating. You should take special note of these items to be sure you do not overlook them in your own writing.

Voice

For most of the writing in this book, you are attempting to write in an academic and formal voice. Producing this means reading a lot of the type of writing you are trying to create and comparing your work with that of others. If your professor has any examples of exemplary work, read those before you start and think about how they sound. What is the balance of original to quoted material? What kinds of headings and subheadings are there?

Changing voice may include removing informal words and replacing them with more formal ones. This could also include varying sentence length by shortening some and lengthening others. You should rely on the ear you have developed from reading similar writing to find the appropriate balance between long and short sentences. Another revision that can help with voice is structuring active sentences. Passive sentences often sound more academic; however, a captivating voice includes an active presentation.

Structure

While the structure will vary depending on what you're writing (see Chapter 5 for more information), you should be sure to be consistent once you have chosen your structure (or had it assigned to you). If you are supposed to go from an introduction to a literature review, methods, results, discussion, and conclusion, you should make sure to do that properly and smoothly. You should also make sure that each section includes the appropriate type of information. Your subheadings should make sense as the name of a section and as a stop on the path through your paper. Some people advise that section titles should not simply be a suggestion but, rather, should be clear and directly referred to in the context of the surrounding section—the more creative a subheading, the less of an academic impression your paper will leave. Subheadings should work together with the content to hold the entire piece together.

Specificity

Check your paper for places where you have used general words such as *them*, *they*, *we*, or *us*. Even words such as *researchers* or *academics* could be more specific. Who, in particular, are you referring to? If you do not change the word to someone (or several someones) in particular, the sentences either before or after should give a specific example of who the people are to whom you are referring. Time periods should also be specified. If you do not know the exact time period, and cannot find it, you should be as specific as you can. This will at least provide your readers with some context.

Quotes

Quotes are the evidence that supports your points. Generally, you want a paper to be no more than 10 percent direct quotes from secondary sources (this does not include quotes from qualitative research you have conducted). You should be careful not to overburden your writing with direct quotes from other people, but you also must take care to provide enough evidence to support your arguments.

You should also be sure that the quotes you have used are well explained (a sentence before or afterward will usually accomplish that) and are the best possible quotes to make your point. If you remove the quote, can a reader still make a connection between the point you are making and your explanation of the evidence? If not, change the quote or rethink the connection. This is something you may have to check and recheck several times. Do not forget to reread your quotes as you revise your piece. While the quote will not change, the context that follows it might. You may have removed the point you made but forgot to remove the quote supporting it.

Each quote should be properly referenced in American Sociological Association, American Psychological Association, or some other assigned formatting style, and every paraphrase should be indicated with the proper citation. Any time you do not do this, you are plagiarizing (see Chapter 3 for information on referencing and plagiarism). Additionally, without some indication, switching from your voice to the voice of whoever wrote the piece you are quoting breaks the flow of your work.

Sentences

There are other common mistakes that can be caught as you look back at the sentences that form your paragraphs. Often the relationship between the subject and the verb can be confusing and students might switch between singular and plural or be unsure of which is which. If you have one person doing something then the verb should refer to that one person. If you have two subjects connected with *or*, you should use a singular verb. If two subjects are connected with *and*, you should use a plural verb, and if there are multiple subjects with different types of plurality or singularity, the verb should match the object to which it is closest. This should remain consistent in the sentence and the paragraph as you refer to the same object. Another place that students are often confused about agreement is using the word *their, them, they,* and *themselves*. These are plural; however, they can be singular when referring to someone who is gender nonconforming or transgender, in which case *ve/ver/vis* and *zhe/zher/zhim* are also appropriate.

Paragraphs

As described in Chapter 2, paragraphs should consistently have the structure of small papers with an introductory sentence, elaboration, and a conclusion, and/or transition. This requires your paragraph to cover one topic and to not change topics until completing a thought. Paragraphs should also be well thought out and therefore not too long or too short.

Don't forget to circle back through the paper if you have made any major changes to your work. Few things are more frustrating than putting a lot of work into writing and revising a piece and then ruining the flow or the structure because you didn't have the time to look it over again. As described above, pay special attention to the introduction and conclusion when you circle back through the document. Additionally, you may need to change the title and abstract, if applicable, as they are reflective of the paper as a whole and should reflect major changes.

You should also take time to read your instructors comments on any assignments they have returned to you. While some instructors minimize their comments, others can write extensive amounts. Even if an assignment does not include the possibility for revision, the comments can be helpful in thinking about your general writing or what the professor wants for assignments in the future. You might consider keeping a log of the edits and comments that the professor has given you over the course of the semester and make an effort to work on at least one of them during each assignment you hand in.

The revision process can take a long time if done well. We have given you some suggestions for shortening the process, but if you have the time, you should take it. It is certainly worth it. A detailed revision process can help turn a good paper into a great one.

SUMMARY

This chapter focuses on the process of editing and revising. It covers important topics for writing at all levels:

- First drafts and first revisions
- Quick to extensive revisions
- Revising at the level of the complete document, the subsections/ subheadings, and detail work

While this "Writing in Practice" piece covers more advanced writing, the advice is applicable to all writers. We all go through the process of getting feedback and feeling discouraged about it and/or not knowing how to respond. Professor Holstein's advice is as useful to those preparing to write final drafts of papers for their undergraduate courses as for those who have received a "revise and resubmit" recommendation on an article.

WRITING IN PRACTICE

by James A. Holstein

There isn't a publishing sociologist around who hasn't submitted a paper (seemingly honed to perfection) and subsequently been asked to "revise and resubmit" the paper for further review. It's vital that authors don't take this as rejection but, rather, as an opportunity to enhance, enrich, and otherwise upgrade the manuscript—to make it really good. As faculty regularly go through the editing and revision process, students in their practice must go through it as well.

(Continued)

(Continued)

Over the years, I've submitted dozens of journal articles, but only a couple of these manuscripts were accepted without substantial revision. I've also served as editor of a major sociological journal that considered hundreds of submissions annually. As editor, I never accepted a paper without requiring some form of revision. Most articles go through at least two or three new drafts before publication. Thus, revising a paper—sometimes dramatically—is par for the course, even for the most successful authors. It's an integral part of the writing and publishing process. Journals are typically peer reviewed—that is, critiqued by a number of experts in the field—and, like your professor, the reviewers' job is to offer *constructive* criticism (something you should consider if asked to review a peer's work). Responding to conscientious professional reviews is an opportunity to improve your paper. To that end, I'll offer some suggestions about approaching the revision process from a positive perspective.

Don't (Over) React Immediately or Defensively

If asked to revise a paper, don't be disheartened. Resist the initial impulse to throw the request in the trash. Read the professor's comments, but don't dwell on them. Set the comments aside and let your thoughts "mellow" for a period of time. As emotions subside, read the comments again, carefully assessing what they say.

Take Stock

Make a careful, comprehensive outline of things you need to address. Don't omit issues from your list just because you disagree with whoever has reviewed your paper. The critiques are there; don't kid yourself about being able to ignore or finesse them. If a professor or set of reviewers identifies concerns, you need to deal with them.

Create a Strategy

There are many ways to address criticism, but you need to be clearly responsive to the reviews. Frequently, you can address reviewers' comments straightforwardly, as matters of clarification. Setting emotion and ego aside, develop a list of changes that can easily be made. More problematic issues will require additional consideration. Here are three common approaches that writers take to dealing with major criticisms, with some thoughts about their appropriateness:

- "I didn't say that!" (Or, alternatively, "That's what I said!") If you didn't say what a reviewer claims you did, or if you think you said precisely what a reviewer said you ignored, look carefully at your paper to determine why the reader misunderstood you. Ask how you might have caused the confusion. Was the writing unclear or the logic faulty? Did you assume too much about what readers would or would not know? Clean up your argument and be very explicit about what you mean to say.
- "I don't want to say/do that!" After carefully considering reviewers' comments, you may disagree with some suggestions or criticisms. Rather than ignoring those comments, anticipate them in your text. Engage alternate arguments and potential criticisms, briefly outlining those lines of thought and explaining why.
- "I never thought of that!" When reviewers' comments "make sense," take advantage by exploring the possibilities you may have previously overlooked. Don't be stubborn when new opportunities arise.

Pay Close Attention to the Writing: Make It Crystal Clear!

- Read your paper aloud. This helps identify unclear writing.
- Don't assume anything is self-evident. Make your arguments clear and explicit.
- Explain your analytic vocabulary. Eliminate gratuitous jargon while making sure the reader knows exactly what you mean by the specialized terminology you use.
- Don't skimp on the methods section. This is where you demonstrate that your arguments have empirical merit. It's where you convince readers to believe what you say.
- Streamline! Make arguments and prose simple, direct, and parsimonious. Write in an active voice. Avoid redundancy. You can usually reduce wordiness without sacrificing anything but length. "He said X" is three words. "X was made evident in conversation by him" is seven. Do the math!

—James A. Holstein, PhD, is a professor of sociology in the Department of Social and Cultural Sciences at Marquette University.

CHAPTER 7
WRITING FOR THE PUBLIC

As sociologists, we are often called on to share our knowledge. Sociology professors, consultants, and even students can be asked to examine aspects of society or social interactions, analyze them, and interpret the analysis for those who did not conduct the research. In the case of most of the writing we have described in this volume, the other individuals are usually professors. However, there are times when our expertise is shared with other sociologists and students or to help those who haven't studied sociology as we have and do not see the world from our perspective.

When Michael Burawoy was the president of the American Sociological Association, his 2004 Presidential Address, "For Public Sociology," focused on the theme of that year's conference. This sparked a debate about what it means to be a public sociologist and whether public sociology should be embraced by the academic and professional discipline. While the details of this debate are outside the scope of this book, it's important to note that some debate remains about whether it is the responsibility of sociologists to create this bridge between academia and those outside of it. We include this chapter, "Writing for the Public," because we believe it is an important but underemphasized aspect of the career of a sociologist. We discuss other types of public sociological writing such as newspaper articles and white papers in *Writing for Emerging Sociologists*. Here we examine the public writing that sociology students are more likely to do in a class including writing online and for presentations.

WRITING ONLINE

There are several elements that make writing online unique. Many people who are sociology students now have grown up writing online but, as we discussed in Chapter 2 on e-mails, this does not mean that you have learned how to write in an academic way. When writing casually online, you may drop many of your writing conventions. The use of abbreviations, or text speak, are most useful where words are at a premium and you have to fit your words into a very limited space. The abbreviations that you use online in conversations with friends are generally not appropriate for academic writing. They also require that your audience understands what those abbreviations mean in the same way that you do to avoid confusion.

Online text can also often be filled with exclamation points and angry and uninformed rantings. This runs counter to how we think about academic writing, and that kind of writing takes away from the point you are trying to make. It can also make you seem as though you are naïve and lacking in any particular expertise. This perception could follow you into other arenas of your education and life.

Information has a long lifetime on the web; for some things, it may seem to be near infinite. If you look hard enough, you can probably find unused websites that someone put up 10 years ago and never took down, and your text may be similarly preserved. Search engines continue to collect and hold information long after you are done with the site, so your entries may still be accessible. It is for these reasons that you want to make sure your online presence is what you want it to be. Think of all the famous people who have had messages they had posted in previous lives uncovered by fans or foes and used that against them in their current one. Try entering your name into a search engine sometime and see what you find.

There are a few platforms on which a professor might ask you to participate in an academic discussion or project. Many current students use these all the time but others may be less familiar. Briefly, the most popular platforms for use in classroom are the following:

- Twitter: A professor might use Twitter's limited number of character to get you to present concise points and use hashtags to make them easily searchable.
- Facebook: Professors can use its features to make groups where multimedia information on a particular topic can be shared.
- Instagram: This platform might be used to share images that illustrate sociological concepts or ideas in the real world.
- YouTube: Although it tends to include less writing, a professor might request that a video or a recording of a presentation is posted to be shared with others.
- WordPress, Blogger, or another blogging platform: These generally include much more extensive writing and are likely to be the platform where your writing will most resemble that which we have

discussed in the rest of the book. It will be discussed more fully in the next section.

The advice in handling online interactions that we discuss below can be helpful on any of these platforms. We begin with a discussion on blogs.

Blogs

Despite the fact that the term *blog* was created in the mid-1990s—as a joining of the words *web* and *log*—blogs are still fairly new for academics. There are several reasons for this. Many of the professors teaching the classes are unaware of how best to use them or whether they are academic enough. In addition, since anyone can create a blog, many of them contain writing that falls below the standards of academic writing, and this can show both a lack of professionalism and shrink the distance between the sociologist and the public. For some academics, these can both be problematic.

For other academics, however, the lessening of the distance to the public is the most important aspect of a blog. The ability to take your knowledge from the classroom and share it with those who may not regularly have access to it makes blogs a unique form of communication. Although people who regularly write blogs, or bloggers, are often criticized for their lack of credentials and sometimes questionable sources, some blogs have gained legitimacy. Now, not only do blogs and other social media sources break news before other news organizations, but well-known companies, agencies, organizations, and individuals now have their own blogs to reach a larger audience and to reach them more quickly.

Another important aspect of blogs is the opportunity for immediate feedback. A student can post an idea, theory, or opinion and can immediately hear what others think about it. For some, this can be quite daunting, but for those prepared for the immediacy, anonymity, and, often, idiocy that comes from the participants in the blogosphere, it can be helpful to quickly receive feedback on their work and have the option to make connections, debate issues, and share information with people from all over the world.

For academics, a blog can be like a short, interactive paper. While text is often the main aspect of a blog, they also include links to other sites, images, and videos. Unlike most of the writing we have discussed in other chapters, individual blog entries can be short, and the blog as a whole changes regularly as new entries are posted over time. How often you contribute to your blog will vary based on your assignment and/or your interest, but the more often you post, the more likely you are to gain and hold on to an audience.

Audience

There are a couple of different ways that audience may play a role in your blog. Your professor may ask you to create a closed or private blog or she may create one for the class. In this case, your audience is your professor and the other students, and this section is likely less useful to you. If, however, your professor wants you to contribute to an open, or public, blog, your audience is much broader and some of the information below will be very relevant. In addition to the particular assignment, you may also make a decision to continue your blog and/or to grow its audience; this section will help you in that process.

The audience of a blog is both extremely general and very specific. As an academic blogger, you have the opportunity to take the audience potential of "everyone" and select from it an audience with particular tastes and interests. Unlike almost every other type of writing we have included in this book, you are not writing to fit a preset audience but are deciding what kind of audience you want and creating a piece that would suit them.

Involved in this process is making a decision between writing for "people in the know" and "people who want to know." This distinction is important. In writing for people who do not already have knowledge on your topic, you will need to add much more description and be clear with every point you make. Terms you might not need to explain to other sociology students may have to be broken down in a concise and clear way. If your audience consists of people who are familiar with the topic, certain basics do not need to be explained. All things being equal, unless the blog is for a very specific population who you are certain already knows about your topic (like the other students in your class), it is better to explain, as the odds are high that someone will approach your blog without a deep knowledge of your topic. Your professor may also provide you some specific guidance on this topic.

A blog audience can be thought of as a business person might think about her market. Who are the people you are trying to serve? Who will be interested in what you have to say? In thinking about your audience, you should consider such characteristics as age, gender, sexual orientation, education level, occupation, political perspectives, and/or personal interests. Keep this in mind when you write. If you think your blog's audience should be factory workers in their 40s (perhaps too specific of an audience), consider that although they may understand the concepts, they might not understand terms such as *alienation* or *commodification* and you will have to explain them either before or after you name it.

Topic

Blogs come in many formats but they generally accomplish two tasks: They share an opinion or idea, and they pose a question. The question does not have to be explicit, but the expectation for debate is included in attempting to address many issues. You will likely be given a topic by your professor but also may be asked to develop a particular question within that topic. As you consider this, you should think about what might lead to debate within your topic. The topic should be something that can be broken down into specific subcategories or issues. Each individual post will contain one, several, or part of these subcategories. These varied items of interest are what allow you to find and keep your audience.

Your decision to write a blog may have come with particular assignment and a detailed plan of what you need to say and how you need to say it. But if you knew only that you have to communicate with a public audience and had not thought about the details, you want to think about that early in the process. Most bloggers make that decision before considering audience, but it is certainly acceptable to do the process the other way around. You can even go back and reconsider audience or topic after finalizing the other decision.

Once you have at least a preliminary idea of what your content will be, remember that what makes the blog is what is contained within it. This is where you make your point, capture your audience, and gather your feedback. Generally, a blog entry will focus on one or a couple of interrelated points. Your blog as a whole will focus on a particular topic or area, and you can continue to work on it as long as your blog remains active (often far beyond the class), so there is no need to cram everything into one entry. You should have plenty of time to make other points, and if your intention is to create a dialogue with your readers, your professor or other students, additional points may emerge through the comments or your responses to comments.

Make sure that, as in all your academic writing, you are clear in what you're saying. In this case, clear also usually means free of jargon and technical language. If your audience is the general public, you should speak to them as though they do not know anything about your topic or area, and they should not have to read entries between your first and most recent post to understand the context of your entry and contribute to the discussion. If your intention is to address other students or your professor, then a level of basic understanding can be assumed. However, since you are writing to share something new or different, you may have to explain some of the things you discuss even to those within your field.

Structure

The work of a blog does not stop after you have found that interesting aspect. In a blog you would do for a class, much of the purpose is to share knowledge, so you should be sure to support your claims with evidence. Unlike an academic paper, your evidence may not have to all be from journals or other strictly academic sources (although the point will be stronger if it is) but you should check with your professor about her particular guidelines. You can use your opinion or links to the research and opinions of others to support your claims. The entire digital world is open to you to explore or reference as you wish, and you should take advantage of that by finding new and interesting videos, images, people, and stories to which to link.

The general structure of a blog is slightly closer to that of a newspaper article than to that of an academic paper, which is likely another reason why blogs are not fully accepted in academia. The exact structure can change depending on the specific blogging platform you use, but some generalities are found across platforms.

A blog entry begins with a headline. If you want to bring people to your blog, a catchy yet informative headline is important. It should be written in simple language, and if it is ambiguous, it should not present any perspective you are not willing to explain. Most professors will allow you to use a play on words to keep it short and clear. The purpose of the headline is similar to the title of an article or book, except the emphasis is more equally balanced between being informative and interesting, rather than leaning more in the direction of informative, as for manuscript and essay titles.

From there, the structure differs depending on whether you are going to create a long or short entry. There is no hard-and-fast rule on length, but you should consider your assignment or your audience in determining length. If your audience is older, they may have more time to read long entries, although some of them may not be as comfortable reading long passages on the computer and would prefer a hard copy. With younger groups, it can take a lot of motivation to get someone to read beyond a few paragraphs. In the beginning of your blog's lifetime, you may want to try to keep your entries short. A few paragraphs is probably enough to make your point, and until you build an audience, your readers should be able to avoid scrolling if they can. Again, your professor may provide you specific guidelines on this.

In a shorter blog entry, you need only about a sentence to introduce what you are going to say. You should then get to your point, and if you can close with a question for your audience or a point you'd like them to address, it can be easier for your readers to start commenting. If your entry is long, make sure to remind readers of your point before ending and expecting them to comment on it.

Even in writing a blog, try to obey the conventions of language and structure described in this and other chapters. Read over your blog before publishing it. While your language doesn't necessarily need to be academic and you can often write similarly to how you speak, it should be professional. Try not to be vulgar, and be careful what you say.

A blog can be a great way to communicate with other students, your professor, or other professionals. It gives you the opportunity to more fully understand a topic by breaking it down in a way the general public can comprehend. It can also provide you with a public profile, which can be useful for employment or educational opportunities in the future. As long as you always protect and monitor how people perceive you online, a blog can be a useful and informative tool.

Online Comments

If your professor requires a blog in class, she will likely also ask you to comment on yours and others posts. It is important to treat this and other online writing just as you would treat any writing in this book and follow the general written conventions that we have set forth. There are a couple of ways that writing online is unique which could influence how you should present it and how it is received.

Content

Similarly to much of your other writing but much more obviously, a comment is a response to something and the first thing you want to do in your professional comments is to acknowledge what that something is. If you consider how online comments are structured, their threaded quality means that there may be responses to responses within responses. Therefore, if you are not clear about what you are responding to, the person reading what you write will not be clear either. Generally, this will be to the author of the original piece but sometimes, you may feel you need to respond to one of the other commenters. In the same way that you would ensure that a paper addresses the research question throughout, you should include the name of the person, and the particular point or a quote from the comment or article that you are replying to as you discuss your response. Many comment services will allow you to use a quoting feature, if you are addressing a quote, which indents the quote in your comment or changes its background color. Otherwise, you should make sure to place the quote within quotation marks and use the author's name, username, or handle.

One way comment sections are different from traditional papers are that they are interactive and therefore, mutable. This means that they are constantly changing because people are responding to the original article (which may also be revised because of comments) and to the comments. Although you may have a comment near the top (and, if you respond to the original post or one of the first commenters, it should be), it can quickly move when someone else responds or as other comments are added. This is an additional reason to make sure to be clear about to what exactly you are responding.

Context

There are other considerations for writing comments—such as avoiding writing a vague comment and having a clear reason for writing your post—but these are much more focused on those who are writing comments on their own time, rather than those doing it as part of an assignment. Most likely, the comments you will be asked to write will be on a discussion board as a part of an online, hybrid, or face-to-face course. These usually occur at least once a week and often require both a post and a comment to someone else's post. You can review the section on blogs for some advice that you can also use in writing a post to a discussion board but there are also a few things to keep in mind when you write comments to others' posts.

Make sure you are clear on the assignment before writing your post or commenting on your classmates' post. If there is a particular point that you have been asked to make, be sure to make it. You should use evidence from the original post or from the work that you have done in the class. Your professor is unlikely to be satisfied with a comment that simply agrees or disagrees with, or thanks a previous commenter. While part of the assignment is to show that you have read someone else's post, it is also about your ability to engage with someone else on an issue. Part of how you show that you can do that is by carefully reading the post (see Chapter 3 or information about active reading) and pulling out one or several points that speak to you.

Once you know what the point is that you are responding to, you should support it with evidence. It may be evidence that you referenced in your post; it might be evidence from a class assignment, another student's post, or a reading. You should follow the guidelines in Chapter 3 for using and integrating quotes. If you have multiple points, be sure to make them in separate paragraphs. Once you have completed your comment, review what you have written, make sure you have addressed the assignment and made your point. Then, use the information from Chapter 6 to revise where needed.

Finally, as mentioned previously, many people who use online communication see it as a way to say things that they do not want to say in person. This should not be one of your goals and, especially for a class assignment, you should be as respectful online as you are in person. Do not insult or use derogatory language. Do not tear people down to build yourself up. Remember that every online person is attached to an IRL (in real life) person and, even if they do not follow these guidelines, you should. Online, it can lead to bad feelings, personal attacks and cyberbullying, and stalking. In a class, this can lead to a failing grade, suspension, or expulsion.

PRESENTATIONS

We will conclude our chapter on writing for the public with a discussion of presentations. Even with the other opportunities we discussed in this chapter for sharing your work, most students will share their work with their professors, by handing in assignments, and with their classmates, through presentations. Many courses will include in-class presentations around a particular topic, reading, or assignments. Some students will also have the opportunity to present externally at a conference. Below, we discuss both possibilities.

Talking Points

Much of your written work for a presentation within or outside of the classroom will be in the creation of your talking points. Talking points are an important part of writing for the public, as well as a good exercise for any academic since they involve condensing your work into its essential elements. In the business world, talking points are used to ensure that anyone who speaks on behalf of a company—on television, on the radio, or in a newspaper, for example—is consistent. In academia, talking points may be used differently. Your talking points are the pieces of information in your work that you want to make sure to highlight. Once you have talking points on a particular research project, paper, or article, you can use them for a presentation, interview, or simply your "elevator pitch"—the summary of your research in a minute or so (the length of an elevator ride). Generally, if you are in academia, you are writing talking points for yourself. However, most of the advice in this section can also be used if you are writing for someone else.

In many ways, talking points are an outline of your work, and creating them can help you think about what is important in what you are doing and the points that would be of most interest to your audience. Talking points are neither intended to remain static nor will they include every aspect of your research. Like so much of the writing in this volume, your talking points will change to fit your audience—what is appropriate or relevant for one group may not have the same effect on another.

Talking points are also not intended to be recited word for word. They are usually written as bullet points to remind you (or others) of the points you need to hit during your presentation or interview. They should be short (ideally, only a sentence per point) and should be written without exclamation points or bold text. You don't need to add the emphasis. The whole point of the talking points is that they are your emphasis.

You should arrange your talking points in a hierarchy, starting with the most important and including the secondary points below it. An alternative is to organize them in the order you would like to reveal them. You may find that your work is arranged more by first point/second point than by most important point/secondary point. Additionally, if you find that some of your points break down into several smaller points, you can include sub-bullets that support your main point. The most important thing is to keep your talking points short, so it is better to break your main point into smaller points than to create one convoluted talking point.

In general, three is a good number of talking points. This is few enough that you could probably memorize them while still covering all your points for a particular audience. For a conference presentation, you may want to expand to five points, but keep in mind that you will likely need to include points for each of the sections of your paper (see Chapter 5), so it may be easier for you to simply to expand on your three points rather than adding two more.

As described above, you should keep in mind your audience. While your research as a whole might include more than three important points, you likely have three that are most relevant to your audience. If you are presenting to a group interested in Latin@ issues, you should emphasize the points in your research that most speak to that community. It may make sense to you to create a master list of talking points from which you can select those that apply to your group of interest.

Your talking points should be clear and free of both jargon and derogatory or accusatory language. Remember that you are trying to make your point, not bring attention to someone else's. There are situations where your research is about a dialogue or even an argument with another person, but even in that situation, you can usually avoid attacking an individual and focus on critiquing her work.

Talking points are not just for politicians, pundits, companies, or organizations. Academics can also find them useful in presenting themselves and their work to others. Your talking points should travel with you so you will always be prepared to share your work with those you meet. They are especially useful if you will be attending a conference.

Conferences

After classroom presentations, the most likely place where you will use talking points and publicly present your work is at a conference. Most disciplines in the United States have multiple conferences including one major one—related to its major professional organization(s)—and several smaller regional conferences. There may also be large and small international conferences. In sociology, the American Sociological Association holds an annual conference every summer in large cities in the United States as well as Toronto and Montréal. Several smaller conferences often occur at the same time and place as the national conference. In addition, there are sociology conferences happening in other areas around the country throughout the year. Sociologists also might present at other conferences that are not strictly for sociologists but focus on a particular topic of interest such as education, medicine, popular culture, or gender.

Most academics have one or more conferences that they attend every year and they will therefore look out for the Call for Papers—the announcement of the conference theme—around the same time each year. A Call for Papers includes all the relevant information about the conference including the conference theme, its date, time and location, the types of sessions, the process of submission, and any other important rules or guidelines. At most conferences, there will be several sessions that need to be filled on the theme so focusing your work on it could give you an advantage in acceptance. Conferences will also accept those papers that do not fit the theme but you are then competing against every other submission that is not connected to the theme.

Most conferences have an option between a panel presentation, a roundtable, or a workshop. A panel generally consists of three to six people each presenting on a paper for 10 to 20 minutes. A roundtable is less formal. It can include the same number of presenters as a panel but instead of sitting at a long table in front of an audience, presenters sit around a round table and often the audience is only the other presenters. Roundtables are best for works in progress as it is much more of a conversation and often, if the people who review papers for acceptance do not think a paper is ready for a panel, it might be recommended to a roundtable. Although many conferences have specific undergraduate student sessions, as an undergraduate, you are more likely to find yourself at a roundtable or a poster session (see below). Conferences may also hold workshops which are much more interactive. There is an expectation that those who attend a workshop session will actually be doing something during the session. You might attend one of these as an undergraduate, but it is unlikely that you would be asked conduct to one.

The submissions for conferences are generally in the form of abstracts or full papers. Some conferences ask for the submission of an abstract early on and a paper later and others only require an abstract. Even if the conference only needs an abstract for submission or acceptance, there are certain session types where a paper may be requested. If a panel includes a discussant, for example, their job is to discuss the connections between the different papers and they may ask to at least see a draft of your paper before the presentation so they can begin to form their synthesis. A panel might also include a presider, who will introduce each presenter and act as timekeeper and/or a facilitator, who will run the discussion. Either or both of them may ask for additional information from you.

Slideshow Presentations

Although there are many options available for creating visual presentations, most presenters use PowerPoint, Google Slides, or some other type of slideshow software. Whatever information you include in your slideshow should not replace what you say during your presentation, it should be used as a supplement or an outline, not as a substitute. Keep in mind that the audience's eyes will naturally be drawn to whatever visuals you have on the screen so you should make sure they are not taking away from what you are saying—in either their message or their format.

With that in mind, edit your text just as you would any text that you write and know that any misspellings or grammar errors will be large and obvious as the audience stares at them while you speak. One main difference between this and other writing that we have spoken about in this book, however, is that you should avoid writing full sentences in a PowerPoint presentation. Write the word, phrase, comment, or question that you need to anchor the information in the minds of your audience but, again, you do not want them to be reading while you are speaking.

Another good use for a slideshow is if you have visuals—such as a table, chart, or pictures—that help to illustrate what you are saying. For the most part, slides such as these will capture the audience's attention for a moment but then bring it back to you when you are not referring to the diagram. Any bullet point that is longer than three sentences means that the audience is reading, not listening, and then, why are you there? The one exception to this is when you are including qualitative data. Some presenters will excerpt it so that it fits within the length of the rest of the slideshow text. When this is not possible, full quotes, with your main points bolded or underlined, is usually acceptable.

The first thing that you want to do when preparing a sideshow for your presentation is to finish your presentation paper. You may have already had to submit it for acceptance or to the discussant but, if you didn't, you will need to finish it before creating your sideshow. A paper that you are presenting does not need to be the same structure as one that you might have handed in for an assignment. A spoken paper can be different from one that is read so there are sections you might want to emphasize more or less. For example, your literature review might be summarized theories rather than the details of exactly how you arrived at your theoretical perspective or research questions. Similarly, your methods might be abridged and you will generally not speak your in-text citations but might include them as references on your slides instead.

Once you have your paper, you should create a reverse outline (see Chapters 3 and 6), illustrating the structure of your paper and the important ideas and findings. This will likely be the structure of your sideshow with one or two pages per section, depending on the importance or new information in it. If you're not using the talking points as described above, know that it takes about two minutes per one double-spaced page and you should not keep a slide on the screen for more than a minute.

Many people caution against using an elaborate design template or any kind of animation but a blank slideshow page can look just as unprofessional. The best way to handle this is to use the premade templates and to do limited customizing as these templates generally follow a color scheme that is easy to read. What you probably should avoid are the templates that are designed to look like something else, like a notebook, blackboard, or a busy street. These should only be used if they add to your presentation. Similarly, a timed animation (with the changes set to occur "on click") can be a useful tool for the slow reveal of information but they shouldn't be too elaborate or take too much time. While a slide turning into a paper airplane and flying off the screen can look very impressive, it will distract your audience from what you are saying. Your text should also be at least 18 point and should be in an easy to read font such as Times New Roman.

In general, your slides will be organized in the traditional structure with the introduction, literature review and context, methods, results, discussion, and conclusion. Each slide should include only a few bullet points and should not make more than two major points. Your introduction will serve to set the stage for your paper. Your literature review will likely compress each aspect of the literature into one sentence or phrase (followed by the references that support it) and your context will be similarly structured. Depending on how complex your methods are, you may need two pages to describe them. The bulk of the presentation should be the results, discussion, and conclusion. These are the important points of your work and they should be emphasized. Make sure to include references at the end and a slide about the limitations or possibilities for future research as well as your contact information so people can reach you if they have any additional questions or comments about your work.

Finally, make sure that you are prepared. All conferences do not have access to audio/visual equipment, especially laptops and projectors, in all rooms. If you think you will need it, you will usually need to inform the conference organizers during the application or acceptance process. However, make sure you show up with a backup—such as handouts—in case the technology is not working.

Poster Presentations

In addition to a panel or plenary, most conferences include space for posters, and this is often a good place for undergraduates to share their work. The conference application usually includes someplace for you to express your interest in a poster session. Unlike the application for a panel, your paper is generally not pushed into a poster session, like it might be into a roundtable, if it is not accepted the first level to which you apply.

A poster presentation is a little different from a panel presentation in a few ways. First, panel presentations are generally on a particular topic, and the discussant or presider reads all the participants' papers and finds the common threads to share with the audience. In a poster presentation, you are likely in a room with many other posters on a diversity of topics. This means someone could enter the room not because they are interested in your topic but because they have an interest in an area of sociology that you know nothing about.

Therefore, as a poster presenter, part of your responsibility is to engage people in your work and draw them in regardless of what they came to see. Posters are usually hung up in one or two large rooms with the presenters standing in front of them. In some situations, if the topic is digital media, a table for a laptop or screen might be available but generally, you must rely on a single, albeit large, page to provide all the needed information.

Another difference is that for some conferences, the poster is displayed for the entire time of the conference. This gives attendees the time to get an in-depth look at your work and then make a decision about whether they want to return during your designated "session" time to ask questions. For this and other reasons, you should make sure that your contact information is clearly presented in your poster. There will be many who will see your poster and want to follow up before you arrive or after you leave.

Finally, the goals of a poster presentation are often a little different than that of a panel presentation. Like a panel, your primary purpose is to share your work. However, secondarily, a poster presentation is useful for getting feedback from colleagues from a range of disciplines. It is for this reason that some presenters might use a poster to present a work in progress but it's also why engagement is so important.

Poster Format

You should check the guidelines for the conference that you are applying for to see if there are any size or column restrictions or suggestions. Posters come in several different sizes and the conference will usually let you know either the size of the poster or the size of the space.

ASA generally provides each presenter with a 4' x 8' (48" x 96") bulletin board on which to display their poster, which means that is the maximum size for your poster but you might also choose to go smaller. In order to print something of this size, you will need access to a poster printer, which means either printing through your institution or going to a print shop such as FedEx Office. You can find these companies online. You also now have the ability to print your poster on a large sheet of fabric, which will allow for easy transportation and storage. It is important to remember that you cannot wait until the last minute to complete your poster. At the very least, most print shops require at least 24 hours to complete something like a poster, and if you use an online service, it can take up to two weeks. You should give yourself a few weeks to ensure you are able to get it done in time. Some of the print shops will also ship the poster directly to the hotel where you are staying and the conference is being held. Most will allow you to send a file directly from your home e-mail and then pick it up on-site when it's ready.

Posters are either three or four columns wide and many conference organizers will provide a preference or restriction. In that space, you should be able to share a significant amount of information, but you do not need to include everything. As your contact information should be on your poster, attendees can contact you for more information or revisit the poster during your session.

The poster should be a mix of text, graphics, and white (or color) space. Graphics should predominate, followed by the whitespace and only about a quarter of the poster should include text. Remember that what you most want to do with your poster is to show, rather than tell. This also means that you want the poster to be clear, uncluttered, and professional. You may want to map the entire poster out beforehand to confirm the spacing. This drafting process should also include looking at printouts of the images for your poster. Keep in mind that some of your images may become blurry when grown to the size of your poster, so you want to make sure that your original images are large enough or have a good enough resolution so they remain professional looking on your poster.

Title

Conference posters may have up to 10 pieces, but they are likely to be organized into five or six areas on the poster. The first piece is likely the last that you will write and that is the title. This is located across the top of your poster, across all of your columns. Below this, you should include the name and affiliations of all the presenters.

As described in Chapter 5 and above, a title serves two purposes. It informs the reader what your piece will be about, and it catches their attention. This is even more important with a poster because for most of the conference attendees, it is the title that will make them stop to see what you're doing. Remember that there will be different kinds of people in the room, so you want your title to be free of unnecessary jargon.

The title of your poster is probably closer to that of a newspaper headline than it is to a paper title. Because many attendees will decide if they want to stop based on the title, it can be very important. A catchy title uses active, rather than passive, verbs and is written in present tense. Readers should feel as though there is urgency to stopping at your poster—as though the issue or problem is currently occurring (and in many situations, it is). The title should also be clear and simple but provide enough information to tell the reader what the poster is about. Make sure you do not misrepresent your article through the title, however; it should be honest and straightforward.

A good method for creating your poster title is to start with your elevator pitch and then slowly deconstruct some of the larger words and concepts until you have something extremely clear. Make sure to consider the significance of your topic in your elevator pitch. It is in this short piece that you will find your title. In fact, in the tradition of other academic writing, your main title might be the significance of your project with the subtitle of a short, clear elevator pitch.

For example, take this paper abstract:

The ideals of empowerment and service have been integral to the African American struggle for education as evident in the schooling opportunities during the civil rights movement. This article examines the ways in which concepts such as culturally relevant pedagogy and service-based learning have been implemented in the past and how such engagement can continue to be used in current schooling. The contemporary model is Central Park East Secondary School, a public school in New York City, serving predominantly minority and low-income students. Seventy-eight former students of the school were surveyed to assess the school's effect on civic participation. Among this group of former students, 81 percent voted in the 2004 presidential election and 70 percent had participated in civic activities. Models such as this have the potential to alter the lives of African American students and their levels of participation in American democracy.

The first step is to pull out the essence of your research and its larger significance. You do not need to worry about being grammatically or structurally correct:

This article examines the ways in which concepts such as culturally relevant pedagogy and service-based learning have been implemented in the past and how such engagement has been used in current schooling. Models such as this have the potential to alter the lives of African American students and their levels of participation in American democracy.

With a little rearranging, you have an interesting significant title with an informative subtitle:

Changing Students Lives: Culturally relevant pedagogy and service-based learning for Black students in the past, present, and future

You may want to spend some time refining the title and changing the words to something catchier, but by just paring down the abstract, you have a good start.

Poster Text

The text of your poster is organized into the same sections as a formal sociological paper: an introduction, methodology, results, discussion, conclusion, and references. In addition, some posters might include, or conferences might request, an abstract, limitations, implications, and acknowledgments. However, as it is a poster, there should be a larger focus on the visual elements of the work. Rather than describing your data, for example, a colorful chart or graph should be used. You might also include photos or diagrams related to your work.

Instead of the complete paragraphs you would use in a paper, posters generally have text in very short paragraphs or bulleted lists with phrases. In total, the poster should include 300 to 800 words. Your readers should have a clear pathway from one block of text to the next, and some presenters even use arrows to direct the reader's eye. The blocks of text should be situated uniformly, using a formatting tool like a table or a guideline, rather than drawn by hand. Your text should not be smaller than 18-point font with most of it in the 30 range, subtitles between 50s and 70s, and titles no larger than 95. This varies, however, so check with your professors and other classmates and look at all of your text in relation to each other. Unfortunately, it may not be possible to print out a sample of your poster to check the sizes, but you may be able to print out just a portion of it to see whether the size of the text works once it is on a poster. The combination of the background box and the text should also be easy to read. This likely means eliminating some color groupings. Yellow on white, for example, would not be advisable. The background of your poster should not have more than three colors.

In composing your text, you should make sure to present the important aspects of your research, and if there are interesting findings or ideas in opposition to your work, you may want to present them as well and explain how your work addresses them. Once you have your text together, think about which pieces of information could be replaced with or supplemented by images.

The Presentation

In addition to the poster, you should be prepared to talk during your scheduled poster session. You will first want to engage attendees as they walk by to encourage them to stop and take a look at your work. If they ask you questions, you should be able to answer them. You should also be ready with a short presentation or some talking points to share when attendees stop to read your poster. Part of this could point out some of the important findings on the poster, but this is also your chance to add any information that you were not able to include on the poster. It should not be longer than five minutes, and you may need to stop and engage those around you or repeat as people stop and move on. You might also consider sharing a handout with some of your data and your contact information.

Not all sociologists believe that writing for the public is an important part of their role as academics. However, making your ideas, analysis, opinions, and suggestions clear to those beyond your professor provides the opportunity to expand the realm of sociology and explore the depths of your knowledge. This chapter provides you with the information you need to do just that.

SUMMARY

This chapter examines the different types of writing a sociologist might participate in to speak to those outside of academia. The chapter covers the following topics:

- Guidelines for creating academic blogs
- Compiling talking points from your research
- Creating a slideshow for a presentation
- Displaying a poster

In his "Writing in Practice" piece, Professor R. L'Heureux Lewis-McCoy describes his own experiences with speaking to the public through his appearances on television and writing for blogs and newspapers. This is interesting for students who have been asked to write blogs for more public audiences or those who want to continue their blogs beyond the limits of their classroom. Professor Molly Vollman Makris shares her experience working with and being a student at a conference. Finally Professor Mary Gatta describes her use of social media in the classroom.

WRITING IN PRACTICE

by R. L'Heureux Lewis-McCoy

While I have successfully passed through the ranks and earned a PhD and tenure, I am well aware that many of the academic articles I write will seldom reach masses of people. When I decided to go into sociology, my goal was to contribute to discussions about race, ethnicity, and education to generate social change. Soon after arriving in graduate school, I learned that it is rare for mainstream American sociologists to contribute actively to public discourse. While one of my professors told me, "My journal publications are my activism," I found myself wanting to tap into a different tradition. By reading about the Black sociological tradition—a tradition that prided itself on both scholarships and activism for the public good—I found a place where authors wrote across publications and audiences. Borrowing from this model, I forged my own path that serves the demands of academic publication while creating the opportunity for pushing public conversations via public sociology.

As a graduate student, I began my first blog, "Black at Michigan," where I discussed what was happening with Black students on the University of Michigan campus, as well as with Black folks within the state of Michigan. Not long after this, I began to contribute editorials to local papers and was soon receiving calls from local media to talk and write about issues of race in the area. From this point forward, I had to work on making complex ideas accessible in a short space.

Writing for public audiences is very different from writing for academic journals and books. While academic audiences are often familiar with subtle nuances and research literatures that span decades, public audiences rarely come to a subject matter with that depth of background. This does not mean that public audiences are naïve—far from it. Rather, their background is usually linked to the experiential, not research based. This is an important point from which to begin, because

(Continued)

(Continued)

while jargon is often seen as the major issue with academic writing, not clearly explaining terms and concepts is more often a central issue for the masses.

Public writing is more than "translation" or "boiling down" ideas; it involves connecting to the needs and worldviews of one's audience. Choose the number of ideas you present wisely. Most times, when I begin to write on a topic, I feel I should unload a full literature review so the reader knows I'm qualified to speak on the topic and to provide the reader with a common vocabulary. This may make for good thesis writing, but it makes for very poor public writing. Instead, I try to think of two, at most, central points that I want the readers to take away from the piece. Within the first two lines, I have to make my points clear and then unpack them in the few remaining paragraphs. Think about your opening as if it contains the two most important lines of your abstract. For me, this tends to mean

(1) what people think they know (null hypothesis) and

(2) what I found that counters that (alternative hypothesis).

Just like an academic article, I try to make sure each of my pieces makes a distinct contribution to the dialogue around a subject matter; if it doesn't, I'm not sure why I would write it.

There are many theories on what the role of an intellectual who does public work is, but I tend to believe a central role is exchanging ideas with those beyond the confines of academia. This, at the same time, carries challenges, the least of which is that, public writing is often not considered in a tenure evaluation, but with good mentorship and advocacy, it can be, as it was in my case.

Writing for public audiences is a practice that is reemerging and continues to be redefined by each author's initiatives. Ultimately, you will have to find your own public voice, preferred writing venues, and topic range—which is part of the fun of doing it. Public sociological writing inevitably should point readers to deeper revelations than does reporting or opinion sharing and should facilitate unlikely, yet attainable, connections for readers. Doing public writing in company with academic writing helps me bring my original goals nearly full circle.

—R. L'Heureux Lewis-McCoy, PhD, is an associate professor of sociology and Black studies at The City College of New York, City University of New York.

WRITING IN PRACTICE

by Molly Vollman Makris

Presentations at conferences, or in the community, are a great way to share research with others and contribute to the scholarly conversation. It is also a good way to build confidence in your own research and to receive feedback and learn from others. It is never too early in your academic career to start attending conferences and even presenting at them.

Presenting With Faculty

As a graduate student, I was privileged to attend a conference in Florence, Italy, where I presented an ethnodrama alongside one of my professors and another graduate student. This experience helped me to grow personally and professionally. While there, in addition to the experience gained from presenting, I also spent valuable time with my professor putting together a proposal for another conference and was able to watch her network and benefit from her experience and connections.

As a professor, I had the opportunity to work with my community college students on a research project and present alongside them at a national conference. This was a wonderful way for my students to become comfortable conducting high-level empirical data collection but also to recognize that they have expertise to contribute.

In order to prepare for this project, I had my students create a list of possible research questions and then choose their favorite to pursue. I then assigned readings for the class, which we would eventually use in our literature review. In class, we discussed the importance of the Institutional Review Board (IRB) and the students went through IRB certification. The students themselves created and distributed a survey and conducted ethnographic observations. Together, we conducted the data analysis and put together the PowerPoint presentation using some of their photography. We met with a researcher from another university who specialized in the topic and we practiced the presentation multiple times in advance of the conference.

At the conference, the students received good questions and accolades from audience members. They also began to understand the importance of networking. A few of my students had a very positive experience and left inspired with copious notes and business cards in hand. While not every student who attends an academic conference with a faculty member will want to be an academic, all can learn something from the experience.

(Continued)

(Continued)

As a student, if you are presented with an opportunity to conduct research or present your research with a professor or independently, take the opportunity. If one does not come up, then seek it out. Ask your professor for advice on conferences to attend or to which you could apply. Do not be shy about asking professors for advice about attending a conference; if they know you are going, they can help you network at the conference. If you are particularly interested in a class or the work of a certain professor, attend their office hours or send an e-mail asking if you can assist with their research in any way. Students can participate in data collection and bring their own expertise, which is often very different than that of the professor, to the table. In my research, I try to include the voices and experiences of young people through a variety of formats such as their photography and map making, interviewing them, or having them as researchers interviewing, or surveying others.

The 4 Ps of Presenting

Once you find an interesting conference at which to present, you must consider how to make the best possible impression so that you and your research can have an influence. I find that as an academic, my background in the performing arts often comes in handy. This background helps me in the classroom but also when doing presentations. A good presentation is much like a strong performance on stage: the presenter must be **prepared, practiced, passionate,** and **poised**. I am often surprised to find that at academic conferences, early career academics and students frequently give the strongest presentations. I believe this is because they are just starting out, enthusiastic about their topics, and feel they must prove themselves. It is important that at any stage in your career you do not become complacent about presenting.

Be *prepared* and know the time limit for your presentation and what equipment will be available; check the formatting of your presentation on the screen before it begins and back your presentation up in multiple formats. Edit your presentation thoroughly in advance and do not complete it at the last minute. Trust me, you need to go back to review your presentation multiple times on different days to really fix all issues.

Practice your presentation aloud using any notes you will need and time yourself. Nothing is worse than a presenter only making it through a quarter of his slides or ignoring the moderator while taking another panel member's time.

Be *passionate*. Even if you are given the early slot the morning after St. Patrick's Day at a conference in New Orleans with a very small (possibly hungover) audience (true story—it happened to me at one of my first conferences), you should present with passion and charisma. If you are not excited about this research, no one is going to be. Be creative with your presentation when possible and appropriate; use pictures, sound, interesting quotes. I have seen respected academics bring props, rap, and present with high school students—all of these were memorable and academically rigorous.

Have *poise*. Take a deep breath and recognize that you have a valid contribution to make and are there to receive helpful feedback. Speak slowly, stand up, make eye contact, and do not become defensive during question and answer sessions. Many newcomers to academia experience what is called "imposter syndrome"; this can prove especially challenging to overcome for women and/or people of color. Remember that you belong and use your voice (loudly, clearly, and slowly) to share your contribution.

—Molly Vollman Makris, PhD, is an assistant professor
of urban studies at Stella and Charles Guttman
Community College, City University of New York.

WRITING IN PRACTICE

By Mary Gatta

As a professor, I use many forms of social media—such as Twitter, Instagram, and Facebook—in order to extend the sociology classroom beyond the physical walls on campus. Depending on how I'm structuring the social media components of my sociology course, you may be sharing posts with just your classmates and me, or your post may be shared with a larger public online audience. In either case, I ask my students to write their posts in a casual, yet professional manner. When you are interacting on social media as part of your class, you are representing yourself as a sociologist and your post may be read and shared within the larger sociology circles. While your writing does not have to present the concepts used in a course paper in the same way, you do need to be sure to write in a manner that is professional and clear. I remind them that their audience is other sociology students, professors, and intellectuals and that they should want to write accordingly.

(Continued)

(Continued)

There are several ways I have had my students engage with sociological ideas in the social media worlds. I have asked them to locate a news article, video, or other multimedia artifacts related to a topic we are discussing in class and then post the news artifact in a Facebook group to share with your classmates or post on Twitter. My students then include a few sentences with the post to succinctly explain how the artifact relates to the topic at hand. Often, they pull a few sentences out of the article or video to highlight how it is illustrative of the sociological concept they are studying.

I have also asked them to generate the sociological content themselves. In these cases, we mostly use Facebook, although students could also be asked to use Instagram. For instance, I have asked students to find an example of a sociological concept in their environment, take and post a picture of it, and explain how it illustrates sociology. One example was the secularization of Christmas. A student chose to take a picture of the Christmas tree in Rockefeller Center, posted it, and then explained how it illustrates the secularization of the holiday in a few sentences.

We also often use of hashtags in our posts in my class. This allows for its categorization. For one assignment, I asked students to use an existing hashtag that other individuals are using such as tweeting the gender wage gap for #EqualPayDay. A sociology colleague of mine even created a unique hashtag for her class and asked students to include that hashtag with all their posts. In this manner, students can search on that hashtag to see what their classmates are posting and be able to see and respond to them. One important point that you want to remember is that when you use hashtags, it will also allow other individuals to find your posts in a hashtag search. Your posts become part of the public discourse on the topic.

Students in my class have also been asked to tweet a concise comment about a piece of sociology that they are reading or discussing. In this case, they included the Twitter handle of the author of the piece. This is a great way to begin a Twitter discussion with the author and to be part of a larger sociological discussion. If you engage on Twitter with other sociologists, you want to be respectful and constructive in your posts. The person may or may not respond to you, but if they do, congratulations, you are engaging in sociology!

—Mary Gatta, PhD, is an associate professor of sociology at Stella and Charles Guttman Community College, City University of New York.

CHAPTER 8

WRITING BEYOND THE COLLEGE CLASSROOM

Not only is sociology a fun and fascinating area of study, but students of sociology also have many excellent graduate school and career options. Sociology provides scholars with an array of insights into human behavior, group dynamics, community involvement, and social relations. Sociology also provides unique theoretical perspectives and research skills that will aid in one's understanding of social and cultural interactions. As a result, sociology—and the skills sociology majors and graduates learn and develop—is an asset to a number of career fields, as well as to master's and doctoral programs. There are so many different career options for sociology majors, and we cannot begin to cover all the types of writing you may encounter in the careers that attract sociology majors, as the career determines the writing style. This chapter does not focus on career or graduate school guidance but, rather, reviews the writing needed in preparation for advanced studies in sociology as well as the typical writing types and styles involved in preparing for careers where your sociological training can be applied. First, since graduate studies are often the next step for sociology undergraduate majors, we will examine the different types of writing needed to become a master's or doctoral student.

GRADUATE SCHOOL: MASTER'S AND DOCTORAL PROGRAMS

Many students who major in the social sciences in college intend to continue their education with graduate school and doctoral studies. Since sociology covers so many different areas of study, sociology students often apply to a wide array of graduate and professional studies programs, such as the following:

- Anthropology
- Applied sociology
- Criminology
- Education
- International relations
- Law school
- Political science
- Public health
- Public policy
- Social work
- Sociology
- Urban studies

This section will begin with a brief discussion of the differences between master's and doctoral programs in sociology. It is important to first note that students do not necessarily need to major or even minor in sociology to apply for master's or doctoral studies in sociology. Having an undergraduate major in sociology certainly helps, but most master's and doctoral programs supply their students with the necessary skills in theory and research methods for their respective programs.

Master's Programs

A master's degree signifies that the scholar has mastered the material in a particular area of study. This mastery may include an advanced understanding of readings, research, or theories in the scholar's field. Those interested in pursuing a master's degree in sociology can choose between two different types of sociology master's programs: sociology and applied sociology.

A master's degree in sociology, typically a Master of Arts (MA) or a Master of Science (MS), requires that students develop an advanced understanding of sociological theory and research methods. Ideally, the student should be able to apply what she learns in class and discovers through her research to real-world situations.

Applied sociology master's programs have become a lot more popular as career opportunities for social science majors have increased with the rise of research institutes, think tanks, and academic research centers. These master's programs spend substantially more time on research methods, quantitative in particular, and on the application of theory to real-world settings and programs. Those with a master's degree in applied sociology often go on to work in research and evaluation offices or programs. These sociology programs do not simply focus on studying and understanding the social world but, importantly, on how sociology can be used to advance the social world.

Master's programs in sociology typically require that full-time students complete about 2 years of coursework, or 36 units, as well as some kind of concluding project, such as a thesis, exam, or capstone project. Unlike undergraduate programs, master's programs in sociology have few required courses beyond theory, research methods, and possibly an internship or co-op course. One of the great benefits of both master's and doctoral programs is that students have not only the opportunity to select their courses but also ample opportunity for independent and advanced scholarship.

A master's degree in sociology provides numerous career opportunities, such as teaching in some community colleges or part-time teaching at a 4-year university. (Doctoral degrees are most often required for teaching sociology full-time in a 4-year university.) Master's programs also can help gauge one's interest in sociology and in advancing to a doctoral program.

Doctoral Programs

Although a bachelor's degree in sociology is not needed to be considered a successful candidate for many sociology doctoral programs, the more experience one has with sociology, such as a sociology major or minor, or even employment in a setting that utilizes sociological skills, the more prepared she is for advanced studies.

Doctoral degrees are the highest degree a person with a focus in sociology can attain. The PhD, or Doctor of Philosophy, signifies that the scholar is able to apply theoretical concepts and thinking to a particular area of research, with the ability not only to master the material but also to produce work that advances the particular area of study. Doctoral programs consist of coursework (typically around 60 units) and qualifying exams to advance in the program. These exams include oral examinations where students must demonstrate an understanding of sociological terms and concepts, as well as written exams that test theory and its applications. Doctoral programs culminate in the most well-known and often-feared part of every doctoral program: the dissertation.

A master's degree is not needed to apply to all doctoral programs. While in a doctoral program, after a certain number of credits in coursework are completed and often a large paper or exam, students can be eligible for an "en route" degree. This means that the required amount of coursework or exams has been completed to qualify for a master's degree. This helps doctoral students who need to have a master's degree for employment while still in school.

Doctoral programs in the United States are typically housed within larger colleges and universities. These programs often provide ample opportunities for doctoral students to engage in the work of the discipline, both funded and unfunded, such as experience with research or serving as teaching assistants or part-time/adjunct course instructors.

It takes the average sociology doctoral student between 7 and 8 years to complete her program. Some students complete the program much more quickly; however, they often come in with a master's degree and transfer their credits into the doctoral program, reducing the amount of classes they have to take while in the program. Those who finish more quickly are often also fully funded, meaning that the university or a fellowship covers tuition and provides a stipend, so they can focus on their studies and not work.

WRITING TO GET INTO GRADUATE SCHOOL

For most scholars, the first introduction to sociological writing begins when they are undergraduate students, but writing is even more integral to graduate studies, as students learn about advanced theory and research methods through their writing. Many graduate students have often remarked that writing is much more enjoyable in graduate school than in their undergraduate experiences. Graduate school writing is outside the scope of this book but is discussed in more detail in *Writing for Emerging Sociologists*. Graduate students have more flexibility in selecting their own courses and research interests, and, therefore, graduate studies provide more options for studying topics independently. The first major hurdle in the writing process for someone wanting to pursue advanced studies in sociology is the application process for master's and doctoral programs.

Application Process

The graduate school application packet typically contains letters of recommendation, a statement of purpose, transcripts, a writing sample, and Graduate Record Examination (GRE) test scores. Between researching programs and funding opportunities and preparing your application packet, you could spend up to a year preparing to apply and applying to graduate school, particularly if you are interested in doctoral programs. The more time you give yourself, the more likely you will be successful in the application process. We will briefly examine what is often required in graduate program application packets as well as provide advice on preparing them. For additional information on applying to graduate programs, you should make appointments with your sociology professors and advisors.

Statement of Purpose

With the increase in students applying to graduate school, it is imperative that you write a well-organized and well-prepared statement of purpose to separate you from the rest of the applicants. Most graduate program applications require that students write about themselves as well as their career and research interests. Examples of statements of purpose essay prompts are provided in the Appendix.

Graduate programs use a variety of different essay prompts and instructions. In addition, the way each applicant approaches and responds to the prompt will vary based on the individual student, program, research interest, and career interest, for example. As a result, the best advice we can offer is to be honest and forthcoming in your essay. This is the most personal piece of writing—and, for many of you, the only piece of writing—you will write as part of your application packet. Be honest in your description of your research interests and career intentions. You may be applying to be at this institution for several years. It is important that you and the program are a good match.

Spend time writing your personal statement and do not rush the writing process. Think about your research and career interests, why you chose sociology, and why you want to attend this particular program. We would suggest seeking out help from a career or study center on campus, as well as from a sociology department advisor and/or professor, on composing and revising your statement of purpose. The keys to a good statement is writing and editing multiple drafts as well as getting feedback from "reviewers." The more time you spend on your essay, the better it will be.

Writing Sample

Graduate program application packets routinely require writing samples as an example of your level of writing. Look through the different papers you've written while in college. The paper you select should show that you are an effective writer with strong critical thinking and analytical skills. The writing sample should, ideally, be a social science paper but, if not, it should be something the admissions committee or panel will understand. For example, a mathematical paper written for a calculus course would not serve as an appropriate writing sample for most graduate or doctoral sociology programs.

Make sure you edit the writing sample before turning it in. Even if an application requires that you submit a writing sample that was a course paper, you can still edit it before turning it in. As an undergraduate student interested in furthering your education in sociology, you should keep in mind that you may need a writing sample for graduate school, and try to produce work while you are an undergraduate student that could serve as a writing sample in the future. You should not submit a paper with edits, a grade, or your professor's comments marked on it. Remember, it is a writing sample, not a sample of a graded course paper. Ideally, you will have a digital version of the paper saved, but if you do not, either choose another paper or retype it so you are submitting a clean copy to the admissions committee.

Transcripts

Graduate programs require a record of the courses you took as part of your undergraduate study, as well as the grades earned in said courses. Importantly, your transcripts contain your grade point average, or GPA. Graduate programs routinely set minimum GPA requirements for their applicants. The GPA requirement for admissions into a doctoral program (3.5 or B+/A–) is typically higher than for master's programs (3.0 or B). The higher your GPA, the more likely you will not only get into school but obtain funding as well.

Graduate Entrance Exams

There are two entrance exams graduate programs often require of their applicants, with both being offered through the Educational Testing Service (ETS): the Graduate Record Examination (GRE) and the Major Field Test (MFT) for Sociology. Despite the controversy over using this test as a measurement of a student's success in graduate school, almost all American sociology doctoral programs and many sociology master's programs use the GRE to gauge an applicant's potential for success in graduate education. This 4-hour, computer-based exam measures quantitative and verbal reasoning, as well as analytical writing skills. The GRE is created and administered by the

ETS, the same nonprofit testing service that conducts the Scholastic Assessment Test (SAT). It is important to note that the GRE changes its format every few years, so you should check with ETS for updated information. However, the GRE tends to consist of the following four sections. You will take six of them over the 3 hour and 45 minute exam:

1. The *analytical section* includes two timed essays where test takers evaluate a logical argument and express their views on a critical issue. Responses are measured to ensure the test takers' ability to apply critical thinking and writing skills to the response. Test takers have 30 minutes to complete each essay.

2. The *verbal reasoning section* measures a test taker's reading comprehension skills and ability to apply her reasoning skills. This section no longer includes antonyms and analogies. This section also consists of text-completion questions, which test the student's ability to interpret and evaluate what she has read. The GRE general test includes two 30-minute verbal reasoning sections, with each section containing 20 questions.

3. The *quantitative reasoning section* examines math skills such as algebra, statistics, geometry, probability, arithmetic, and data analysis. It also focuses on reasoning skills and provides real-life scenarios. This section of the exam includes a number of multiple-choice questions. No writing is involved in the quantitative reasoning section. The GRE general test includes two 35-minute quantitative reason sections, with each section containing 20 questions.

4. The *research section* consists of either a verbal reasoning section or a quantitative reasoning section, and does not count toward the test taker's score. ETS uses this to measure whether or not the section should be included as a scored section in a future GRE test. So while the test taker might complete six specific sections in total, only five will count toward the GRE score. You will not have any indication of which section is the research one. Though the analytical section comes first, the quantitative reasoning, verbal reasoning, and research sections could come in any order.

There are many benefits to the computer-based GRE General Test as opposed to the older paper tests. You aren't required to use the full time provided to complete each section; you can, instead, immediately move to the next section once you are finished. Within each section, you will be able to identify the questions you would like to go back to review and answer. However, once you submit that section, you will be unable to return back to that section. Immediately after the GRE General Test is completed, you will have the option of scoring or not scoring the exam. If you chose to score the exam, this score will be recorded and included on all GRE records sent out to the schools that you identified. However, if you chose not to score the exam, you won't receive a score for the exam at all and your performance will not be stored with ETS. You must make this decision carefully and consider how well you feel that you performed on the exam, as well as considering the cost of the GRE General Test, the availability of test preparation courses, and graduate school application due dates, among other things. This provides you with the option of using it as a "practice test" if you feel that you didn't perform well (although, you will not know your score). If you chose to have this test scored, you will be able to immediately see unofficial scores for the verbal reasoning and quantitative reasoning sections, scored on a scale of 130–170, with one-point increments. At this time, you will have the option of sending the score for free to four schools, with the option of sending the most current score, or the scores of all of the exams taken with ETS. The scores from GRE General Test are reportable for five years following testing.

The score for the essay portion of the test, as well as percentile scores (from 0–100) which indicates how well you perform on the essay relative to everyone else who took the General Test, will be available on your ETS account after the test is complete but not immediately accessible. The essays are scored together, on a scale of 0 to 6.

A vast majority of sociology graduate/doctoral programs that require the GRE require only that students take the GRE General Test; however, some programs require the ETS Major Field Test (MFT) for Sociology. The MFT for Sociology consists of 140 multiple-choice questions that evaluate the test taker's knowledge of sociological concepts, terms, and theories—such as deviance and social stratification—along with statistics, data, and methods. The MFT for Sociology is graded on a scale of 120–200. Subscores are given for core sociology and critical thinking groups, with each on a 20–100 point scale, and each of these scores are reported in percentiles.

Letters of Recommendation

Although you don't write your own letters of recommendation, you can take steps to ensure that you receive good letters from your recommenders. Seek out faculty members, employers, mentors, and other people who know you very well personally, academically, or professionally. You want to find someone who not only *can* write you excellent letters of recommendation or provide you with great references but *will*.

It is useless to spend all your time trying to get someone to write you a letter when you know that person is unreliable or will not do it.

Most programs require three letters of recommendation or the names and contact information of three people who can provide you with a reference. Even though those writing you letters of recommendation always have great intentions, you should be certain to have at least five people in mind who you are certain will be able to write you a letter, in case one person backs out or cannot write the letter for a particular reason. This also gives you the option of selecting an appropriate person to write a letter for a specific school.

To ensure good letters of recommendation, you want to make sure you spend some time with the person writing you the letter. If you are seeking a letter from a professor, you should be certain to visit her office hours so she can write a letter that focuses on you as a whole and not only on your classroom experience. If you can, try to get a teaching or research assistantship while you are still an undergraduate student. This provides valuable experience you can put on your curriculum vitae (discussed in more detail later in this chapter) and provides the writer of your letter with something to write about. As an undergraduate student, if you find a professor you like, you should also try to take multiple courses with this professor, as many will write letters only for students they have gotten to know over several courses. This may go without saying, but you should make sure to participate in their classes and present the professor with quality work. Also, be sure to give all your recommenders time to write your letters. The rule of thumb is to give at least a month.

You should provide each recommender as much information about you as possible and all the information he needs to write your letter. This may include a highlight sheet (see the Appendix), which underscores you, your interests, and the program (or job if you need a reference for an employment opportunity) you are interested in. It can be as simple as a bulleted list. If the recommender is your professor, tell him what aspects of the course you have done well in, what is important to you about the school or program you are interested in, and how you fit those elements. You may also have recommendation sheets from the school to give to your recommenders, as well as the address, e-mail address, or website where the letter should be submitted.

Although you do have the right to view your letter of recommendation, as it is part of your academic file, master's and doctoral program applications always offer applicants the option to waive their right to view the letter. Whether or not you decide to do this is a personal choice, but our advice is to waive your right to view the letter. If you do so, chances are that the person writing you the letter of recommendation will be more honest and forthcoming in her description and analysis of your work.

CAREERS

Sociology is a fascinating area of study that provides skills applicable to many career choices. You will have different career options depending on whether you hold a bachelor's (BA), MA/MS, or PhD in sociology. Even an undergraduate major in sociology will provide you with a wide array of sociological insights and opportunities. Sociology offers skills in research methods, problem solving, editing, advising, and critical and analytical thinking.

Before you decide to pursue a degree in sociology—or in any field, for that matter—you should first ask yourself what you want to do with the degree. Although many students take sociology courses or select the major because it addresses many interesting issues and topics such as religion, sexuality, disease, and crime, for instance, we advise students first to decide what they are interested in doing and what social problems they hope to address in their work once they have completed their studies and then to determine if a sociology degree will help advance that particular career choice.

The American Sociological Association (ASA) website (www.asanet .org) is a great resource for students looking to pursue a career where they get to apply the skills they learned in their sociology courses. ASA provides the following career areas where a degree in sociology is helpful:

Figure 8.1

- *Social services* → in rehabilitation, case management, group work with youth or elderly, recreation, or administration
- *Community Work* → in fundraising, for social service organizations, nonprofits, child-care or community development agencies, or environmental groups
- *Corrections* → in probation, parole, or other criminal justice work
- *Business* → in advertising, marketing and consumer research, insurance, real estate, personnel work, training, or sales
- *College setting* → in admissions, alumni relations, or placement offices
- *Health services* → in family planning, substance abuse, rehabilitation counseling, health planning, hospital admissions, and insurance companies
- *Publishing, journalism, and public relations* → in writing, research, and editing
- *Government services* → in federal, state, and local government jobs in such areas a transportation, housing, agriculture, and labor
- *Teaching* → in elementary and secondary schools, in conjunction with appropriate teach certification

Source: American Sociological Review: Manuscript Submission. Washington, DC: American Sociological Association. Retrieved April 2, 2012.

Since there are so many career choices for sociology majors, it is futile even to attempt to explain the different types of writing one may encounter as part of a particular career. The important thing is to use the lessons you have learned in this book to create the types of writing that are appropriate for the career you have chosen. Additionally, to apply to these career choices, you will be required to have at least a letter of interest/statement of intent/cover letter and a curriculum vitae, which will all be discussed in the following sections.

Curriculum Vitae

A curriculum vitae, or CV, is an academic résumé. CVs are used similarly to résumés in Europe, although in the United States, they are primarily used within academic and research institutions. In American academic institutions, we are much more likely to use a CV as opposed to a traditional résumé; as such, we will focus more on writing CVs than on writing résumés.

While the traditional résumé primarily focuses on your previous work experience in the area in which you are applying, CVs focus on your research and teaching experience within academia or in an applicable area. Unlike résumés, which usually have the few subsections of contact information, education, work experience, and references, CVs provide much more information. CVs can contain the following subheadings: address/contact information, current employment, education, papers published, conference presentations, courses taught, research experience, grants, awards, fellowships, professional memberships, research/teaching areas of interest, languages spoken, specialized skills, and references. Keep in mind that there is no one right or wrong way to structure the CV, but the section that is most important to the place where you are submitting it should be near the top, below your name and contact information.

First, all information in your CV should be in chronological order, with the most recent information closest to the top. We suggest putting the month and year the CV was last updated at the top or bottom of your CV, possibly under your name or in a footer, so that you and the reviewer know that the CV is updated and, if the reviewer holds on to it, when it was last updated. Keeping track of dates is very important since you will need to provide timelines for attendance in educational programs and dates of publications and conference presentations. You should add items to your CV immediately after they happen. Many job applications will also ask you for this information.

In constructing your CV, you want to make sure it looks both professional and well organized. We suggest first laying out the various headings for each section of your CV and then using a formatting tool, such as a table, to organize them. Once you have completed constructing your CV, you can hide the table borders. You can do this in any edition of Microsoft Office Word, as well as in most other word-processing programs. As previously mentioned, CVs contain the following information.

Name/Contact Information

Begin with your name, in larger font than the rest of the text, in bold, and centered or at least separate from the other text on the line. Beneath your name, include your current address. If you are a current graduate student or affiliated with a university and can receive mail there, you should include your sociology department address. You can also include your home address if you like. Separate the university address from your home address by placing them on opposite sides of your name or on different rows. You should include your home or mobile phone number, as well as your e-mail address. It goes without saying that you should use your university e-mail address or a professional e-mail address (see Chapter 2 for more information on e-mail addresses). If you plan on posting your CV online, you may want to reconsider including your home address/personal telephone number. For example, it is unlikely that you will see the home addresses and personal telephone numbers of faculty on their CVs; however, home contact information may be the primary contact for people who do not have an office. Make sure it is clear whether you are providing your personal information or university information.

Employment

Typically, those with academic appointments or research-related positions include employment experience within academic or research institutions before educational experience. The title and name of the institution will be listed, as well as the dates the position was held. Some people with academic appointments will also include a section titled "Current Position" if they want to highlight a current experience. However, most students will skip over this section when writing and begin with education.

Education

Provide your educational background and begin by listing all undergraduate institutions attended as well as major, year of attendance, and degrees completed. List each institution, from your first undergraduate institution to the present. If you started at a school but did not receive a degree there, you should only include it if its absence leaves a gap in your education or you feel including it will provide some kind of advantage. If you earned any special honors, such as Magna Cum Laude or a particularly high GPA, you may want to make note of that. Include any degrees you may have earned from certificate programs.

Publications

We realize that, as students, you will likely not have publications yet; however, we will briefly cover this section of the CV. Published articles and books listed on the CV should be written in ASA or American Psychological Association format. Publications are listed in chronological order from the most recent to the earliest. Some separate peer-reviewed publications found within scholarly journals from non-peer-reviewed publications. If an article, book, or some other work has been accepted for publication and is scheduled to be released or is forthcoming, list that publication first and write "forthcoming" where the date would appear.

Some opt to include separate headings for manuscripts under contract, manuscripts under review, and manuscripts in preparation. These potential sections are particularly important for students, as they will likely have items to list under these headings but few or no complete publications. Provide references—without the date of publication and volume number, if applicable—for each manuscript that is under contract with a publisher.

Under the review section, list only those articles, books, or other writings that have been submitted and are still under review. There is some small debate over whether you should list the name of the journal while the manuscript is still under review, in the unlikely event that the reviewer may see your CV and recognize your work or because of the possibility that the journal may not accept your manuscript, which would then force you to continually change the name of the journal. However, many people do opt to include the place the manuscript is being reviewed, as it adds legitimacy to your "under review" claim.

In listing your manuscripts under preparation, make sure to include only those manuscripts you plan on submitting to journals or presses within the next few months. If any of your publications are coauthored, you should list the names in the order that they appear in the official citation of the article and bold your name if it does not appear first.

If the place where you are sending your CV is more interested in other experiences, those should come before publications.

Professional Presentations

List all your panel, poster, and roundtable presentations, including those you conducted at conferences and at your own institution. Provide your name, the year of the presentation, and the title of the work being presented, along with the institution and location where the presentation was held. This information should be provided in chronological order.

Teaching Experience

This section can appear under a separate subheading from employment as it focuses on and highlights your teaching experience. Again, you may not have information to include in this section; however, with more students working as teaching assistants, many of you will be including this in your CVs. Under teaching experience, list your official title, the name of the course, and the year and semester it was taught. If you served as a teaching assistant, also include the name of the instructor, and you may want to briefly list some of the responsibilities you held in the course. If you are applying for something that emphasizes teaching, this should be placed before publications.

Fellowships, Grants, Honors, Awards

List all your fellowships, grants, honors, and awards in chronological order, beginning with the most recent award given. List the name of the award, the year of the award, and who distributed the award. In the case of monetary awards, such as grants, you also may want to include the amount awarded. If you are going to be doing fundraising work, you might consider listing your grants near the top.

Other Work Experience

List all the different positions you have held in while in college and relevant non-academic and volunteer work. These include any research experience, paid or nonpaid; conference work; editing work; volunteer work; committee work; and internship or co-op work. Provide your title, making sure it is clear what role you performed and the date you performed it. These should be listed in chronological order from most recent to earliest. Again, unless you accomplished some amazing task while in high school and you are currently an undergraduate student, focus on work you have done since you entered college. You should also avoid listing any work that does not support your academic goals. While you might be proud of the time you spent working retail in the Adidas Originals or Disney stores, it is not relevant to your academic experiences.

Professional Memberships

If you have any active memberships in professional organizations, such as ASA, list the name of the organization as well as any special sections or organization committees you may serve on. All professional sociology organizations encourage student involvement and allow students to present their research and papers on special panels during conferences. Again, these organizations generally offer discount prices for membership and conferences for students.

Languages/Special Skills

If you know or are fluent in any other languages besides English, list the language and the level of fluency you have in writing, reading, and speaking that language. Also, list any statistical or qualitative programs or software packages you may be well versed in, such as SPSS and ATLAS.ti.

Areas of Interest

List your areas of research interest in sociology. In Chapter 3, we discussed and listed the different sociology sections and areas of study within sociology. Look through this list and select the areas that interest you most or you have particular expertise in, and include any other areas of study within sociology that are not included in the list of sections.

References

You should have professional associations with at least three people who can provide you with a reference. Provide each reference's name, title, institution, institutional address, telephone number, and e-mail address. Those who act as references are typically professors or professional colleagues, mentors, supervisors, or employers. These should be the same people you have approached for letters of recommendation. Be sure to look for any guidelines you may receive concerning who your recommenders should be. There are some graduate schools that ask for a combination of professional and personal recommenders or academic and professional. Some people list up to four references on their CVs. These references should be able to speak to your research and career interests. Each person does not necessarily need to be aware of all aspects of your experiences, but you should make sure that, as a whole, whomever you are sending your CV to is provided with a complete picture. If you are not applying for a particular position and plan on posting your CV online, you may want to avoid including the names and contact information of your references and should simply write, "References furnished on request."

As students, you are not likely to have a very long CV, as you won't have much research or teaching experience. However, it is important to begin developing a CV while in school and to make sure you keep it updated.

There are two types of CVs: the abridged CV and the regular CV. A regular CV covers all your research and any teaching experience you may have participated in since you began your academic career—typically, this starts with college. Be certain to list all panel presentations, papers presented, publications, and relevant volunteer experience. You should keep track of everything you will include on your CV so you do not forget to include it all later. Some seasoned academics have CVs that are dozens of pages long. Your full CV will probably only exist as a record of your work; it is unlikely that you will ever submit it.

An abridged CV, on the other hand, is a shortened version of your regular CV. For this, you should include information from your two most recent institutions. Abridged CVs are often tailored for the particular position, omitting all nonrelated positions and experience, and are typically only a few pages in length. When writing an abridged CV, it is important to let the reader know it is abridged. The reader will assume it is not abridged if not explicitly indicated. If the CV is abridged, write "abridged" in a smaller font under your name or in the header, along with the month and year when the CV was last updated.

Focus your CV on your current and most recent educational experiences. As an undergraduate, you can include on your CV any appropriate work you performed in high school. For example, if a sophomore in college won an award for a psychology paper she wrote in high school, she would include that on her CV. However, once she enters a doctoral program, she should no longer include what she did in high school, or even mention her high school under education on her CV. If she were to become an assistant professor, she would list information that only goes as far back as the start of her doctoral study. She would list her undergraduate degree but would no longer include her undergraduate work (unless this work included a major grant, fellowship award, or publication).

Since space is such an issue in constructing and organizing your CV, the font style should be Arial, Times New Roman, or some other standard font. With the exception of your name, the font size should be between 10 point and 12 point (for readability). Try to keep the margins about 1 inch all around. See the appendix for sample CVs.

Résumé

Unlike a CV, a résumé focuses more on professional, non-academic work experience. There are typically three different types of résumés: those written in chronological order (chronological), those based on skills (functional), and those that are more of a hybrid model—a combination of the two. You may want to do a search for résumés in the career you are interested in to make sure you create one that fits the position for which you are applying (see the sample résumé in the Appendix).

Chronological Résumé

In your chronological résumé, you should cover your relevant work experience for the position to which you are applying. For example, if you are applying for a job at a research institute and have a lot of work experience as a paid research assistant but spent a summer working at a fast-food restaurant, you can leave off your fast-food job. The résumé should generally be limited to one page, should be one-sided, and should cover all relevant work experience over the previous 10 years. Résumés provide similar information as CVs but in a much more condensed fashion. Even though space is typically an issue in constructing and organizing a résumé, you still need to make sure your résumé looks professional. The font style should be similar to that of a CV—Arial, Times New

Roman, or some other standard font style—with the font size generally between 10 point and 12 point.

Name/Contact Information. Center your name and be sure to make the font larger than the text in the résumé. The idea is to make sure your name stands out. Below your name, provide your address, e-mail address, and telephone number. Since this is a résumé and not a CV, you should include your personal address; you will not necessarily need your university-affiliated information.

Objective. Your objective is the reason why you are applying for the position—in essence, the goal of the résumé. In fact, it is becoming increasingly popular to leave this objective section off of the résumé. However, choosing to include this in the résumé and referring to the position to which you are applying shows the employer that the résumé was especially tailored for that position. The decision on whether or not to include an objective is up to you. You may want to check what other people who have applied to a similar position have done.

If you plan to include an objective, it should be a short sentence describing to your potential employer your objective for pursuing this position. You will likely need to tailor your objective for the different jobs to which you are applying. Is your objective to find a position that will let you utilize your research analysis skills? Are you looking for an internship or co-op opportunity? This section shows the employer not only that you are interested in the position but also how you fit the position. The objective describes a little about you to the employer.

Education. The education section comes after the objective statement or, if an objective is not included, below your name and contact information. Potential employers need to know your educational experience. Provide your degree, program/major, minor (if you have one), and the month and year you graduated or expect to graduate. Also list the name of the academic institution. List all the colleges or academic institutions you have attended since high school. If you attended several different colleges, you may want to limit your list to those from which you have obtained degrees or certificates. Your educational experience should be listed in chronological order, starting with your most recent educational experience or your most recently earned degree.

If you are applying for an academic position or a position that requires specialized training or a degree, you may want to highlight any educational qualifications and added experience you have. For example, you may want to include a short blurb in this section if you have earned a high GPA or graduated with honors.

Related Experience. As résumés are rather short, you want to focus this section only on your related experience. If you do not have a lot of experience, you can call it simply "experience." List your relevant work, volunteer, internship, and co-op experiences. Provide your title/position, making sure it is clear what role you performed and the date you performed this work. These experiences should be listed in chronological order from most recent to earliest.

Honors/Awards. List any honors, awards, or fellowships you may have received that relate to the position to which you are applying.

Skills. Here, list any skills and certifications you may have. If you know or are fluent in any other languages besides English, list them here along with the level of fluency you have in writing, reading, and speaking each one. If you know any particular software programs or are well versed in Microsoft Office, for example, inform the potential reviewer what this skill set is and how advanced you are in it.

Functional Résumé

A functional résumé is generally used for someone who has limited experience or is attempting to move into a position she has not worked in previously. Rather than focusing on the position, a functional résumé focuses on the relevant skills you may have gained over several different positions. Functional résumés are compiled in different ways, but they typically include the following sections.

Contact Information. Your name should be centered, in bold and in a slightly larger font, at the top of your résumé. Your personal contact information, including your address, e-mail, and telephone number, should follow.

Objective. Explain why you are applying for this position. What is the purpose of this résumé? How do you fit this position?

Summary of Qualifications/Profile. In this section, either called summary of qualifications or profile, you should include a quick summary of your skills. What stands out in your experience that you think a potential employer would be interested in? Write in quick, short sentences. This should not be any longer than two paragraphs.

Professional Skills. Without necessarily naming the particular positions, describe in detail the skills you gathered during your work experience. If you are interested in finding a job in a nonprofit office and you've worked as a record keeper in several different retail locations, you can talk about your skill with word processing, strict record keeping, and communication with clients. You should include three or four categories of skills, detailing beneath each one how it applies to you.

Skills Summary. If there are additional skills you think are important, you can include them in a list of bullet points.

Education. Finally, you can include your educational information, beginning with your most recent school.

References. Try not to include your list of references on the résumé itself; instead, you should include the phrase, "References will be furnished on request." An interested potential employer will contact you for a list of references. If you do want to or are required to include references on your résumé, provide each reference's name, title, institution, institutional address, telephone number, and e-mail address. Those listed as references are typically professors or professional colleagues, mentors, supervisors, or employers. Your reference list should consist of people who will provide a positive evaluation to a potential employer.

Hybrid Résumé

A hybrid résumé begins the same way as the functional résumé but, above the education, includes a related experience section and lists the few positions you have worked where the experience is relevant to the position to which you are applying. You might also include volunteer and community service experiences.

As you can see, writing plays an integral role within sociology—it helps us become sociologists. A couple of very helpful books can get you started on the variety of career options sociology students have. *Great Jobs for Sociology Majors* by Stephen Lambert and *Careers in Sociology* by W. Richard Stephens Jr. both provide useful resources that will help you if you are interested in a career where you can apply the skills you developed as sociology student.

SUMMARY

This chapter examined professional as well as graduate school writing. We focused not only on the major writing assignments found within most sociology graduate programs but also on the writing involved in the graduate school application process. Additionally, this chapter examines the writing necessary in the beginning stages of a sociology career. More specifically, this chapter reviews the following areas:

- Master's and doctoral sociology programs
- Letters of recommendation, letters of intent, the GRE, and other aspects of the application process
- Course papers and culmination papers, such as dissertations
- How to write a CV and résumé, as well as the differences between the two

This chapter contains a "Writing in Practice" essay by Christina Nelson, a recent Marquette University alum with a major in sociology, who explains how she went about the process of applying to graduate schools.

WRITING IN PRACTICE

By Christina Nelson

I entered Marquette University as a first-generation, low-income student through the aid of Student Support Services (SSS), a federally recognized program to help marginalized students succeed in higher education. As a "Trio Student," as those of us receiving support were called, SSS provided me with an advisor, tutoring services, mentorship by staff, and opportunities to discover what I was passionate about, throughout my undergraduate career.

As a second-year student, I was strongly encouraged to apply to the Ronald E. McNair Scholars program, an offshoot of SSS, focused on getting first-generation college students on the pathway to earning a PhD. The McNair Scholars program at Marquette started as a summer program and was focused primarily on research, graduate school preparation, and enhancing writing ability. Not even knowing what research was at the time and having little idea what I would do following graduation, I applied to the program. I was accepted and through McNair became exposed to research for the first time.

(Continued)

(Continued)

Thanks to funding from the McNair Scholars program, I was able to focus on research during the summers following my junior and senior years. This proved to be essential to helping me decide upon graduate school and a career in sociology after I complete my doctoral studies. I was exposed to both quantitative and qualitative research, wrote research proposals, worked on research papers for publication, developed my curriculum vitae, and was taught how to present in front of a large audience. I was also given responsibilities including coming up with interview questions, scheduling research-team meetings, facilitating focus groups, assisting in conducting interviews, and transcribing, coding, and analyzing data. Furthermore, being exposed to the stressors, rewards, and accomplishments of research allowed me to see that research would be a major focus in my future career, particularly in my planned area of focus, medical sociology. Knowing this, the next step was for me to apply to graduate school.

Applying to graduate school is, hands down, the most intimidating act for a young researcher and student. In order to be successful, I had to be well organized and proactive in the application process. I decided to make a timeline of when I needed to complete individual tasks for my application, beginning the summer before I started my senior year of college. I considered the following things: the GRE, my statement of purpose (sometimes known as a personal statement), my letters of recommendation, what type of program to apply for—masters or doctoral—and how I could make the entire application process go as smoothly as possible. To help, I made the timeline below.

Before I could even start on applications, I needed to know what schools I wanted to apply to. I decided to narrow the selection of schools to areas I would be happy living in and where I would also have access to a large research population. As someone wanting to do sociological research, the second of these is an important consideration—for qualitative researchers like myself, not living near a potential research population means that research is harder to conduct. From there, I looked at schools to which I would have a pretty good chance of being accepted. I decided to apply to half masters programs and half doctoral programs, so as to give myself options, and to be able to continue with my schooling regardless of whether or not I was immediately accepted to a doctoral program. I used the timeline below.

I decided to take the GRE in August, because it would give me time to retake the test in case I did not get high enough scores for the schools to

Table 1 Applying to Graduate School Timeline

July	-Study for GRE -Work on a list of graduate schools to apply to
August	-Study for GRE/Take GRE -Begin reaching out to faculty of interest (assistant/associate) -Start working on a template of personal statement
September	-E-mail/meet with faculty to ask for a letter of recommendation -Polish personal statement -Reach out to faculty of interest (assistant/associate) -Retake GRE (optional)
October	-Retake GRE (optional) -Customize each personal statement -Submit applications
November/December	-Submit applications
January/February	-Reach out to current graduate students at institutions
February/March	-Start hearing back from schools

which I applied. Over the summer, I worked on a draft of my statement of purpose; this allowed me time to have it revised many times over by my peers, my university's writing center, and those writing my letters of recommendation. The two aspects that you can change to improve your application are your letters of recommendation and your personal statement. Your personal statement should be extremely well written and lay out who you are as a researcher and where you want your future to take you. Each department looks for something different in the statement of purpose; however, for sociology, it is important to keep it focused on the research you have conducted, leadership in the university, any teaching you have done, publications you have up for revision, presentations, and any awards you have received for the service you have done at your university. You would want to avoid telling stories about your personal life unless they answer the prompt, but do give examples of past academic achievement. With my personal statement, Marquette University's writing center was an incredibly useful resource for me, and most universities have similar resources—I highly recommend taking advantage of the one in your

(Continued)

(Continued)

school, as it can help improve your writing skills and has staff available to assist in editing papers. With the assistance of the writing center, I had my writing sample revised multiple times before I included it in my application. Most, but not all, graduate schools require one.

My next step was gathering letters of recommendation. I knew they could make or break an application, so I needed to ask the right people. To be courteous of your recommender's time, it is important to ask early—for me, this meant at least two months before they were due. I decided to ask at the beginning of the fall semester and asked three individuals: two members from the research team I had worked with, both of whom were professors at another research institution, and a tenured faculty member from my university with whom I had also worked. It is important to keep in mind that you want individuals who will write positive letters; they need to be carefully chosen to show the graduate admissions committee that the people who recommend you have complete faith in your abilities. It is worth keeping in mind the knowledge base of your recommenders—if they have the degree you are seeking, they have a better idea of whether or not you are also capable to handling the work to obtain it. To help my recommenders write an effective letter of recommendation, I created a folder for my recommenders, which included a letter thanking them, a copy of my transcripts, a draft of my personal statement, a list of positive and negative qualities as I saw them, my CV, a list of schools I intended to apply to, and the date by which the letter needed to be submitted. You also want to always waive the right to view your letter of recommendation, as it shows the admission committee the recommender was not influenced by you.

Once I requested my letters of recommendation, I knew that I should make contact with schools to which I would be applying. Despite the efforts of acceptance committees to be impartial, doing this could help influence the acceptance committee; they would know my name, my research interests and abilities, and my willingness to work hard for what I wanted. I made a list of all the doctoral programs I would be applying to, chose three to four faculty whose research interested me and fit my career trajectory, and e-mailed them. Some faculty would respond to my e-mails, while some did not. Of those who did respond, some would tell me about their research at length, others would want to have a phone conversation with me, and others would say that I did not need to talk to them unless accepted. Regardless of their response, I thanked them and learned whatever I could from the interaction.

As I worked on completing applications throughout the month of October, I also worked on expanding upon my CV, to emphasize that I was serious about presenting at conferences, publishing, and contributing to my university. I applied to present my research at about five conferences I could find and I submitted my paper for undergraduate paper competitions. I found that a lot of notable research associations accepted student research, not only for presentations, but also for publication within undergraduate journals. By the end of October, I was ready to submit most of my applications. I had set personal submission deadlines of November 1 and December 1, for doctoral programs and masters programs, respectively.

For me, the key to applying to graduate school was staying organized from the beginning. As a prospective student, you need to know when everything is due, and have it completed at least a week before then. Furthermore, beginning your first year of college, you should assume that you will be taking the post-graduation path that will take the most work— often, this will be graduate school. Because the foundation of your graduate school application is your cumulative GPA and research experience, it is important to think about them long before you begin to apply; neither is easily changed during the first semester of your senior year, when most of your applications will go out.

Once you have gone through the application process, you then have the most stressful part: waiting to hear back. I am currently in this part of the process, which is sometimes extremely rewarding and sometimes heart-breaking. I have heard back from about half of the 19 schools to which I applied (yes, that is a lot!), and I am eager to hear back from more. Then, hopefully, I can start making concrete plans about the future—a future I am incredibly excited about! If you are considering applying to a graduate school, good luck. Give yourself credit for all the work you have done, and get ready for a lot more in graduate school!

—Christina Nelson is the program assistant at the Center for Gender and Sexualities and has her undergraduate degree in sociology from Marquette University.

APPENDIX

CHAPTER 2

Often Mistaken Words

These are a few examples of words that are commonly mistaken for each other. We have not included every example, nor have we included every definition of each word. Our intention is to provide you these samples with the hope that they can assist you to become better writers. You should follow up with a dictionary or thesaurus for further information.

Then	vs.	**Than**
adv. At that time OR soon after that		*prep.* In comparison with
He remembered that he had jumped the turnstile and then run into the train.		She hoped to make him jealous by being more beautiful than he remembered.
Advice	vs.	**Advise**
n. A suggestion meant to assist		*vb.* To give advice
My sister's advice convinced me not to see him anymore.		Please advise me on these investments.
Affect	vs.	**Effect**
vb. To produce a material influence on or alteration in		*n.* Something that inevitably follows an antecedent (a preceding event, condition, or cause)
The paralysis affected his limbs.		The effect of the change in food on the animals was lethargy.

Your	vs.	**You're**
Adj. Possessed by yourself		Contraction of "you are"
This is your mail.		You're missing my point!

Accept	vs.	**Except**
vb. To receive willingly		*prep.* With the exclusion or exemption of
I'll accept the box for my neighbor.		I'll eat anything except eggs.

Desert	vs.	**Dessert**
n. An area of land with no or little water		*n.* A food served after a meal
Being in the desert is like standing behind a bus.		Orange sherbet was my favorite dessert as a kid.

Its	vs.	**It's**
Adj. Possessed by itself		Contraction of "it is"
The house looks great. Its door frames are solid oak.		It's too late for dinner.

Lay	vs.	**Lie**
vb. To put down		*vb.* To be in a horizontal position
Please lay your coat down on the bed.		Just lie quietly until nap time is over.

Past	vs.	**Passed**
adj. Occurring in a time before this		*vb.* To have moved by
My childhood is all in the past.		The car quickly passed us.

Their vs.	They're vs.	There
adj. Possessed by them	Contraction of "they are"	*adv.* A position away
Scarlett and Carlos are their friends.	They're going to head over to the party soon.	You don't have to come here; just stay there.

To vs.	Too vs.	Two
prep. Movement toward	*adv.* Also or excessively	*adj.* One more than one
Please move to the right.	I made too many cookies.	There are two of us.

Lose vs.	Loose
vb. To miss or fail to win	*adj.* Not tight
I tied it on so I wouldn't lose it.	The screw was too loose.

Cite vs.	Site vs.	Sight
vb. To quote or refer to	*n.* A location	*n.* Ability or something to see
Don't forget to cite your references.	I visited the site of the new school.	The bird was a beautiful sight.

Sample Job Cover Letter

123 S. Louis St.
New York, NY 10023
September 18, 2012

Dr. Christopher McCoy
6000 Morrell Ave.
New York, NY 12345

Dear Professor McCoy,

I am writing to apply for the position of college assistant at The College of the State of New York. I am currently working on my bachelor's degree in sociology and have spent the past year as a student worker at New York College. I am confident that my experiences in the organization, record keeping, and scheduling will serve me well in this position.

I have also assisted in planning several workshops for students, including arranging speakers, ordering food, and ensuring supplies are available. My evaluations have been at good or above for all of these events.

During my time in college over this past year, I have also had the opportunity to participate in several community-based organizations. I have worked closely with neighborhood children and their parents and have strived to make them comfortable to speak to me about their needs and how I can help them get access to the services they require.

I want again to express my interest in a position at The College of the State of New York. I have enclosed a copy of my résumé and several references you may contact. I look forward to speaking to you further.

Sincerely,
Adriana Fuller

Sample Request Letter

123 Electric St.
New York, NY 10023
September 18, 2012

Dr. Joey Amaya Milan
6000 West End Ave.
New York, NY 12345

Dear Dr. Milan,

I hope you are doing well and that the summer has been enjoyable for you. I am writing this letter to let you know that I am applying for a position at New York College and to ask if you are available to write a letter of recommendation for me for this position. I recognize that this is a busy time of year, and, as such, I have attached a copy of my résumé, my cover letter, and a brief note highlighting my recent experiences. I can also meet with you if you need to speak with me. Please let me know if you require further information from me before beginning. Thank you again for your help.

Sincerely,
Naima Marable

Sample Thank-You Letter

Dear Dr. Bassett,

It was really great to meet you yesterday. I am writing to thank you for the opportunity to interview with you. It was wonderful to hear more about New York College and to speak to you about how I might become a part of it. I hope to have the opportunity to work with you in the future.

Sincerely,
Serena King

Sample Shorthand

Shorthand

Hints:

- Leave out vowels
- Leave out unnecessary verbs
- Leave out little words
- Use only the first syllable
- Use an apostrophe for eliminated letters

Vs	Against
& or +	And
A	Answer
≈, Approx., ~	Approximately
@	At

b/c,	Because
b/4	Before
C	Century
Δ	Change
Cf.	Compared to
↓	Decrease
Def.	Definition
Diff.	Difference
⟩	Does not lead to
=	Equal to
Eg. or ex.	Example
;	Feet, minutes
Fr.	From
>	Greater than
* or Imp. or (Circling) or underlining	Important
+	In addition to
"	Inches, seconds
↑	Increase
→	Leads to
<	Less than
↔	Linked, related
♂	Man
Max.	Maximum
Min.	Minimum
$	Money
≠	No equal to

!	Not
No.	Number
#	Number
¶	Paragraph
/	Per
%	Percent
Q	Question
Re.	Regarding
1st, 2nd	Sequence
∴	Therefore
K	Thousand
?	Uncertain, question
v.	Very
w/	With
w/o	Without
♀	Woman
✓	Yes

CHAPTER 5

Sample Syllabus Review

Class:
Professor:
Office hours:
Office location:
Contact information:
Preferred method of contact:
Course website:

Assignments:

Due Date	Assignment

SAMPLE ASSIGNMENT SUMMARY FORM

Semester: Year:

Assignments

Month: _____

Due Date	Class	Assignment

Month: _____

Due Date	Class	Assignment

Month: _____

Due Date	Class	Assignment

Month: _____

Due Date	Class	Assignment

Month: _____

Due Date	Class	Assignment

SAMPLE HOMEWORK WORKSHEET

Background Information

❑ This assignment is due _____ at _____ am/pm
❑ This assignment includes ___ drafts
❑ The assignment includes an outline
❑ This assignment is worth __% of my total grade
❑ This assignment is part of a larger assignment,___ of ___

Preparation

❑ To complete the assignment, I will need to talk to:
❑ To complete the assignment, I will need to research:
❑ To complete the assignment, I will need to watch:
❑ To complete the assignment, I will need to read:

I will also need to:

❏ Analyze	❏ Describe	❏ Justify
❏ Apply	❏ Discuss	❏ Outline
❏ Argue	❏ Elaborate	❏ Relate
❏ Assess	❏ Examine	❏ Research
❏ Clarify	❏ Explain	❏ Respond
❏ Compare	❏ Explore	❏ Review
❏ Consider	❏ Evaluate	❏ Show cause
❏ Contrast	❏ Identify	❏ State
❏ Define	❏ Illustrate	❏ Summarize
❏ Demonstrate	❏ Interpret	❏ Synthesize

Format

❏ The assignment should be ___ pages
❏ The assignment should be double/single spaced
❏ The assignment should have a cover page
❏ The assignment should be in _____ font
                                    (size) (color)

Progress

Completed

Completed Step

❏ _____

❏ _____

❏ _____

❏ _____

❏ _____

❏ _____

CHAPTER 8

Sample Statements of Purpose

The University of Chicago

A candidate's statement of academic purpose should discuss your academic and career objectives in a concise, sharply focused, and well-crafted essay. This statement must be completed online as part of the Online Graduate Student Application. Admissions committees are particularly interested in this statement, so it is considered a vital part of your application. Therefore, you should be as specific as possible in discussing your academic objectives and research interest. There is a 2,500-word limit for the statement of purpose on our online application.

Stanford University

The statement of purpose should describe succinctly your reasons for applying to the Doctoral Program in Sociology at Stanford; your preparation, study and research interests, future career plans, and other aspects of your background and interests which may aid our admissions committee in evaluating your aptitude and motivation for pursuing a Ph.D. in Sociology.

The University of North Carolina, Chapel Hill

Please provide a personal statement that describes your reasons for seeking a PhD in Sociology at UNC, your major intellectual interests and career goals, the sort of research and scholarship you hope to pursue, and the most important aspects in your background that have prepared you for graduate study in Sociology. The statement should be not more than three pages long.

University of Illinois at Chicago

The Personal Statement is a short statement (2–3 pages) detailing how and why you decided to pursue a PhD in sociology, including personal, work, and research experiences. Applicant should indicate their present research interests as well as any information they want the graduate committee to consider in their deliberations. The personal statement should be sent directly to the department.

The Ohio State University

A statement of purpose, which should outline the applicant's relevant training, research experience, academic goals, plan of study, career objectives, and reasons for choosing sociology at Ohio State. Any special circumstances that need explaining should be noted as well.

The University of Wisconsin–Madison

We'd like to know the kinds of topics and approaches that interest you. The statement should make us understand that you are really interested in a scholarly life as a sociologist. Why sociology? Why Wisconsin? Are there particular faculty or program areas of special interest to you? Do you see your research interests as well-defined or fairly open at this point? Based on your knowledge and thinking now, what research problem(s) would you hope to pursue while here.

University of California, Los Angeles

A statement of purpose, not to exceed three typewritten double-spaced pages outlining reasons for pursuing graduate work, interests within sociology, and any pertinent intellectual and career experiences and interests. The Admissions Committee considers a strong applicant to have well-conceived research interests, past research accomplishment, and intellectual biography.

Sample Highlight Sheet

Dear Dr. Fitzpatrick,

Here is a summary that highlights the work I have accomplished this year. In the past 8 months, I have done the following:

- Worked as a teaching assistant for three courses in the Sociology Department at New York State University in New York, New York, which were highly rated by the students and Dr. Andrea Orman. I worked with:
  - Introduction to Sociology (1 section)
  - Race, Class and Gender (1 section)
  - Social Statistics (1 section)
- Worked with the faculty member to prepare a course for next semester
  - Sociology of Work
- Revised a paper previously submitted in your class on the ways racial tensions played out in a public park, for which I received an A
  - "Race in the Park"

- Had a paper accepted for a conference presentation
  - Seth, Gwen and Jarvis, Lillieth. 2011 (forthcoming). "Race in the Park," to be presented at the American Sociological Association Annual Conference.
- Submitted my dissertation manuscript to Paradise Publishers for review
- Your letter will be sent to
  - Dr. Lori Nembhard
    Nick R. Bocker Fellow
    New York State College
    1 Penn Plaza
    New York, NY 10001

In my letter for the position at New York State College, I decided to highlight the following:

- My research experience and scholarly work on race
- My teaching experiences at the school
- My experiences with advising students

Please let me know if you have any questions or need any further information. Thank you again for all your help.

Gwen Seth

Sample Curriculum Vitae

Betty A. Deas
abridged as of September 29, 2016

Work Address
Sociology Department
University of North America
New York, NY 10036
bdeas618@unorthamerica.edu

Home Address
77 W. Monticello Ave. #3931
New York, NY 10023
(212) 555-7270 (home)
(626) 555-8245 (cell)

Education

PhD	2017 (expected)	Sociology	The University of North America
MS	2007	Applied Sociology	Stand College
BA	2003	Sociology, magna cum laude, honors in sociology	Port Charles University

Doctoral Dissertation

Title: An Intersectional Analysis of State-Funded
              Welfare Programs

Committee: Chair: Rajaun Rodriguez
              Members: Arielle Rasmussen, Roberto Sanchez, Nikisha
              Welcome

Research Interests

Historical Sociology, Sociology of Science, Race/Ethnicity, Sex and Gender,
Sexualities, Immigration, Class, Quantitative Research Methods

Fellowships, Grants, and Awards

2012   Dissertation Fellowship, The University of North America

2010   Graduate Research Grant, The University of North America

2007   The University of North America Teaching Fellowship

2007   Stand College Master's Thesis Award

2002   Port Charles Student Leadership Award

Teaching Experience

2010   Instructor, The University of North America, "Historical Sociology"

2009   Teaching Assistant, The University of North America,
           "Introduction to Sociology," under Anisa Cribb

2008   Teaching Assistant, The University of North America,
           "Statistics," under Richard Hahn

Publications

Adams, Roxsan and Betty A. Deas. 2010. "Challenges in Qualitative
Research: Meeting Respondents."

Deas, Betty A. 2008. "Review of The Housing Crisis: A Social Problem."
Journal of Social Issues 42(4): 371.

Manuscripts Under Preparation

MacEachern, Conrad and Betty A. Deas. "Mexican Nationalism and Racial
Perceptions in the United States." *Revise and resubmit.*

"'Show Me the Money': Funding Nonprofit Organizations." *In progress.*

Professional Presentations

2011   "'Show Me the Money': Funding Nonprofit Organizations."
            American Sociological Association, Las Vegas, NV.

2009   "Mexican Nationalism and Racial Perceptions in the
            United States." Society for the Study of Social Problems,
            San Francisco, CA.

Related Experience

Research Assistant, The University of North America, Sociology Department,
under Dr. Nikisha Welcome, 2009–Present

Research Consultant, Society of Religious Institutions, 2007–2009

Professional Organizations

The American Sociological Association

The Association of Black Sociologists

Sociologists for Women in Society

Society for the Study of Social Problems

The Society of the Study of Symbolic Interactionism

Association for Applied and Clinical Sociology

Eastern Sociological Society

References

Nikisha Welcome, PhD
Department of Sociology
The University of North America
299 W. 12th St., New York, NY 10012
(212) 555-2343
nikisha.welcome@unorthamerica.edu

Arielle Rasmussen
Department of Sociology
The University of North America
299 W. 12th St., New York,
NY 10012
(212) 555-8462
arielle.peterson@unorthamerica.edu

Roberto Sanchez
Department of Sociology
The University of North America
299 W. 12th St., New York, NY 10012
(212) 555-2853
robert.williams@unorthamerica.edu

Sample Résumé

Louise Miller
27 W. 128th Street Apt. 2
New York, NY 10027
(917) 555-1142
louisemiller@gmail.com

Objective: To utilize my office skills, customer service experience, and academic knowledge in a library position at The University of North America

Experience: Kaplan, Inc.   New York, NY   January 2007–present

Technology Procurement

- Currently working in the Technology Procurement Department
- Utilizing Microsoft Outlook and BMC Magic Client Services software, fulfilling technology order requests by creating and updating service tickets, and tracking shipments through vendor websites

Anthropologie   New York, NY   May 2003–January 2007

Sales Associate, Loss Prevention Specialist

- Provided friendly, attentive customer service at the busiest location in an upscale clothing, furniture, and housewares retail chain
- Handled multiple-line phone system, cash register, multitasking in high-pressure environment
- Maintained and restocked two-story sales floor; rapidly carried, sorted, and replenished large volumes of clothing and merchandise

Cycle Count Specialist   March 2005–August 2005

- Improved accuracy of store's estimated merchandise loss due to theft or error ("shrink") from more than 4% previous year, meeting goal of 1.0% dollar loss
- Responsible for thoroughly searching sales floor and two separate Manhattan stockrooms for missing items; involved some heavy lifting/moving boxes

- Communicated updates to corporate office via telephone and Microsoft Outlook

New York City Ballet   New York, NY   June/July 2002

Telefundraiser

- Conducted persuasive telephone calls in high volume, encouraging Ballet attendees to contribute to the nonprofit Ballet Guild

Account Resource   Oak Brook, IL   2000–2001

Temporary Office Support Staff

- Worked for United Parcel Service, American Pharmaceutical, MTI Globetrotters
- Developed spreadsheets and documents using Excel, Word, IBM OnDemand
- Performed extensive data entry tasks, reorganized and maintained filing systems

Education:

City College of New York   New York, NY   2005–2007

- 3.89 GPA; BFA in studio art

School of Visual Arts   New York, NY   2002–2003

- Worked toward BFA in illustration

Beloit College   Beloit, WI   1998–2000

- Worked toward BFA in studio art with a minor in Asian studies
- Studied at Kansai-Gaidai University in Osaka during fall semester 2000
- Intensive summer Japanese course at University of Chicago, 1999
- 1998 National Merit Finalist, Beloit College Presidential Scholarship recipient

Skills:

- Adept in both PC and Macintosh platforms
- Microsoft Word, Outlook and Excel, Adobe Photoshop and Illustrator
- Familiar with PowerPoint and HTML
- Excellent math, grammar, and proofreading abilities
- Proficient in Japanese

References available on request.

Biographies

Angelique Harris is associate professor of sociology in the Department of Social and Cultural Sciences and Director of the Center for Gender and Sexualities Studies at Marquette University. Her research and teaching interests include the sociology of health and illness, race and ethnicity, gender and sexuality, media studies, religion, and social movements. Dr. Harris has written numerous books, articles, chapters in edited volumes, book reviews, and encyclopedia entries.

As a doctoral student, Dr. Harris served as a writing fellow for the Writing Across the Curriculum (WAC) program at Queens College, City University of New York (CUNY). WAC is a program that encourages colleges and universities to incorporate more writing into coursework to improve both student writing and learning. As a writing fellow, Dr. Harris aided faculty in developing writing assignments for social science students in writing-intensive courses. She also conducted workshops, worked one-on-one with students, and met with faculty to address the writing needs and concerns of their students. After earning her doctorate from the Graduate School and University Center, CUNY, and before working at Marquette University, Dr. Harris worked at California State University, Fullerton, where she regularly taught the Writing for Sociology Students course—a writing course geared toward sociology undergraduate students.

Alia R. Tyner-Mullings is an assistant professor of sociology and a founding faculty member at Stella and Charles Guttman Community College (formerly The New Community College at City University of New York [CUNY]), the first new college to open in the CUNY system in 40 years. Her areas of interest are the sociology of education, the sociology of communities, the sociology of sports, and cultural studies. Dr. Tyner-Mullings's coedited volume, *Critical Small Schools: Beyond Privatization in New York City Urban Educational Reform* (Information Age Publishing 2012), includes 10 chapters describing the strengths and challenges of small public school education in New York City. Her most recent book, *Enter the Alternative School: Critical Answers to Questions in Urban Education* (Routledge 2014), includes in-depth research on one of these schools, Central Park East Secondary School, how its model worked, and the ways in which that model spread across New York City's critical small public schools.

As a writing fellow in the Writing Across the Curriculum program at Hunter College, CUNY, Dr. Tyner-Mullings worked with students from the social sciences and humanities on their course writing, as well as coordinating a statistical study on the ways writing is used in under-graduate courses on campus. Dr. Tyner-Mullings taught the writing component of CUNY's Pipeline Program, which prepared advanced undergraduate students for writing at the graduate level. Most recently, she taught a sociology course at an Early College High School, which included a 10-page research paper as a culminating assignment. Additionally, she has given multiple presentations on academic writing at the graduate level, facilitated workshops and been an invited lecture on organizing academic work and has conducted several career workshops for undergraduates covering résumé and cover-letter writing.

Dr. Tyner-Mullings and Dr. Harris also published *Writing for Emerging Sociologists* (SAGE 2013), which covers writing activities for sociologists ranging from those who have just discovered sociology to those who are beginning a career as one.

"WRITING IN PRACTICE" CONTRIBUTORS

Chapter 2

Barbara Katz Rothman is professor of sociology, women's studies, and public health at the City University of New York (CUNY) and has held visiting professorships at the Charité Universitätsmedizin Masters in Health and Society in Berlin, the International Midwifery Preparation Program at Ryerson University in Toronto, Canada, and the Department of Sociology at Plymouth University in the United Kingdom, and others. Her books include *In Labor* (W. W. Norton 1982); *The Tentative Pregnancy* (Rivers Oram Press 1994); *The Book of Life*; *Recreating Motherhood* (W. W. Norton 1989); *Weaving a Family* (Beacon Press 2005), and most recently *A Bun in the Oven: How the Food and Birth Movements Resist Industrialization* (New York University Press 2016) and have been translated into German, Japanese, and Finnish. She has developed a course in writing for publication, which she teaches to doctoral students in sociology at the Graduate School and University Center, CUNY, and has led workshops on the topic for midwives in the United States and Canada.

Chapter 3

Cynthia W. Bruns is Information and Instruction Head at the Pollak Library at California State University, Fullerton. She specializes in teaching research methods to sociology and criminal justice classes, as well as assisting individual students with their research questions and locating the materials the students need. Cynthia Bruns has a master's degree in library and information science and a master's degree in American studies. Her thesis for American studies was "Into the Wilderness: The Rise and Decline of Backpacking in America During the Years 1965–1977." This study reflects her long-term interest in backpacking and her love of exploring the wilderness. Cynthia Bruns wrote about the explosion of appreciation for backpacking in the United States that coincided with the development of the environment movement during the 1960s. During this period, backpacking became a vacation fad among Americans as concern over the deteriorating state of our environment grew. One of the advantages of working in a university library is the endless array of research possibilities continually being presented. She finds the research process fascinating and is currently exploring the topic of our changing attitudes toward the environment.

Chapter 4

Thurston Domina is associate professor of educational policy and sociology at the University of North Carolina, Chapel Hill. Dr. Domina earned his doctorate in sociology from the Graduate School and University Center, City University of New York, in 2006. His research pairs cutting-edge empirical methods with sociological theory to better understand the relationship between education and social inequality in the contemporary United States, with a particular focus on student transitions from middle and high school into higher education. His work has been published in *American Educational Research Journal, Child Development, Educational Evaluation and Policy Analysis, Journal of Higher Education, Social Science Research, Sociological Science,* and *Sociology of Education,* among others.

Randol Contreras is an assistant professor of sociology at the University of Toronto, Mississauga. He received his doctorate from the Graduate School and University Center, City University of New York. As an urban ethnographer, he studies social inequality and crime while seeking to uncover the pain and suffering of marginal populations. His book *The Stickup Kids: Race, Drugs, Violence, and the American Dream* (University of California Press 2012) is based on field research in his old South Bronx neighborhood, where he followed the lives of Dominican Stickup Kids, or drug robbers, who robbed wealthy drug dealers storing large amounts of drugs and cash. He is currently doing field research on the Maravilla gangs in East Los Angeles in order to explain the suffering in urban areas.

Chapter 5

Daniel Balcazar is a graduate student in the master's of public health program at Emory University. He earned his bachelor's degree in 2016 from Marquette University in sociology. He won an award for the Best Research Paper for the College of Social and Cultural Sciences at Marquette University and was on the Dean's list for the fall of 2015. He published a chapter in a book on *Global Perspectives in Disability* on the topic of "War and Disability." His interests include Latino studies and the sociology of health and illness.

Chapter 6

James A. Holstein is professor of sociology in the Department of Social and Cultural Sciences at Marquette University. His research and writing projects have addressed social problems, deviance and social control, mental health and illness, family, and the self—all approached from an ethnomethodologically informed, constructionist perspective. He has authored or edited more than 40 published volumes, as well as dozens of journal articles. In collaboration with Jaber F. Gubrium, much of Holstein's work addresses the relation between theory and method in qualitative inquiry. Recently, his attention has focused on the interactional production of narrative realities. Holstein has served as editor of the journal *Social Problems* and the research annual *Perspectives on Social Problems*. He received his doctorate from the University of Michigan.

Chapter 7

R. L'Heureux Lewis-McCoy is associate professor of sociology and Black studies at The City College of New York, City University of New York. His research and advocacy focus on the areas of education, race, place, and gender justice. In the area of education, he studies how diverse school districts address equity and demographic change. He regularly comments in national media, including *Ebony* magazine and The Root, and has been a guest on national television programs such as the O'Reilly

Factor and Al Jazeera. He holds a doctorate in public policy and sociology from the University of Michigan.

Molly Vollman Makris is assistant professor of urban studies at Guttman Community College, City University of New York. She is the author of the book *Public Housing and School Choice in a Gentrified City: Youth Experiences of Uneven Opportunity* (Palgrave Macmillan 2015). Dr. Makris holds a doctorate in urban systems with concentrations in urban educational policy and the urban environment from Rutgers University and New Jersey Institute of Technology, where she was advised by sociologist Alan Sadovnik. She began her career as a social studies teacher in a NYC public high school and then worked for a nonprofit youth development organization. Her current areas of research are urban education reform, charter schools, school segregation, public housing, and gentrification.

Mary Gatta is a sociologist and associate professor of sociology at Guttman Community College in the City of New York (CUNY) system. Recently, Dr. Gatta explored the experiences of women as they navigate one-stop career centers, which led to her new book, *All I Want Is A Job! Unemployed Women Navigating the Public Workforce System*, released from Stanford University Press in April 2014. Dr. Gatta is also the author of *Not Just Getting By: The New Era of Flexible Workforce Development* (Lexington Books 2005) and *Juggling Food and Feelings: Emotional Balance in the Workplace* (Lexington Books 2001), and is the editor of *A US Skills System for the 21st Century: Innovations in Workforce Education and Development*. Dr. Gatta received her doctorate in sociology from Rutgers University. Prior to her appointment at CUNY, Dr. Gatta served as a senior scholar at Wider Opportunities for Women in Washington, DC, and as Director of Gender and Workforce Policy at the Center for Women and Work at Rutgers University. In addition, she was an assistant professor in the Department of Labor Studies and Employment Relations at Rutgers.

Chapter 8

Christina Nelson received her bachelors of arts in sociology from Marquette University in 2016. Her research interests include health and illness, race and ethnicity, urban studies, gender and sexualities, environmental studies, and social movements. Nelson works as a program assistant for the Center for Gender and Sexualities Studies at Marquette University. While working, she is taking classes part time in working toward a doctorate in sociology.

INDEX